INFORMATION
RETRIEVAL
MANAGEMENT

EDITED BY

LOWELL H. HATTERY and EDWARD M. McCORMICK

LSL
PROF
Z
699
.H34
1962

651.5
H36i

LIBRARY
FLORIDA STATE UNIVERSITY
TALLAHASSEE, FLORIDA

© 1962 American Data Processing, Inc.
All rights reserved.
Library of Congress Catalog Number: 62-18060
First Edition

Printed in U.S.A.

About the Library Series...

The DATA PROCESSING LIBRARY SERIES was inaugurated in 1962 to answer a widespread need for reference information in depth about selected subject areas in the field of business data processing. To provide this information, American Data Processing, Inc. sought out leading authorities in these subject areas and arranged for their assistance not only in the collection of material, but also to help ensure that the contents of the Series are held to exacting standards of quality and timeliness. With the Library Series, the manager or researcher in business data processing is assured a continuing supply of authoritative and definitive reference books covering all important aspects of the subjects they explore.

About the Publisher...

AMERICAN DATA PROCESSING, INC. (formerly Gille Associates, Inc.) began research on its first data processing information service in 1950. The resulting publication, The Punched Card Annual, became the first regularly published national reference on data processing systems.

Since that time, American Data Processing has continued to lead the way in making available the newest data processing information in the most usable forms.

These now include:

DATA PROCESSING — a monthly magazine.

DATA PROCESSING EQUIPMENT ENCYCLOPEDIA — detailed standard descriptions and specifications for all office data processing equipment.

COMPUTER APPLICATIONS SERVICE — case histories issued semi-annually in hard-bound form.

DATA PROCESSING LIBRARY SERIES

DATA PROCESSING YEARBOOK — a reference guide.

PUBLISHED BY AMERICAN DATA PROCESSING, INC.
2200 BOOK TOWER   DETROIT 26, MICHIGAN

Publisher	FRANK H. GILLE
Editor	ALAN D. MEACHAM
Assistant Editor	VAN B. THOMPSON

Advisory Committee

To The American University for the Fourth Institute on Information Storage and Retrieval

SAMUEL N. ALEXANDER
  Chief, Data Processing Systems Divisions, National Bureau of Standards

LEA M. BOHNERT
  Chief, Information Retrieval Section, Library Branch, Federal Aviation Agency

GEORGE P. BUSH
  Emeritus Professor of Government and Public Administration, The American University

VERNER W. CLAPP
  President, Council on Library Resources, Inc.

LOWELL H. HATTERY
  Professor of Government and Public Administration, and Director, Center for Technology and Administration, The American University

KARL F. HEUMANN
  Director, Office of Documentation, National Research Council

PAUL W. HOWERTON
  Vice President, Information for Industry, Inc.

CHAUNCEY D. LEAKE
  Retiring President, American Association for the Advancement of Science

EDWARD M. McCORMICK
  Office of Science Information Service, National Science Foundation

CATHERYN SECKLER-HUDSON
  Dean, School of Government and Public Administration, The American University

Contents

Preface

THE PAPERS IN THIS VOLUME are adapted from the proceedings of the Fourth Institute on Information Storage and Retrieval presented in February, 1962, by the Center for Technology and Administration, School of Government and Public Administration, The American University.

One purpose of the Institute and these papers is to present a broader systems approach to the handling of technical information. A complete systems approach must include many elements sometimes neglected, including the user and, particularly, the manager. The manager is responsible for the input to science information centers and for utilization of the output from these centers. Management is therefore so intimately associated with the scientific information problem that its role in the system must be studied and rationalized.

With what level of management are we concerned? It certainly includes the managers of technical information activities, but it must go beyond that level. Upper levels of management are often "unsold" on the importance of the scientific information function. Although executives are providing increased support to these activities, from their point of view the science information function must be judged and weighed in competition with many other demands on the resources they control. There is general reluctance to give all the support that enthusiastic directors of scientific information centers would like to have. This function is not alone in making a case for increased support; generally, there isn't enough to meet all demands. Management must decide what can be supported, by how much, and what must be cut back.

Implicit in this consideration of the management aspects of science information centers is the assumption that technical information is valuable, in that it is rather directly related to a commercial product or is valuable to our defense efforts. Further, it is assumed that a substantial portion of the cost of the item is the cost of the scientific effort involved in its research and development. If this cost itself is not significant, then we presume that the value of the time is significantly dependent on the contribution made by scientists. In addition, we presume that the effectiveness of scientists can be substantially enhanced by more effective communication of scientific information. Even in considering the cost of scientific information we have much yet to learn; in considering value we know even less. Yet, managers are and must be quite cost and value conscious.

Another aspect of the cost versus value of scientific information is contained in the objection expressed by managers that their activities are considered to be expendable. Whenever there is a cutback, the library is the first to get a cut. This attitude is reflected in the fact that the costs of such services are generally taken up in "overhead" accounts. Sometimes an even more suggestive term is used synonymously with overhead, the "burden". This could be interpreted as a negative attitude toward the value of technical information. When management is in a position to consider technical information to be a major resource, rather than a burden — a valuable resource it is willing and able to allocate in a positive sense towards the goals of the company — then we will have made a significant advance in the scientific information area.

In every organization, in addition to information for the scientist, there is obviously a substantial class of information which the manager needs for his own use. Although this managerial information is outside the scope of this volume, there are areas of overlap. Often there are common approaches to these two classes of information. Sometimes the same organization, the same personnel, and the same equipment are involved. Thus, although we cannot and do not always want to separate them, the emphasis is intended to be on management aspects of science information activities as needed by the scientist, not by management.

The chapters in this book tend to fall into five subject categories. Each represents an area of management interest.

The five sections are:

The General Problem. Leake, Hattery, Heumann, and Gorn consider technical information in broad, general terms. They examine various aspects of the historical, social and cultural backgrounds of the problem, and the general factors significant to date and of probable significance in the future.

The Management Problem. Cahn, Howerton and Hillier set the stage for the management situation with respect to science information centers. They consider various aspects of the management problem and some of their interrelations. In these chapters, the presentation does not consider specific areas in detail.

McCormick, in the final chapter, summarizes the material on information retrieval management.

Communications Aspects. These four chapters, by Luhn, Brownson, Anderson and Kehl, are directed toward an important aspect of management, i.e., communications. They consider the facets of communications which are peculiar to science information centers. Luhn considers the general business intelligence system. Brownson indicates the nature of the scientist. Anderson studies the compatibility of these new information services with other information activities, and some problems involved in integration of these services. Kehl considers the rather specific problem of cus-

tomer communication with a digital computer information retrieval system.

Problem Definition. This section of three chapters provides specific approaches to certain areas of interest to management. Myatt reports on a survey technique used to determine design information for an information center. Newman presents criteria for the economic justification of a science information center. Gull gives guidelines for the decision to mechanize a technical information activity.

Systems Experience. This set of three chapters, by Sherrod, Dennis, Asbury and Moise, reflects the operating experience of one government and two industrial environments. In each case, they consider in some detail the situation in which each exists, the types of services provided to the customers, and problems associated with the operation of the centers. Dennis particularly emphasizes the problems of financing an industrial technical information center.

As is evident from reading the papers, we are in the developmental stage of a new dimension in science information. No seminar and no collection of papers at this stage can define and solve all the problems of information storage and retrieval and associated managerial problems.

Nevertheless, we are progressing in the ability to meet the challenge. It is hoped that this volume will contribute to a better understanding of the science information process and provide guidelines for managers and information specialists. Our objective is to present points of view and reports of experience. The state of the art does not support a single philosophy, approach, or set of conclusions. Therefore, divergent points of view and opinions are presented. We believe this is appropriate to the stimulation of thought, experimentation and progress.

—The Editors

The Contributors

HATTIE T. ANDERSON is the Librarian at W. R. Grace and Company, Clarksville, Maryland. Her professional background is in chemistry. Mrs. Anderson has made a study of the relationship between the technical library and the other technical information activities within the company.

W. S. ASBURY is Vice President of Esso Research and Engineering Company for the Legal Patent and Information Division. He joined Esso Research Laboratories in Baton Rouge in 1927 and served in various posts in the United States and abroad. In 1947, he was appointed Vice President and a member of the Board of Directors of Esso Research and Engineering Company.

HELEN L. BROWNSON is Program Director for Documentation Research, Office of Science Information Service, National Science Foundation. Mrs. Brownson has been in scientific information activities at the National Science Foundation since its inception. Prior to that, she was Secretary of the Special Committee on Technical Information, Research and Development Board, Department of Defense. She also served with the Committee on Medical Research of the Office of Scientific Research and Development.

JULIUS N. CAHN is Project Director of the Subcommittee on Reorganization and Internal Organizations of the Senate Committee on Governmental Operations. He has had many professional Senatorial assignments.

BERNARD K. DENNIS is Manager, Technical Information Center, Flight Propulsion Division, General Electric Company, Evendale, Ohio. His professional training was in education. He has been concerned since 1954 with technical communications, and has been Manager of the Technical Information Center since 1957.

SAUL GORN, Ph.D., is Associate Professor of Electrical Engineering, Moore School of Electrical Engineering, and Director, Office Computer Research and Development, University of Pennsylvania. His background is in mathematics. He is an authority in the digital computing field. Dr. Gorn is engaged in formal language design and learning models.

C. DAKE GULL is a Consulting Analyst, Information Processing Unit, General Electric Company, Bethesda, Maryland. Mr. Gull is a librarian with extensive experience in mechanized information systems. His experience includes assignments at the Library of Congress and with Documentation, Inc. He is a past president of the American Documentation Institute (ADI) and is chairman of the U. S. National Committee for the International Federation for Documentation (FID).

LOWELL H. HATTERY, Ph.D., is Director of the Center for Technology and Administration, The American University. The Center's activities include institutes on information storage and retrieval, research administration, and electronic data processing. Professor Hattery also directs academic programs in these areas in the School of Government and Public Administration, The American University.

KARL F. HEUMANN, Ph.D., is Director, Office of Documentation, National Academy of Sciences. An organic chemist, Dr. Heumann's scientific information experience includes Minnesota Mining and Manufacturing Company. He was Director of the Chemical Biological Coordination Center, National Research Council, and was Director of Research for *Chemical Abstracts*. Dr. Heumann is a past president of the American Documentation Institute and is a vice president of the International Federation for Documentation.

JAMES HILLIER, Ph.D., is Vice President, RCA Laboratories, Princeton, New Jersey. Dr. Hillier is a physicist who was a pioneer in developing the electron microscope. Since 1953, he has been concerned with the management of research activities. Dr. Hillier is also on the faculty of Princeton University.

PAUL W. HOWERTON is Vice President and Director of the Communication Sciences Division of Information for Industry, Inc., Washington, D.C. Mr. Howerton is a chemist and a linguist. His experience in organizing and managing large information centers includes service as Deputy Assistant Director for Central Reference of the Central Intelligence Agency.

WILLIAM B. KEHL is Director of the Computation and Data Processing Center and Associate Professor of Mathematics at the University of Pittsburgh. Mr. Kehl has developed an information retrieval system using a digital computer. This has been used for legal information retrieval at the Health Law Center of the University of Pittsburgh, and has also been applied to other information problems in a university environment.

CHAUNCEY D. LEAKE, Ph.D., is Professor and Assistant Dean of the College of Medicine, Ohio State University. His professional background is in pharmacology, but his interests in science are manifold. He is past President of the American Association for the Advancement of Science, and was responsible for establishing the section on Information and Communications Science in the AAAS.

H. P. LUHN is a documentation consultant recently retired from the International Business Machines Corporation. During his career at IBM, Mr. Luhn had been engaged in design and development of special purpose machines for information storage and retrieval, and has been identified with several significant innovations including Keyword-in-Context (KWIC), Auto-Abstracting, and Selective Dissemination of Information (SDI).

EDWARD M. McCORMICK is with the Office of Science Information Service, National Science Foundation. He is engaged in activities concerned with the use of digital computers in documentation systems. His experience includes management of a digital computer and data proc-

essing activity for the Navy. Mr. McCormick's background is in mathematics, and he has held positions as an electronic engineer. He is the author of *Digital Computer Primer*.

J. E. MOISE is Acting Manager, Technical Information Division, Esso Research and Engineering Company, Linden, New Jersey. From 1933 to 1958 he was on the staff of Esso Research Laboratories in Baton Rouge. He was appointed Assistant Director of the Laboratories in 1951 and served in that position until his transfer to the Department of Refinery Liaison of the Esso Research and Engineering Company in 1958.

DEWITT O. MYATT is President, Science Communications, Inc., Washington, D.C. Mr. Myatt is a chemical engineer with experience in technical information with Atlantic Research Corporation, The American Chemical Society as Managing Editor of *Industrial and Engineering Chemistry*, and the Tennessee Valley Authority.

SIMON M. NEWMAN is a documentation consultant. He has served the U. S. Patent Office for over 30 years. Trained as a chemist and as a lawyer, Mr. Newman had considerable experience as a patent examiner. He worked in the Research Department of the Patent Office in developing systems for storing and retrieving information for use in patent examination.

JOHN SHERROD is Chief of the Science and Technology Division of the Library of Congress. Prior to joining the Library of Congress in 1952, Mr. Sherrod's professional activities were in meteorology at Pennsylvania State University.

By Lowell H. Hattery
The American University

1. The Systems Concept in Documentation[1]

IN THE FIELD OF SCIENCE INFORMATION we are faced with confusion in terminology. Librarianship, documentation, science information, technical information, science communication are all used to identify areas of concern which may be identical, partially duplicative or exclusive depending on the user of the term and the situation.

Not only does the obfuscative practice of inexact and unstandardized terminology make communication difficult — it also tends to insulate against detailed probes into the nature of operational science communication. Yet, a direct look at situational objectives and processes is needed sorely at the present juncture. The look must encompass the total of a given situation. Implications to be drawn from description of a science information center if the center is the only agent serving a group of scientists are quite different from those to be drawn if a library also exists to serve independently or in concert.

Libraries and information centers are not the only agents to serve the science information function. Nor are the needs and processes the same from one science discipline to another, from one science problem to another, from fundamental research to development and testing, from one organization to another, from one point in time to another, or from one group of scientists to another.

Although there are many variables in science communication, and many conditions which may contribute to confusion, it is possible to develop an orderly approach to science communication in any given situation. The approach is based on the concept of science communications, as a system in which information is produced by Researcher$_1$ and transmitted to Researcher$_2$. (See **Exhibit 1**.)

The next step is the production of information from Researcher$_2$, which may be transmitted to Researcher$_1$ among others, thus closing the loop (**Exhibit 2**).

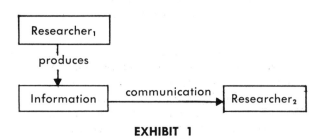

EXHIBIT 1

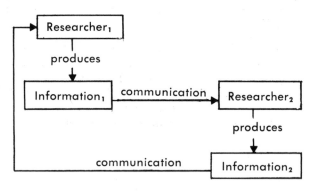

EXHIBIT 2

Complexity is added to this scheme when all researchers are substituted for Researcher$_1$ and Researcher$_2$. Not only are numbers added, but communication must pass barriers of distance, discipline, proprietary interests, patent rights, language and political boundaries. Each of these and other barriers is a matter of concern in the study of science communication.

The barrier of language, for example, suggests such problems as translation, automatic translation, research in syntax, international exchange of literature, and the potential of universal languages such as Interlingua. Illustrations of the characteristics of the language problem are shown in **Exhibit 3**. Yet this diagram only begins to suggest the facets of communication across the language barrier. Who shall do the translation? How will it be financed? What media should be used for the original publication and for publication at subsequent stages? If an abstract only is translated, what arrangements are to be made for full text available to Researcher$_2$? What is the loss in accuracy and subtlety in translation? What is the comparative loss in machine v. individual translation? Are competent translators available? If so, at what cost to more direct contribution to science? We might spin out many more questions or problems related to language in science communication.

MEDIA

In transmitting information from scientist to scientist, various media may be used as illustrated in **Exhibit 4**. It is obvious that the list of seven media is not complete. The medium of professional journals itself can be subclassified into several significantly different groups. As one does so, many related questions arise — questions of editorial policy, financing, distribution, publication time lag, condensation, abstracts, reviews, etc.

Relatively little written information goes direct from scientist to scientist even through the media just referred to. For example, a scientist cannot read the many journals which may be related to his research interest — not only language barriers but the sheer volume of journals in his own field and in related disciplines make it impossible. He must depend heavily on intermediary repositories where information can be stored and later retrieved through classification and index systems. The nature and role of the repository varies according to needs of the person served, nature of the information handled, media, available means and other factors. (See **Exhibit 5**.)

Not only does the matter of repositories or stores of information raise a large number of questions about organization, media, financing, personnel, acquisitions, physical facilities, and dissemination; it also carries with it the necessity for effective systems of classification and indexing. Traditional library classification must be modified or supplemented to meet special needs. Since the primary need is *information* and only secondarily a document, indexing systems take on great significance. As methods and equipment for searching indexes are developed, improvement of indexing systems becomes more important. Effective information storage and retrieval depends very largely on indexing systems and the quality of indexing.

THE SCIENTIST

Thus far the discussion has been directed to what happens *between* researcher and researcher — events from origin to destination. Yet of transcending importance is the scientist himself — the user and producer of information.

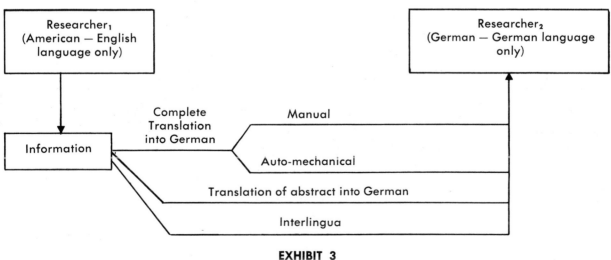

EXHIBIT 3

As a producer, the scientist's thoughts, observations, and findings must be placed into transmissible form. It is interesting to speculate how many useful ideas are not recorded and transmitted and how many potentially useful experimental results never progress beyond the mind of the scientist-observer or beyond his undecipherable notes.

Turning to the user in the system, it is a truism to say that information is useless unless used. "Availability" to the researcher is not achieved unless it is brought into the scientific activity of the researcher in his efforts to produce new information. When, how, and in what order of importance is information utilized by different kinds of researchers on different kinds of problems in different kinds of research situations? Some assumptions and some understanding of this question are fundamental to the purposeful development of science communications systems.

THE CONCEPT OF THE SYSTEM

All of the diagrams shown might be placed into a single complex scheme. The effect is to show the interrelationship of media, libraries, storage, retrieval, translation, indexing, abstracting, electronic sorting, financing, personnel, and other component elements to the simple ordering objective of transmitting ideas and information from one research scientist to another. Science communication is a single, international, multi-lingual, multi-disciplinary, multi-process system.

Planning one element in the system, therefore, is likely to affect another. A change in translation programs may affect the role of libraries. A different mechanism for searching indexes may require a modification of the index. Changes in media affect problems of financing. The system concept in science communication is particularly significant because of the understandable practice of specialists who attempt to solve the problems of an element without reference to the complete system.

LOCALIZED SYSTEMS

We have extended our concept of system to all science communication. We may also focus it to a laboratory, or to a corporation, or to a Federal bureau. Though the number of individuals involved may be reduced to a few thousand, a few hundred, or even a few dozen, much of the detail of a total system concept remains relevant. The set of elements, processes and relationships is sufficiently complex to demand explicit enumeration and description and sets of running rules, understandings, and limits.

As for any administrative study, objectives

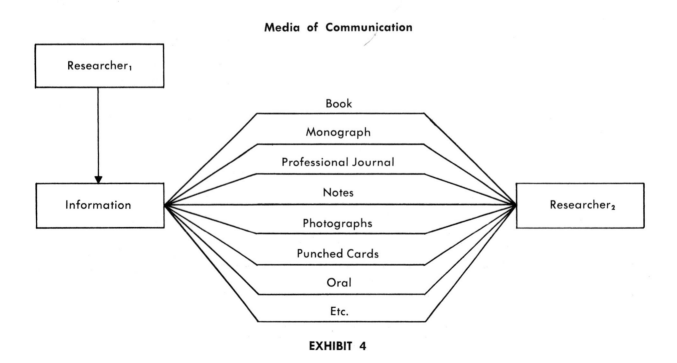

Media of Communication

EXHIBIT 4

and needs set the frame of reference for defining an optimum local science information system. Once these are established, organization, methods, and techniques for achievement are defined. The present resources are assessed. Present limitations and barriers are identified. Desirable changes and additional resources are specified. These steps are well known and accepted in principle. They are not so well known in practice.

This approach immediately establishes the relative roles of libraries and science information centers, formal and informal programs, media, machines, and people. The contribution of a central library is put into perspective along with the contribution of a special or branch library.

An interesting approach to defining the roles for libraries and science information (or documentation) centers has been developed for Russian mechanical engineering industries.[2] Within a "technical information bureau" are: "the technological information group; the technological library; the technical office; and the system of technical information representatives and correspondents in the plant's departments."[3]

Processing the input to the technical information bureau is classified into: "library processing, bibliographic processing or information processing".[4] A detailed table of processing functions is presented for books, periodicals, and other documents. The processing actions for each major activity are as follows:[5]

Library Processing
1. Inclusion in acquisition plans
2. Cataloging
3. Classification and filing of cards
4. Processing and shelving of publications
5. Notification of publications received

Bibliographic Processing
1. Bibliographic description
2. Filing of cards in reference and bibliographic files
3. Reproduction of cards
4. Notification of individuals

Information Processing
1. Distribution of literature and documentation at request of departments
2. Information notification
3. Preparation of reference cards and filing in reference information file
4. Preparation of abstract
5. Making of technical translation
6. Microfilming and photoreproduction
7. Reproduction of material
8. Ordering of material needed
9. Assembling selections on particular topics
10. Inclusion in work plan, amendment of plan.

This illustration suggests an approach to a definition of functions and assignment of responsibility which is an essential first step to the development of an orderly, complete library-information program.

COSTS OF SCIENCE INFORMATION

For advance planning, budgetary controls and evaluations, cost estimates of the science

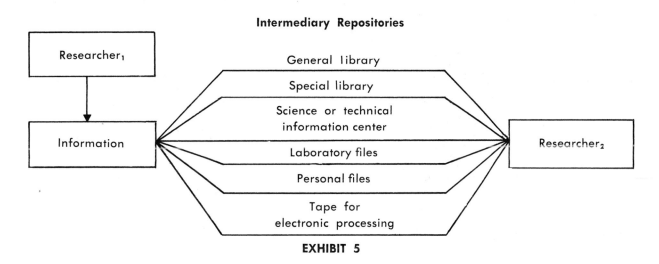

Intermediary Repositories

Researcher₁ → Information

General library
Special library
Science or technical information center
Laboratory files
Personal files
Tape for electronic processing

→ Researcher₂

EXHIBIT 5

information system are needed. Cost analysis should include resources directed to informal as well as formal processes. Cost evaluation should take into account the penalties attached to lack of information as well as the values of the information program provided.

As an increasing number of persons point out, trends in expenditures for science information services run far behind other support for research and development activities. It is probable that one reason for this disparity is that the need for experimental equipment such as a new laboratory instrument is more readily demonstrable than the need for information. This situation makes better cost analysis of the science information function more important.

RESPONSIBILITY FOR SCIENCE INFORMATION

There are several factors identified or implied in the preceding discussion which relate to the location of responsibility for science information, planning, and operations. Scientist producers and users continue to be key elements in the system. But the complexity of the system, the extension of information processes beyond those of the traditional library, an extraordinary concern with a multitude of external relationships, the availability of new machines and techniques for information storage and retrieval, and an increasing tendency to develop and define non-science information systems within organizations, all tend to push upward prime responsibility for the science information system.

Precisely where this responsibility should lie depends on many special conditions. The slow but inevitable rise in status of the administrative information function has led to the designation of a vice president or the equivalent for internal information systems. Although this arrangement does not ordinarily include the science information system, it does include information processing machines and personnel essential to some aspects of a modern, effective science information system. It includes the systems analysts who can contribute to definition, plans, and operations for the science information system.

Substantive planning and operational control, however, are properly assigned in part to professional personnel associated with the scientific and technical program, reporting typically to a vice president for research and development.

It is a short step to recognition that the science information problem requires the joint contribution of professional knowledge, understanding and skills of the scientist, the systems analyst, the librarian, and the information or data processing specialist. This combination forms the basis for defining a new professional field of science information (or documentation). Several universities are developing curricula designed to train science information specialists to meet modern needs of documentation. The American Institute of Biological Sciences has recently announced a program, supported by the National Institutes of Health, to train science information specialists in biology in a cooperative arrangement with The American University. Selected trainees undertake internship projects under the direction of the Biological Sciences Communications Project of the AIBS and enroll for Master of Arts or Doctor of Philosophy degrees in Public Administration at The American University with special emphasis on documentation and related fields. Several schools of library science are extending their curricula to include special training in science information and data processing.

SUMMARY

The science information function can be conceived and designed as a system. The nature of the current science information problem calls for high level organizational attention. The planning and operation of a science operation system and many of its elements calls for a combination of knowledge, understanding and skills which is bringing a new profession into focus — the science information specialist or documentalist.

REFERENCES

[1] Exhibits 1 - 5 and some of the descriptive material are taken from Lowell H. Hattery, "Information and Communication in Biological Science — A Report Prepared for the Biological Sciences Communication Project," *American Institute of Biological Sciences*, December, 1961.

[2] Aram S. Melik-Shakhnasarov, *Technical Information in the U.S.S.R.* Translated from Russian by Boris Gorokhoff. Massachusetts Institute of Technology Libraries, Cambridge, Mass., 1961. 122 pp.

[3] *Ibid.*, p. 36.

[4] *Ibid.*, p. 25.

[5] *Ibid.*, pp. 26-35.

By **Chauncey D. Leake**
The Ohio State University

2. What Must Give in the Documentation Crisis?

SOMETHING HAS TO GIVE in our current crisis in documentation. Like an overblown balloon, science is ready to burst its conventional bounds. If something does not give, we are going to be drowned in the flood of our scientific knowledge.

A moratorium on the publication of scientific findings has been proposed. This suggestion comes snidely from uncomprehending humanists who claim to want time for people generally to be able to absorb what science is all about. This is not a satisfactory answer to the problem. We must continue the prompt publication of the results of scientific studies in order to accumulate that verifiable information about ourselves and our environment which is essential for wise policy decisions, whether private or public. Clearly the conventional methods of documentation are not adequate to the task of handling the current flood of scientific information. What gives?

The bare statistics, whether for scientific periodicals, for abstracts, or for indexes, are discouraging in their mountainous size. Thanks to various mechanizing devices, we are beginning to see a little hope of being able to handle the necessary indexing of what is being reported. However, in the publication of original scientific information, and in its abstracting and reviewing, we are floundering and desperately wondering what we may be able to do about it.

PURPOSES IN DOCUMENTATION

In order to keep ourselves oriented in our documentation problem, let us consider what it is we are trying to do. To begin, I think we can all agree that verifiable knowledge about ourselves and our environment is essential for us so that we may make satisfactory public policy decisions on ways and means of maintaining or increasing our individual and social satisfactions. John Locke (1632-1704) made this clear in his consideration of the psychology of democracy. His point was extended in our country by Benjamin Franklin's insistence on free public libraries. It was extended further by Thomas Jefferson's insistence on free public schools. In both instances, the purpose was to make it possible for people in every community to have access to the same body of "sound information," as Locke called it, and thus be prepared to make wise public policy decisions. On this basis, scientific information, the best of "sound information," must continually be available for our people.

The main function of science documentation, therefore, would seem to be to arrange ways and means by which scientific information can best be collected, preserved, analyzed, indexed, abstracted, reviewed, translated, and interpreted, for two purposes: (1) that scientists generally might know what is going on, and (2) that people generally might understand something of what science is about, and what it may mean to them in comfort, health, convenience, and satisfaction.

The collection and preservation of scientific information is the basic responsibility of libraries. Libraries also have the taxonomic job of classifying it, analyzing it, and indexing it, so that it may readily be found when needed. Is this enough?

The collecting, classifying, indexing, and retrieving of scientific information might seem to be a simple clerical task. In order to be useful, however, whether to scientists or to people generally, the ever growing and changing scientific information must be analyzed so that there may be an effective taxonomic approach for satisfactory indexing.

It is unfair to think of librarians in scientific libraries as being merely clerks. Skilled librarians in good science libraries are really part of the scientific team. They participate in the group research endeavor by anticipating what already published scientific material may be helpful to the scientists who are at the bench. The reference function of a good science library is an extremely important one in modern scientific effort.

It is always interesting to watch capable scientists work in a library. More and more it is becoming necessary to have the current scientific material right out on shelves where it can readily be found. This is the prime function of the current periodical room, which is increasing in size every year. The rapid scanning of periodicals by individual scientists, even if they are well acquainted with their respective fields, is an increasingly time consuming and difficult task. Such a device as *Current Contents* gives an opportunity for quick weekly scanning of major scientific journals as they are published, so that scientists can title-scan the current reports as they appear. They may then quickly note what it is that they may wish to examine.

Increasingly, libraries must make readily available the large and growing indexes to current scientific information, so that scientists may be able to find quickly what specific references they may wish. The library card catalog requires continual revision and analysis, with cross reference, in order to aid in quick retrieval.

No matter how carefully a library may maintain the current periodical room and index references, there may still be frustration for the scientists who do not know exactly what it is they wish to find. This is why it is becoming increasingly important that current monographs and reviews, particularly those for the last ten years or so, be kept on open shelves where browsing scientists may see the title that will give them the idea of where they may find what they seek.

The essential purposes in science documentation are to handle the flood of scientific publications in such a way that specific factual data may promptly be found, as well as analyses of their significance. Adequate science documentation also should include syntheses of scientific trends, with indications of relations to other factual data, or to significant applications.

INDEXING AND ABSTRACTING

Indexing always seems to be a compromise. Most scientific publications contain much more significant information than can ever be indicated by a title. Titles are often deceptive. If an effort is made to be precise in a title, it may become too long. Then it becomes difficult to index satisfactorily, especially if adequate cross reference is to be given.

Nevertheless, very helpful mechanical devices are being developed for useful indexing, and these are being utilized by *Chemical Abstracts*, *Biological Abstracts* and *Index Medicus*. These are meeting many of the objections to the older hand labor indexes. At least they can appear contemporaneously with the material that is being indexed. Are these mechanical devices to be adequate as scientific reporting doubles in another decade?

Chemical indexes have a definite taxonomic advantage over indexes to biological and medical reports. Chemistry has an exact system of nomenclature, precisely organized so as to be able to handle any conceivable chemical compound. It is taxonomically stable, even with the introduction of new chemical concepts.

On the other hand, biological and medical terminology is subject to great change. This occurs with improved etiological understanding of disease, and with new insights regarding the relationships of various kinds of living material. This causes many taxonomic difficulties. With inevitable changes in terminology, the systems of indexing for biology and medicine can have little stability. Much confusion results on attempted retrieval of past information, which may be indexed under different terms than those which are used now. Much potentially valuable scientific information may thus get lost.

There is much speculation about the possibility of computers being used for medical diagnosis. This will be practically impossible until there is a stable taxonomy for disease, and this may be a long way in the future. The best that could be done now, even with our most advanced concepts and mechanization, would be to give the probabilities that a particular set of symptoms observed in a patient might be diagnostically indicative of a specific disease concept. Information on the key symptom for an accurate diagnosis, however, might be lacking completely.

It is particularly important in effective retrieval of scientific information to study indexing in depth. This has been well attempted by Dr. Isaac Welt, first under the auspices of the National Research Council, and now working through the Institute of Medical Communication. Indexing in depth is applicable only to relatively circumscribed areas of scientific interest, such as cancer, or drugs acting on the cardiovascular system.

Indexing in depth involves the careful reading of original articles and noting whatever scientific information or data of possible significance is included, and making cross references so that this information can be retrieved. For example, in compiling an index in depth on the effects of drugs on the cardiovascular system, one may list all drugs in the literature examined against the biological effects produced by these drugs. One can also list various biological effects which are possible, and then place against such a list the various drugs which produce these actions. There is thus provided a cross-index of great power and usefulness. The bulk of this sort of information is not to be derived from the titles of the articles, so ordinary indexing by title would not give the information that is available.

Many of these problems of indexing were recognized a couple of decades ago in what is now the National Library of Medicine. Under the leadership of the late Colonel Wellington Jones, General Joseph McNinch, and now Dr. Frank B. Rogers, the National Library of Medicine has exhaustively studied the indexing problem and set up a highly efficient mechanized system for compiling the *Index Medicas*. Nevertheless, this is under strain. A computer center system is being devised. It is called MEDLARS (not the dictionary's "crabapple" but an acronymn for "Medical Literature Analysis and Retrieval System").

MEDLARS is scheduled to begin operation in another year or so. With it, *Index Medicas*, which now indexes 130,000 articles a year from 1,800 periodicals, should be able within a few years to handle 250,000 articles annually from 6,000 journals. Subject headings which now run about 5,000 can be increased to 12,000. The articles will have to be coded by human analysts, but this coded information can be placed in computer storage, so that on command the computer can print out a compendium of whatever set of entries are desired in a format ready for publication. This can compile bibliographies by subject.

Dr. Rogers is quite specific about what MEDLARS can do: "It is not a system for picking out and reproducing the articles themselves . . . Something else is called for which no computer can supply. This is intelligence — human intelligence. MEDLARS will respond to questions which are asked as precisely as possible in terms of the system. Frankly, many people don't know how to ask questions at all. A person who walks in and asks for a bibliography on diabetes will have to decide exactly what he wants to know about diabetes. He may even have to define what he means by diabetes. If he knows what he wants, we can help him."

Here is the scientific situation in a neat capsule: Ask the right kind of questions, and scientific effort may be able to provide the answers. It is the appropriate kind of questions that we need to bring up for consideration in respect to indexing, abstracting, and other aspects of documentation. When we ask these questions in an appropriate manner, we may be able to get fitting answers that may help solve our dilemmas.

Abstracting is an art. It is particularly well developed in chemistry, medicine and psychology. It is dependent entirely upon human judgment, usually the judgment of experts in the particular field that is being abstracted.

The flood of articles worthy of being abstracted is, however, becoming so vast that the system shows signs of cracking. There are many practical and theoretical reasons for looking carefully into the whole proposition of abstracting scientific publications. The abstracting process may break down in practice because of sheer bulk; theoretically, it may be questioned whether or not even a "good" abstract is much better than the title of the article in a "good" index. Frequently the original articles must be consulted by the scientists who need specific information, unless the indexing has been in depth.

Abstracts may be unsatisfactory because they are too brief and do not give all the essential information, or because they are as detailed as the original article itself. Quite often one will find an abstract in *Chemical*

Abstracts which will run to a column and a half of fine print, when the original article itself may only be a couple of pages.

Abstracts themselves must be indexed if they are to be useful, and this is a problem equally as difficult as indexing original articles. There is another trouble: an index to abstracts is by no means a comprehensive index of the field. Abstracts are selective. For some reason or other, many original contributions may not be abstracted anywhere. Worthiness for abstracting is usually an individual judgment: who may say when some other individual may find something quite worthwhile in the article that has not been abstracted?

Nevertheless, abstract journals do have one great function: they do bring together at one time and place the important contemporaneous contributions that are being made in any particular scientific field. They thus can save a great deal of time in scanning. Certainly the great success of *Chemical Abstracts, Biological Abstracts, Excerpta Medica,* and *Psychological Abstracts* testifies eloquently to their usefulness and need. Those who have been responsible for developing these great abstract services deserve the abiding thanks of all scientists.

An exceptionally well organized and standardized abstracting system, with effective cross-indexing, has been developed by the Federation of American Societies for Experimental Biology, under the direction of Milton O. Lee. Nearly 3,000 abstracts for the great annual meeting are assembled, classified, indexed, and distributed within 10 weeks time. The resulting publication runs well over 500 pages of double column offset, but it serves as an indispensable adjunct to the meeting program (of 212 pages itself!), which is classified by titles and cross references to the abstracts.

One might think from the increasing excellence of our scientific indexing and abstracting services that we are well on the way to solving the documentation crisis. This is by no means the case. The best possible indexing and abstracting of scientific literature is not enough to make this verifiable information about ourselves and our environment available for appropriate application in bringing us the satisfaction we want. No matter how skillfully indexed and abstracted scientific information may be, it still has to be analyzed, digested, correlated, and prepared in such a way that it can become the basis for wise individual public policy decisions.

REVIEWS

From my own personal experience in trying to handle scientific information, I am becoming more and more convinced that we need to put particular effort and emphasis on critical reviewing. I have had experience as a librarian of medical school libraries, as an abstracter, and as a bench and working scientist. Over the course of many years, I have found that I can orient myself best into a field of science in which I am working, or am expecting to work, by reading carefully such critical reviews on the subject as may be available. I've had experience in attempting critical reviews also, and I can testify directly to the very strenuous effort involved.

We have critical reviews in such fields as physics, chemistry, biology, physiology, and pharmacology. Many of our better medical journals also include carefully analyzed reviews on practical medical problems. Many of these reviews become classic starting posts for the most effective kind of scientific endeavor. We need many more critical reviews.

It is interesting that *Annual Reviews* is aware of the necessity of critical analysis and correlation. It is not enough merely to list each year the important contributions that the reviewer thinks may have been made in a particular subject. Annual reviews in any subject must be critical, analytical and correlative, in order to be helpful. The great success of *Annual Reviews,* and of other special review journals, again is direct testimony to the long range value and importance of this type of documentation activity.

My own feeling is that the scientific research team is incomplete without a competent library scientist. Such a person should have equal status with the bench and working scientists. Such a scientist requires special training and background.

The library scientist should be familiar with basic scientific principles and concepts. Library scientists should know how to judge the scientific validity of scientific reports. They should know how to appraise data, and they should have wise judgment in regard to the soundness of conclusions drawn from scientific data. Furthermore, they should be able to show significant correlations between individual scientific reports, so that trends and developing concepts may promptly be recognized and utilized.

Library scientists would need much training in judgment. This comes best from intensive study in the humanities, including languages, literature, and history, including the history of the fine arts as well as the history of science. They should have a broad acquaintance with general philosophical concepts. Furthermore, library scientists should be able to write easily and succinctly.

It is clear from this outline of the appropriate qualifications for the library scientist in a research endeavor that the position is a challenging and worthy one, and that it deserves full status, salary and recognition. If library scientists really do have the kind of judgment which I have indicated, they might well become the scientific reporters for the scientific research effort. Some improvement thus might follow in the literary quality of our scientific publications.

If satisfactory reviewing of scientific contributions can be developed, it might diminish the pressure to extend our abstracting services. Actually, I think our abstracting services would be wise to include review articles as a regular feature of their respective periodical publications.

Library scientists could well become those who are particularly familiar with scientific literature and the ways and means by which it may most effectively be handled. It would be their responsibility to tell the working scientists in the group what information may be pertinent to the problem at hand, and what actual data may already be available on it.

It is well recognized that teamwork has become an essential aspect of our scientific research endeavor. It is not likely any more that any single individual will be able to make a major scientific contribution alone. Certainly under economic and national pressures, the teamwork approach will expand, and it will be necessary for the scientific research team to meet together, perhaps daily, to go over the work as it proceeds, to coordinate it, and to continue to supply that enthusiasm and curiosity that is essential for success in scientific effort. In this kind of increasing teamwork in scientific research, the library scientists may become among the most valued and respected members of the team.

If library scientists have the appropriate judgment for correlating isolated bits of scientific information and determining trends and significance, they may be well qualified to act as interpreters of scientific advance for the people at large. Library scientists could well serve as the point of contact with professional science writers, so that all aspects of the scientific research program could be presented in such a way that intelligent people could understand what it's about.

I think there is a great and challenging opportunity for library scientists in our future scientific advance. If we can successfully develop such a group of qualified workers, in the increasingly necessary division of labor in scientific research, we may provide a background for aiding materially in our documentation crisis. Critical reviews can certainly help. They can point clearly to the status of the scientific development in any particular field at that particular moment. They can indicate the gaps to be filled. They can show the inadequacies of previous approaches. They can stimulate to fulfill the promise of indicated trends.

IN PROSPECT

In his interesting *Science Since Babylon*, Derek de Solla Price has a chapter devoted to "Diseases of Science." The most significant disease of modern science seems to be an exponential increase in number of publications. This is reflected in the logarithmic growth of scientific journals, which may approach 1,000,000 in another half century. The data so vividly arranged by Doctor Price are frightening.

Many proposals have been made about collecting scientific data in regional repositories, with brief abstracts appearing in scientific journals, so that scientists may know what information is accumulating. This device, even though it might cut down the number of publications in scientific literature, would still require effective indexing and reviewing in order to be useful.

Whatever device may develop to reduce the number of scientific publications would be a welcome respite, provided that we could be certain that the scientific information accumulating would not be lost.

All indications point to the increasing significance of library scientists in handling our documentation crisis. It may be that the crisis will yield to the development of an effective technique for critical reviewing by specially trained library scientists. Library scientists may be increasingly expected to become a significant part of research team effort. Library scientists might just as well be trained and encouraged to undertake critical reviewing, so that the general status of an area of science can quickly be estimated.

Here, as in any other aspect of science, much depends on the responsibility which can be developed by those who are concerned with any phase of handling scientific literature. Library scientists, of the type I have been advocating, would have a heavy burden of responsibility in accurate, non-biased, and comprehensive appraisal of the scientific information accumulating in their fields of interest. Further, the working scientists would have to repose a great deal of trust and confidence in library scientists, in order that the mutual division of labor could proceed smoothly. This all takes a high level of individual self-discipline oriented toward the collective social good.

Various aspects of automation will aid in the documentation crisis. We will be certain to get more satisfactory and comprehensive indexes. We will develop indexing in depth, so that the conventional abstracting service may again be challenged. The current crisis in scientific documentation may give quite a bit, without bursting, if we can develop a successful method of critical reviewing, with competent review scientists, who would have status, and in whose efforts both working scientists and the general public would have confidence.

With international concern over the crisis in science documentation there is much talk and some progress. A well attended international congress on scientific information was held in Washington, D.C. in November, 1958, and a huge volume of discussion resulted. Jesse H. Shera is editing for International Publishers of New York and London an important serial on *Advances in Documentation and Library Science*. H. P. Yockey edited a helpful *Symposium on Information Theory in Biology* (Pergamon Press, London, 1958, 418 pp.). Communication theory is developing with elaborate mathematical analyses, and cybernetics is an established scientific discipline with vast applications in computer technique. The American Association for the Advancement of Science established at its Denver 1961 meeting a Section on Scientific Information and Communication. Very significantly, the Committee on Government Operations of the United States Senate has a keen staff studying and reporting on documentation, indexing, and retrieval of scientific information. With these many pronged attacks upon it, it would seem that there is certain to be some yielding in our science documentation crisis.

By Julius N. Cahn
Staff, U. S. Senate Committee on
Government Operations

3. A System of Information Systems

RECENTLY THERE HAS BEEN increasing discussion throughout the nation on the subject of national goals. More and more observers have expressed the view that, in this perilous age, the United States cannot afford to drift in any phase of science and technology. These observers have suggested that we need to select our national objectives for the years ahead. Only then, they contend, can we:

(a) establish the *priorities* of the respective goals,

(b) set a *time-table* for accomplishment,

(c) allocate our limited *resources* accordingly, and

(d) *monitor* our progress.

It is the purpose of this statement to urge that a national goal be established for a System of Information Systems. This goal would consist of two complementary objectives:

(1) A *Federal* System of Information Systems linking the information activities of agencies of the United States government.

(2) A *national* System of Information Systems linking, to the extent which they may voluntarily regard as feasible and desirable, as many of the *non-governmental* information resources as possible.

Attainment of both objectives requires a greater degree of voluntary collaboration than has ever before been achieved. This includes collaboration within government, among governmental and private groups, and among private groups themselves. Both objectives can be fulfilled; indeed, they must be fulfilled, if other national goals are to be achieved.

AN ORGANIC UNITY OF INTERRELATED PARTS

But fulfillment requires, first, understanding. A system, as it is used in this regard, implies an organic unity of inter-dependent operations. It implies effective organization for optimal input and output; a logical flow of work, step by step; feedback from part to part; fulfillment of *separate* purposes by each part and of *common* purpose by all parts.

A System of Information Systems is required because information is, in effect, a national resource. The resource can be maximized only if it can be made more than a jumble of fragments. Information must be assembled for the good of the republic. (Certainly, enemies are determined to use our pool of information for the detriment of this nation; we can hardly afford to ignore their diligent use or to under-organize or under-utilize our own information.)

All types of information in our nation cannot be generally utilized; some information must necessarily be withheld on national security or proprietary grounds. But tax-supported, non-classified, non-proprietary information is the property of the American people.

A POSSIBLE INFORMATION NETWORK

As a substitute for the concept of a "System of Systems," some observers have suggested different analogies. Some have used the concept of an "Information Network". It would consist of a series of "stations", each of which would serve a particular audience, but which would transmit over the equivalent of "coaxial lines" or "microwave" the best of centrally prepared material as well. Still other observers have used the concept of a "central information switchboard", such as serves independent telephone companies, or of a "grid" such as electric utilities provide, feeding power from one location to another at times of peak loads. Whatever the analogy, an urge for togetherness can be observed, a will to explore the possibility of common answers to common problems.

The time appears ripe for a bold plan to fulfill the urge, to make a System of Systems a living reality. The times offer many "signs and portents" that an historic opportunity is now available.

What are these "signs and portents"? Some are material — strong actions taken by a variety of Federal, professional, commercial and other organizations.

Leadership — the indispensable prerequisite for action — is being demonstrated in deeds.

Much of the evidence, however, consists merely of comments by key individuals, indicating that they are in a mood for cooperative action. Many leaders of scientific and engineering societies, for example, now seem to recognize that present and foreseeable circumstances have made information needs acute; remedial programs which they might have viewed with quick misgivings only a few years ago would apparently now receive more sympathetic consideration.

Such recognition is not universal and it is not uniform; but it does exist in many places. Here are a few of the straws in the wind:

INTEREST AT HIGHEST FEDERAL POLICY LEVEL

The most important single sign is the deep interest which has been manifest at the highest policy level within the executive branch of the United States government.

The Office of the Special Assistant to the President for Science and Technology has been giving intensive attention to the information problem. The Special Assistant, Dr. Jerome Wiesner, has empaneled an expert group on science information in the President's Science Advisory Committee, under the Chairmanship of Dr. Alvin Weinberg, Director of the Oak Ridge National Laboratory.

THRUST FROM FEDERAL RESEARCH AND DEVELOPMENT OUTLAY

The thrust of scientific and engineering research and development on the part of the United States government has inevitably brought about a quickening of interest in information problems.

In the 1963 fiscal year, it is estimated that Federal agencies will request authorization for $12.3 billion of expenditures in research, development, testing and evaluation.[1]

Of this vast sum, $7.1 billion are being requested by the Department of Defense for military functions, $2.1 billion by the National Aeronautics and Space Administration, $1.1 billion by the Atomic Energy Commission.[2]

For medical and health related research and research facilities of all types, $1 billion are being requested in the 1963 fiscal year, including $756 million for the Department of Health, Education, and Welfare. Of this latter sum, $679 million are being requested for the National Institutes of Health.[3]

Perhaps the most dramatic thrust derives from the nation's space effort. President Kennedy had proposed, and the Congress had approved as a national goal, a ten year program of expeditions and experiments in outer space.

Over $5.4 billion in new obligational authority are being requested for Federal space programs in the 1963 fiscal year. Of this sum, N.A.S.A. would receive $3.7 billion, D.O.D. $1.5 billion, A.E.C. $193 million, the Weather Bureau in the Department of Commerce $47 million, and the National Science Foundation $1.7 million.[4]

N.A.S.A.'s information needs probably represent the most urgent, the most comprehensive, the most complex such needs of any civilian agency in American history. Timely, efficient achievement of N.A.S.A.'s 10 year program will, in my personal judgment, require a virtual revolution in the processes of storage, retrieval and dissemination of scientific and technical information. The implementation of N.A.S.A.'s blueprints for its information program will have a profound impact on other governmental agencies, as well as on non-governmental organizations.

In turn, the effectiveness of N.A.S.A.'s programs depends upon the fullest cooperation of information resources outside the agency.

IDENTIFICATION OF PART OF INFORMATION EXPENDITURES

A third sign is the Federal government's identification, for the first time, of at least part of the total of government-wide expenditures for scientific and technical information.

It is estimated that for the 1962 fiscal year, at least $98.6 million will be obligated for Federal support of certain scientific and technical information programs. This estimate includes what the National Science Foundation regards as "reasonably sound" determination of obligations for intra-mural performance.

But, N.S.F. carefully notes, the estimated data relating to extra-mural scientific and technical information "exclude-[s] obligations for such informational activities performed as a supplemental service under a contract or grant primarily for research and development or scientific education and training."

N.S.F. states, too, that "Authorities in the scientific information field have estimated that this amount may exceed $100 million for fiscal year 1962."[5]

Now that these first estimates have been made, we may expect increased legislative and executive branch attention to the efficiency and economy of in-house and extra-mural information outlay. Particular attention is likely to be given to that vast portion of the latter area of spending for which accounting is not now available.

MECHANIZATION OF
INFORMATION SERVICE

The trend toward mechanization continues throughout major Federal agencies. This trend makes possible, indeed it renders essential, efforts to assure reasonable compatibility between the machine systems.

Each of the three great national libraries has mechanization very much in mind. The National Library of Medicine is scheduled to bring into operation two years hence its precedent-making "MEDLARS" (Medical Literature Automatic Retrieval Service.)

The Library of the United States Department of Agriculture will be part of a Task Force on Automation to consider the problems of all of U.S.D.A.'s documentation. The task force may work under the auspices of the Office of Management Appraisal and Systems Development.

The Library of Congress has had the benefit of the services of a team of experts in computer technology, data processing systems, operations analysis and information storage and retrieval, through a grant from the Council on Library Resources.

To this list could be added similar studies, surveys and plans for new or strengthened mechanization on the part of other Federal agencies. Federal officials are naturally noting similar trends abroad, particularly on the part of Soviet scientific and engineering installations, including activities in machine translation.[6] The pace in the international information race continues to accelerate.

DIRECT CALLS FOR COORDINATION

The clearest evidence of what may be the "shape of things to come" may be seen in the direct calls for more coordinated governmental and Federal-private programs.

Lt. General Arthur Trudeau, Chief of Research and Development for the Department of the Army has, for example, called for:[7]

"S.A.T.I.C. — a Scientific and Technological Information Center — a national clearing house for the most complete and comprehensive acquisition, translation and exchange of information that we can get from all segments of our nation and from the rest of the free world."

An engineering journal has stated:[8]

"Above all, in this country we need a central agency to coordinate the overall information effort; winnow the total production; and pick up the loose ends like foreign publications, research bulletins, graduate theses, government reports and papers delivered at conferences. Organizing and operating such an institution would be an effort no bigger than others we have made, no more ponderous than others the government has shouldered and carried home. It would deserve to be called investment rather than extravagance."

It should be recalled that four years ago, experts at the School of Library Science, Western Reserve University, Jesse H. Shera, Allen Kent and James W. Perry, had proposed that:[9]

" . . . a national center for the coordination of scientific and technical information be created, which will achieve an effective balance among centralized processing of the world's published literature, cooperative activity with other processing centers, and provision of direct or indirect services to individuals, research groups, or specialized information centers."

For additional and more recent evidence, we may turn to a specialized area of communication — within medical science. Charles E. Lyght, M.D., noted an appeal by Senator Hubert H. Humphrey for improved information management and stated:[10]

"Sentiments of this kind deserve applause. Any knowledgeable medical research worker knows how slow and faulty communication lines can be at embarrassingly crucial moments . . .

"Perhaps the best response is to encourage Senator Humphrey and his colleagues to survey the problem immediately, thoroughly, and objectively. Then they might consider approaching the host of independent information-gathering facilities throughout the country with an invitation to pool as much of their know-how as feasible and to pour as much of their own data as permissible into a flexible collaborative storehouse and exchange system. Such cooperation could prove mutually rewarding and would be justified as a wise investment of both public and private funds.

"Through a series of compartmented conferences sponsored by the government, the needs of biomedical researchers, medical writers, editors, abstracters, librarians, electronic specialists, and others could be determined and their invaluable experience utilized toward converting 'medical communications' into more than a high-sounding phrase."

There is by no means agreement on the modus operandi for achieving increased coordination. Particularly moot is the issue of what the ultimate Federal role should be. Many observers express deep concern lest a monolithic Federal information operation be attempted. But the urgent need for increased Federal and for public-private teamwork is now conceded virtually everywhere.

POLICYMAKERS' INCREASED UNDERSTANDING

Within the administrative echelons of government, some policy makers now recognize the varied nature of scientific and technical information and its overall significance.

They appreciate that comprehensive, up-to-the-minute information of all types is crucial for administrative decision making, for budgeting, and for bench purposes.

Many recognize, too, that the inter-agency nature of many Federal research and development programs requires pooling of inter-agency administrative and scientific information to a greater extent than heretofore.

It is probable that these informed policy makers are still in the minority. Most officials still tend to view information in a less significant light and largely in an intra-agency context. They see it as an "auxiliary" service, as a part of "overhead". As such, the operation of a library or an information center may, if necessary, be curtailed — relatively casually — like electric utility or other "house-keeping" service. Officials with this view do not yet regard information as an integral part of research and development.

This view of many administrators is not shared by an increasing number of scientists and engineers. They, by contrast, are articulating a more and more insistent demand for improved Federal and non-Federal information services. The demand is far from universal; it is far from uniform; but it is rising.

RECOGNITION OF NEED FOR NATIONAL REFERRAL SERVICE

The need for a national referral service is increasingly recognized. Fortunately, the need has long been recognized by the National Science Foundation, Office of Science Information Service, and plans for such a service — to be conducted by the Library of Congress — are now in the making.

At present, no Federal source has the responsibility of maintaining central information as to *all* Federal and Federally-supported information resources. The result is that no matter how conscientious and helpful any one information office or library or center may be, it is not in a position to give judgment outside its field of competence and responsibility to an inquirer as to which other sources he might profitably contact.

It has long been felt by expert observers that the nation's scientific and engineering community should be enabled to tap into the total Federal information system at any one or more points and get the benefit of leads to information available throughout the entire system.

It simply cannot be assumed that even the best informed inquirer, in or outside of government, will be familiar offhand with all the many resources which might be contacted on any given subject.

INFORMATION RESOURCES INVENTORY

Only now does the Federal government itself possess a definitive inventory of the nation's scientific information resources.

A landmark study[11] sponsored by the Office of Science Information Service and conducted by the Battelle Memorial Institute, has identified 427 different organizations or projects throughout the nation. Criteria for the listing were carefully applied. All of the listed resources specialize in some subject area; all provide some type of information service beyond the publication of a periodical. All are currently operational and are available to some segment of the scientific community, provided security, proprietary, society membership or other described restrictions are met. Only services indicating some degree of service beyond their immediate organization have been listed.

The 427 groups represent a winnowing from an original potential list of some 10,000 organizations which were identified by response to N.S.F. press releases or by selection from directories, association lists, registers or reference files.

The U. S. Air Force has also recently published a helpful guide[12] to organizations within its area of interest.

With the help of these and other inventories, it is now possible to take many steps which were not previously possible or practical.

These steps include:

(a) comprehensively informing specialized segments of the science and engineering communities of all the services within their particular field of interest; and

(b) encouraging individual services within a given area of interest to open up or strengthen discussion among themselves so as to increase cooperation. Illustration of the types of cooperation would be possible use of a common thesaurus of "key words" or "descriptors" as guides to the information systems, possible efforts to minimize unintended overlapping, etc.

DESIRE FOR ALL TYPES OF INFORMATION

Another phase of increased understanding is a change from the traditional view that the scientist or engineer is allegedly interested only, or essentially, in one type of information, i.e., in the contents of professional journals, in serial articles, or in published proceedings or books, together with their abstracts and index guides.

It is increasingly recognized that many an inquirer would like to have access to much or all of the *total* of information, whatever its nature or format, which may be available on any given subject or subtopic.

"Access" does not, of course, mean that the inquirer wants or could possibly use or digest all the information; but it indicates he wants the assurance that he knows where the information generally is, what it may comprise, and how he or his librarian can get it if he so desires.

In effect, the inquirer may, in individual circumstances, want the published, the unpublished and the prepublished.

He may want:

— summaries of Federally supported research and development projects which are still in progress;

— technical progress reports on such projects;

— completed reports;

— graduate these, in process or completed;

— translations of foreign articles, monographs and books;

— bibliographies, prepared by Federal or non-Federal sources, particularly if annotated;

— reviews, preferably of an evaluative, not merely descriptive nature;

— audio-visuals;

— or any of a variety of other types of information.

SOCIETIES' PROPOSED STUDY OF NATIONAL PLAN

Officers of many of the major scientific and engineering societies have demonstrated that they feel the time is appropriate to plan for a national system.

The National Federation of Science Abstracting and Indexing Services has made application to the National Science Foundation, Office of Science Information Service, for support of a management-type survey of the needs and opportunities for a national system. Many or all of the member societies of the federation are well aware of the enormous costs which implementation of such a national system might entail. Even at present, the principal societies are hard pressed to provide publishing, abstracting and indexing services for their clienteles. But the societies seem more willing today than ever before to come to grips more decisively with the challenge now confronting them and their colleagues and looming in the years ahead.

These, then, are a few of the signs and portents on the national information scene and on the national horizon.

FORTHCOMING SUBCOMMITTEE STAFF REPORT

Other propitious circumstances could be enumerated by way of confirming that now is the right time to initiate vigorous follow-through.

The circumstances are set forth in a staff report scheduled for publication by the Subcommittee on Reorganization and International Organizations of the Senate Committee on Government Operations. The tentative title of the report is "The Crisis and Opportunity in Scientific and Technical Information".

This report will summarize progress in scientific and technical information since the committee and the subcommittee began their review of the problem more than 3½ years ago. The report will pick up from where four previous committee and subcommittee reports and prints left off.

Thus, it will supplement:

(a) the two reports [13,14] on "hardware" and "software" in agency information systems, and

(b) the two reports [15,16] on management of information on *current* research and development (as distinguished from information on *completed* projects).

It is not now possible to preview in detail all of the findings in the staff report. But Senator Humphrey has been anxious to help the scientific and engineering communities move ahead as rapidly as possible in their own plans. Therefore, I am in a position at this time to submit at least a tentative listing of a few of the possible staff recommendations.

1. *National goal.*

The objective of a System of Information Systems should be established as a national goal.

Based on inter-agency agreement and on the consensus of non-governmental organization, there should be formulated, to the extent that it is procedurally and fiscally practical, a national program, national time-table and national allocation of resources.

2. *High level unit.*

Progress toward a Federal System of Information Systems should be monitored at the highest level within the executive branch.

An organization unit specializing on information should be established within the Executive Office of the President. It may be recalled that the Subcommittee on National Policy Machinery, of the Senate Government Operations Committee, has proposed an Office of Science and Technology be set up there.

If such an office is established, it should have an information unit. On the advice of the Director, U. S. Bureau of the Budget; Director, Office of Science Information Service, National Science Foundation, and other authorities, this unit could serve as an influential catalyst toward improvement in Federal information systems.

Simultaneously, there should be set up as a standing committee of the Federal Council for Science and Technology, a Committee on Information.

3. *Inter-library plan.*

The three great national libraries should prepare a memorandum of agreement. It would replace present relatively haphazard cooperation with a plan for optimal division of labor in serving the scientific and engineering communities.

Needless, unintended overlap could thereby be minimized in acquisition, cataloging, bibliographic and other reader services.

Each of the three national libraries is preeminent in its field; each has greater resources than are now being utilized; each can help the other, and the national information community, to a greater extent than heretofore.

4. *Inter-agency compatibility*

Through the technical counsel of the National Bureau of Standards' Data Processing Center, efforts should be strengthened to assure optimal compatibility between the major inter-agency and intra-agency systems.

Illustrations of *inter*-agency systems are: O.T.S., Department of Commerce; Science Information Exchange; etc. Illustrations of major *intra*-agency systems are: D.O.D.; A.E.C.; N.A.S.A.; N.I.H.; etc.

Research should be expanded as to how far individual systems — manual or mechanized — may vary one from the other (as they do vary at present) while still offering reasonable opportunity for compatibility.

5. *Inter-agency modernization.*

Each of the principal Federal agencies supporting research and development should review its information policy, structure and procedure. To the extent which may be necessary, each should make necessary revisions so as to serve more efficiently in-house and extra-mural administrative, scientific and engineering needs, as well as inter-agency needs.

With but few exceptions, Federal agencies' information activities are, at present, neither sufficiently coordinated within departments, nor sufficiently modern and user oriented.

Among the notable exceptions in the U. S. Atomic Energy Commission; it possesses perhaps the most integrated, technical information program of any Federal agency. Building on experience under the A.E.C.'s program, the National Aeronautics and Space Administration has devised a well coordinated organization and blueprints for advanced information activity.

But other Federal agencies have not as yet placed themselves in a position where they can adequately serve their own or others' needs. Many of the principal departments are, by nature, conglomerations of virtually separate agencies; the result is that their respective information activities tend to be isolated, one from the other, with virtually no organic unity. Illustrations of this circumstance may be found in the Department of Defense, De-

partment of Commerce, and the Department of Health, Education and Welfare.

Remedial action is essential. It must be recalled that in the final analysis, the proposed Federal system of inter-agency information systems will be no stronger than its principal *intra*-agency components.

6. *Funding information programs.*

"Line items" for information services should be established in Federal appropriation laws for each of the major research and development agencies of the United States Government.

At present, there is virtually no regular accountability to the Congress efficiency and economy in most Federal or Federally-supported information services. Only a handful of Congressional hearings annually take up the issue of the adequacy of scientific and technical information. Among these exceptions are the hearings on appropriations for each of the three national libraries, for the Office of Technical Services of the Department of Commerce, and for a few others. If a "line item" is written in, there will be assured an annual "dialogue" between information experts and the appropriations subcommittees most directly concerned.

Such a line item should be established, for example, in the Department of Defense appropriation, as an integral part of the funding of research, development, testing and evaluation; for the Science Information Exchange, in the Smithsonian Institution; for the information services of the National Aeronautics and Space Administration; and for the U. S. Public Health Service, as well as for other key agency programs.

7. *Department of Defense planning and policy.*

The Department of Defense should establish central monitoring of its farflung information programs at the highest policy level. D.O.D. should be given a Congressional-Executive mandate to do more than merely respond to information requests from its contractors.

The most logical location for central information surveillance would be in the Office of Director of Defense Research Engineering. Here, policies, plans and programs for the information activities of the respective services should be reviewed, coordinated, and strengthened.

D.O.D. should be given the green light to take the initiative in disseminating its vast reservoir of scientific and engineering information. It should be authorized and directed to change its relatively passive policy.

8. *Strengthening A.S.T.I.A.*

The great asset represented by the Armed Services Technical Information Agency should be capitalized upon to a much greater extent than heretofore.

A.S.T.I.A. represents a powerful instrumentality for the nation's defense effort, as well as for civilian science and technology. At present, however, A.S.T.I.A. does not have the resources to do its existing, limited job, much less to perform the tasks which it wants to and should perform, consistent with its mission.

9. *National Science Foundation.*

The Office of Science Information Service should be given the means to strengthen and accelerate its services for the Federal government and for the nation's scientific and engineering community.

O.S.I.S. has probably served as the most influential single force for progress in scientific and technical information throughout the world. Although its information resources are less in magnitude than those of the Department of Defense, it has been able, from its central vantage point and professional interest, to allocate seed money for the broadest variety of information programs.

If the state of the art in information and communications is to advance at the desired pace within the next decade, O.S.I.S. will require more resources. It will, moreover, have to devote resources to support bolder experiments in *innovative* information systems.

10. *"Institutes of Communication Science."*

Basic research in documentation and communications problems should be provided for by a series of university based "Institutes of Information (or Communication) Science."

An informal suggestion[17] for such institutes, prepared by a group of experts acting as individuals, deserves serious consideration. Fundamental problems in linguistics, and in a variety of other disciplines, represent formidable obstacles to the future of documentation and communication science. A few of these problems are at present under study by some Federal, commercial and not-for-profit private organizations. Systematic, Federally supported study of these problems at a few leading universities might have a profound and beneficial effect. Such study should be part and parcel of a program of postgraduate education, leading to the granting of a degree.

11. *Inter-disciplinary training.*

The supply of manpower, skilled on an inter-disciplinary basis in information, documentation and communication science, should be greatly expanded. Plans of the National Science Foundation for training grants to schools of library science should be implemented at the earliest possible date. The Federal government should establish a career corps of information specialists. The corps should be trained not only in communication science, but also in the information needs of major scientific disciplines, so as to be of maximum service to principal Federal research missions. The members of the corps should be systematically rotated among the agencies as well as in university and other settings. Adequate salary, tenure and other incentives should be provided.

12. *Evaluation criteria.*

Refined standards must be established for purposes of evaluating the performance of information systems. An important contribution toward this goal has been made by the Stanford Research Institute,[18] under the auspices of the National Science Foundation.

Much additional work needs to be done, however, in order to determine sound cost-benefit ratios for centers, systems and services.

It cannot be taken for granted that under all or most circumstances highly advanced computer systems will necessarily pay their way in terms of benefits to end users. Careful scrutiny must be made of actual use to which systems are put, by whom, for what purpose, when, under what circumstances, with what results, as compared with alternative systems.

13. *Author abstracting and indexing.*

Editors of professional journals should consider a policy of requesting abstracting and indexing at source.

An increasing number of organizations have reported successful experience with the procedure of having the author of proposed journal articles prepare an abstract and a list of key index words at the time he completes his paper and forwards it. Many sources feel that whatever the limitations of amateur abstracting and indexing at source, it may still offer an important time saving. Professional abstracters and indexers can thereafter review and polish the author's version much more readily than if they had to originate the effort. The Engineering Joint Council is now actively planning to apply to all of engineering the successful experience of the American Institute of Chemical Engineers[19] in abstracting and indexing at source. A master thesaurus is contemplated which would serve for all of engineering as the Chemical Engineer's Thesaurus now serves that specialized profession. A training program for editorial staffs for source indexing is also planned.

14. *Management information.*

Information systems must be strengthened to provide customized services for purposes of advanced management of research and development. PERT (Program Evaluation and Review Technique), which has made so vital a contribution to the success of the Polaris fleet ballistic missile system, should be adapted in other administrative areas as rapidly as possible.[20]

ADDITIONAL SUGGESTIONS BEAR CONSIDERATION INTERNATIONALLY

Many other suggestions will bear consideration, particularly in the sphere of international cooperation. A world-wide System of Information Systems should clearly be the goal of international scientific and engineering organizations.

As its name implies, the Subcommittee on Reorganization and International Organizations is deeply interested in international action, particularly on the part of inter-governmental organizations.

We have concentrated on Federal and national needs, because the parent committee is the Committee on Government Operations. But committee members are deeply cognizant of the primary role of non-governmental groups both at home and abroad.

The willingness of private groups to co-operate with one another in the common interest will be put to the greatest test in the years ahead.

W. T. Knox, now Chairman of the Science Information Council, and Manager, Technical Information Division, Esso Research and Engineering Company, has stated:[21]

"The major national problems in this field stem from the enormous complexity of the existing system and the reluctance of any organization to give up some of the known benefits of autonomy for the hoped-for advantages of a cooperative effort.

"One [problem] is the urgent need for the professional scientific and engineering societies to take greatly increased responsibility for the development of a unified United States information system. It is the consensus of most groups who have studied the problem that the basic control of the scientific and engineering information system should remain with the scientists and engineers. Yet it is painfully obvious that a number of professional societies are not fulfilling their obligations."

THE CHOICES BEFORE THE NATION

The United States is at a turning point in its program of scientific and engineering information.

We have reached this point by virtue of the dedicated labors of small numbers of pioneers in information and communications. They have laid a firm foundation for future action. But the action must be coherent, not chaotic; planned, not haphazard.

The coherent plan can only come from the cooperative efforts of a vast number of individuals responsible for information offices, libraries, centers, systems and services. Each month, these information resources tend to proliferate further, and the task of linking them grows more difficult.

Inevitably, each would view the problem of a System of Systems from the standpoint of his own mission. Each would view proposed changes, particularly collaborative efforts, against the criterion of what his group stands to gain and what it may lose in terms of independence or increased cost in striving for compatibility.

These are perfectly understandable criteria; they are far from insuperable. A free society is ultimately based on the "engineering of voluntary consent."

The future is rich with opportunity. It is also fraught with hazard if efforts prove too little and too late.

Mere progress in information systems is not enough. Knowledge, particularly at the inter-disciplinary frontiers of science and technology, is growing at an exponential rate. The capacity and flexibility in systems must be strengthened at a tempo and to a degree which keeps pace with, or preferably, surpasses the growth tempo of knowledge itself.

The decision to move ahead with all proper dispatch toward a national information goal cannot be made by only one source, even by the President of the United States.

It can only be made, and be implemented, by the scientists and engineers of the nation, acting voluntarily through their chosen instruments.

The hour is late. The need is great.

The choice is: to drift or to steer; to break through to a higher level of efficiency· or to plod along with antiquated ways; to be content with pro-forma cooperation or to make information teamwork a living reality.

NOTE: The views presented herein represent individual judgment; they are not intended as an official statement of the policies of the Senate Committee on Government Operations or of the Subcommittee on Reorganization and International Organizations, except where specifically stated otherwise.

REFERENCES

[1] U. S. Bureau of the Budget, "The Budget of the United States Government for the Fiscal Year Ending 1963," 1962, Special Analysis G-1, p. 327.

[2] Ibid., pp. 332, 334, 335.

[3] Ibid., p. 330.

[4] Ibid., p. 329.

[5] National Science Foundation, "Federal Funds for Science," Surveys of Science Resource Series, December 1961, NSF 61-82, p. 44.

[6] The attention which the U.S.S.R. accords, in turn, to the problem may be seen in a U. S. translation of five reports published by the U.S.S.R. Institute of Scientific Information, Academy of Sciences. The translation appears under the title "Foreign Developments in Machine Translation and Information Processing," No. 30, distributed by the Department of Commerce, Office of Technical Services, OTS: 61-31, 465, June 2, 1961.

[7] Address, "Industry's Contribution to Military Research and Engineering Programs," American Management Association, New York, N.Y., Oct. 6, 1961.

[8] Editorial, "What's the Price of Information Unlimited?" The Trend in Engineering at the University of Washington, Oct. 1960, p. 2.

[9] "Information Resources, A Challenge to American Science and Industry," based upon the Proceedings of a Special Meeting of the Council on Documentation Research, Western Reserve University, Cleveland, Ohio, Feb. 3-4, 1958, p. 7.

[10] American Medical Writer's Association, Quarterly Bulletin, Feb., 1962, pp. 1-2.

[11] "Specialized Scientific Information Services in the United States, A Directory of Selected Specialized Information Services in the Physical and Biological Sciences," National Science Foundation, NSF 61-68, Nov., 1961.

[12] United States Air Force, DCS/Plans and Operations, Headquarters, Office of Aerospace Research, Washington 25, D.C., "Directory of R and D Information Systems," A Listing of Centers, Services, Sources and Systems Engaged in Collecting, Storing and Disseminating Scientific Data and Information Applicable to Aerospace Research and Technology, Aug. 1961.

[13] "Documentation, Indexing and Retrieval of Scientific Information," A study of federal and nonfederal scientific information processing and retrieval programs, Senate Document 113, 86th Congress, Second Session, June 23, 1960.

[14] "Documentation, Indexing and Retrieval of Scientific Information, Addendum to Senate Document No 113," Senate Document No. 15, 87th Congress, First Session, Mar. 9, 1961.

[15] "Coordination of Information on Current Scientific Research and Development Supported by the United States Government," Senate Report 263, 87th Congress, First Session, May 18, 1961.

[16] "Coordination of Information of Current Federal Research and Development Projects in the Field of Electronics," Sept. 20, 1961.

[17] Joseph Becker, Robert M. Hayes, Klaus Liebhold, Melville J. Ruggles, Roger Sisson, Proposal for an Institute of Information Sciences, Mar. 9, 1961, revised July 16, 1961.

[18] C. P. Bourne, G. D. Peterson, B. Lefkowitz, D. Ford, "Requirements, Criteria, and Measures of Performance of Information Storage and Retrieval Systems," SRI Project No. 3741, Dec., 1961.

[19] B. E. Holm, "Information Retrieval — A Solution," Chemical Engineering Progress, Vol. 57, No. 6, June 1961, pp. 73-76.

[20] Address, "Managing the Fleet Ballistic Missile Program," National Security Industrial Association; Jan. 11, 1962. Excerpted in Aviation Week and Space Technology, Jan. 29, 1962, p. 21.

[21] "The Technical Information Crisis," Industrial Research Institute, Pittsburgh, Pa., Oct. 16, 1961, p. 6.

By Paul W. Howerton
Information for Industry, Inc.

4. Status of Technical Information Centers

IF ONE MAY ADAPT A CLASSIC PHRASE from that great practitioner of the English language, Churchill, it can be said that: "Never in the history of human communication has so much been written by so many which is of use to so few." The question before us is: "Why are these writings of use to so few?" My contribution concerns itself with the status of technical information centers with the word "status" to be understood to mean both "prestige" and "hierarchal position". I shall attempt to avoid confusion of Utopian ideal with reality by discussing status already achieved, but I shall reserve the right to make forecasts at the end of this paper concerning certain pragmatic developments in the handling of technical information in both the short and long range. These forecasts will be made in the general context of the status of the technical information center.

In the course of this paper, a recurrent theme of service to the user will be evident, and the principal thrust of my argument will be that the term "status" is semantically equivalent to "service." The two generic types of technical information centers to be discussed are: 1) the internal technical information center which serves its own parent organization exclusively, and 2) the center which makes its service available to the scientific and technical community without restriction beyond normal administrative rules.

STATUS OF THE USER

The popular assumption that information center users are, by definition, both industrious and well informed, not only about their personal subject interests but also about how the information is retrieved, needs to be dispelled. A symbiosis of user and proprietor of technical information centers results in an advantage to both parties. The user who communicates his total problem to the center's information specialists gains status by virtue of his acceptance of the specialists' talents in solving his problem completely and expeditiously.

There is, however, a more important status gain for the user who understands the capabilities and limitations of the center. He tends to improve the capabilities and reduce the limitations of the service by his active participation with the information specialists in the identificaton of the association of units of information.

On the other side of this partnership, let the technical information center proprietor volunteer his expertise to the scientist. Traditional library practice has been reluctant to allow the client direct access to the stacks and to data or information files. There were good reasons for both of these actions, but in today's world, information services can still defend the integrity of collections while guiding the user through the intricacies of the sophisticated organization of the system.

In other words, the only purpose of a technical information center is to serve its clientele. The improvement of the status of the user by responsive action in the center will be reflected in a concomitant improvement in the status of the center.

THE INTERNAL TECHNICAL INFORMATION CENTER

When a company, a government agency or a component of either operates a technical information center, it assumes a responsibility to supply adequate and useful service to its customers. This responsibility is frequently not met because of lack of status within the organization which is to be served. As the former Deputy Assistant Director for Central Reference, I know that the real success of the central reference facility of the Central Intelligence Agency is largely due to the expertness and ingenuity of its staff; but the fact that Mr. Allen W. Dulles and General C. P. Cabell, as the Director and Deputy Director respectively of the CIA, actively supported the efforts of the staff, guaranteed the status of the facility. If someone dismissed the central reference service as inadequate or incompetent, he knew that the justification for his statements might have to be presented at the highest level of the agency.

The status of any internal technical information center is directly proportional to the support given the effort by top management. It is this statement that must be the keystone of the center. This position leads one into the question of what should be the orientation of a technical information center in an organization. Should there be a horizontal administrative relationship with customer components; that is, should each division head have authority jointly or independently to determine policy for the center? Or should there be vertical administrative responsibility to a top official to whom customer component heads also report? I have no doubt but what the latter course is the wiser, both from the point of view of the center and its clientele.

Let me now refer to my earlier points about user status. I have found that the most effective internal technical information centers had their reference staffs substantively trained in the fields of science of greatest interest to the people using the center, and secondarily trained in library techniques. The so called literature scientist falls into this pattern of preparation for exercising his ingenuity to induce new levels of knowledge from his base of experience, both with the tools of the library and his discipline. Because these internal technical information centers are usually, but with some noteworthy exceptions, defining their scope fairly narrowly, the qualifications I suggest are not difficult to attain. Customer acceptance is much more likely to be easily established in an environment of peers.

THE PUBLIC TECHNICAL INFORMATION CENTER

There has been a deploring of the situation, a wringing of hands and wailing about the inadequacy of technical information centers available to the general public. Long and tedious hearings have been held by the Congress on the subject. The press, both technical and general, has had feature articles or editorial comments on the subject. But when a rigorous, rather than emotional, analysis is made of the use of existing and competent aids to technical documentation, such an apathetic view is held by so many scientists that one is startled by their vocal concern for technical information centers. The findings of surveys made under National Science Foundation auspices support the contention that the present scientific and technical literature of the world is *not* being used by the scientific community as it should be. Why does this condition exist?

I believe the reason lies in the status of these centers and tools in the scientific community. Those who view this situation with alarm do not realize that documentation and documentalists have now reached a professional level commensurate with the other members of the total research team. The establishment of technical information centers is regarded as deflecting funds which could be directed to support of laboratory science.

There are many who believe this technical information center problem belongs to government alone. I do not count myself in this group. Private enterprise, which must provide a satisfactory product or fail, has a strong motivation toward the efficient and useful operation of information centers, just as it does in other marketing enterprises. I have urged that when machine translation becomes an operational capability, the production of translations be turned over to private enterprise.

The task oriented service bureau to which industry, government or education may turn for comprehensive coverage of the literature of the task on a retainer or fee basis, must deliver the goods or fall by the wayside. The status of these privately organized and administered centers will be measured by the service they perform in response to the interests of their clientele.

Small companies, whose budgets cannot justify the establishment of a technical library facility, can command the services of substantively competent documentalists in the centers set up by private enterprise. The integrity of the staff of the center will protect the proprietary interests of the client in relationship to other clients in the same field. Without this assurance, the center's prestige and status will fall into oblivion. For a fee considerably less than the cost of setting up its own information center, a company can have linguistic, substantive and documentation talents applied to its problem which, in many cases, even the largest internal technical information centers cannot assemble.

The compatibility of an information service, such as an abstracting or current-awareness service, with the technological advancement in the mechanical linguistics of indexing, the hardware of storage and the techniques of reproduction, must take into account the interdisciplinary flavor of modern research. The tremendous corpus of technical literature already in being must be tied logically to the generations of research results of the future. The scientific method prescribes that from a data base of the past, extrapolations into the unknown are made followed by the collection of evidential support to change the hypotheses into scientific fact. This retrospective search of the literature of the past has to make a compatible link-up with the handling techniques of the newer reports of today and the

yet unwritten material of the future. To do this thing breeds status.

CONCLUSION

The burden of my discussion can be summarized as follows: Status is a function of service; service depends on alertness to the changing interests of the clientele; and alertness depends on positive efforts to attain the best communication possible between the technical information center user and proprietor. The support of the internal center by top management is essential to the achievement of status and recognition. The so called public technical information center or service, operated by private enterprise, has a dimension of incentive to service not possessed by efforts within the government structure — that of satisfaction of the customer or failure.

Up to now there has been little real effort to let the rules of supply and demand apply to the handling of technical information centers. I believe the time has come when the economics of the literature problem should enter the picture. The adage that things are usually worth what you pay for them, or will quickly adjust to that condition, would be the term of reference for establishing a new approach to our concern for the increase in the technical literature problem.

By John Sherrod
Library of Congress

5. Functions of a Technical Information Center

THREE ASPECTS OF THE modern day technical information center are sufficiently important to single out for general discussion. These are the informational materials serviced, the clientele served, and the operating procedures employed to bring information and user together.

ASPECTS OF A TECHNICAL INFORMATION CENTER

The principal function of an information center, and indeed its only excuse for existence, is to serve the needs of its clientele. In many ways it is similar to the special library. The materials serviced are generally specialized in that they are narrow in subject breadth but comprehensive in depth. The clientele are more often than not sophisticated in the subject matter of concern to the information center, though not necessarily well informed of their own information needs or of the problems inherent in information storage and retrieval. Finally, the methods of information handling are likely to be classed as non-conventional because they usually employ advanced documentation techniques, including mechanization, which are designed to ensure subject analysis in depth for information storage and maximum efficiency in information retrieval.

The unique functions of a technical information center spring primarily from operating procedures based on a policy of aggressive information collection and dissemination. In contrast with normal library service which is more passive in nature, e.g., information may be supplied only on request, an information center can be expected to be continually aware of the present, as well as, anticipate future needs of its clientele and to actively disseminate information to meet these needs. Further, the information center will undertake to educate present and potential users to their need for, and the value of, information assistance.

As the store of information becomes both more voluminous and specialized, there is a growing requirement for bigger collections and better trained subject specialists to serve more adequately the user's needs. To store and subsequently retrieve all existing information on any subject is impossible. A maximum degree of completeness in a subject search requires considerable resources. The expense involved often can be justified only in exceptional cases, such as the national defense.

FEDERAL GOVERNMENT ROLE

Since it is certain that considerable and ever increasing amounts of money will be required to support information centers, the question naturally arises as to the role the Federal government should play in this effort. One of the key questions being debated currently involves the degree to which centralization and/or coordination of technical information centers is desirable or possible.

There are many reasons for not concentrating all or a major portion of this country's activities into a single technical information center. Among these are included the enormous cost of such an undertaking, the effective resistance of some existing centers and other entrenched interests, and the lack of any positive assurance that such a centralized effort would be successful. In fact, even the most critical observers of existing systems here will admit that in most cases a reasonably good job is being done at present.

In spite of these arguments, a gradual increase in the degree of centralization and amount of Federal coordination appears to be inevitable. For one thing, it will never be possible to ascertain that a more centralized effort would not produce better results unless additional steps in this direction are tried. Secondly, one might argue on a purely intuitive basis that there are certain inherent advantages (as well as disadvantages) to bigness. Finally, it is true, certainly, that other countries are doing it. The French and Russians have, to a considerable degree, centralized their technical information efforts; the British are planning an extensive centralized effort.

Against this background of controversy, and lacking positive evidence as to the exact amount of centralization or decentralization that is desirable, existing technical information centers within the Federal complex are developing progressive programs to serve both the interests of their own individual agencies and those of the country as a whole. It is the purpose of the remainder of this paper to trace briefly the program development of one of these information centers.

SCIENCE AND TECHNOLOGY AT THE LIBRARY OF CONGRESS

The activities of the Library of Congress are much broader in scope than a strict interpretation of its name would imply, although service to the Congress is its primary responsibility. It has become, in fact, a national library serving the whole Federal government and, by means direct and indirect, the entire nation.

The Congressional Act of April 24, 1800, which established the Library of Congress provided simply, "for the purchase of such books as may be necessary for the use of Congress at the said city of Washington and for fitting up an apartment for containing them." The first significant material of a scientific nature came with the purchase by Congress in 1815 of the 7,000 volume personal library of Thomas Jefferson, which was the finest private library in the New World and one assembled with a special eye to "natural philosophy". The greatest stimulus to the collection of scientific and technical literature by the Library came in 1866 when, by act of Congress, the Smithsonian Institution's "complete collection of the memoirs and transactions of learned societies throughout the world and an entire series of the most important scientific and literary periodicals" were transferred to the Library of Congress in order

that they might be housed and serviced more adequately.

Today, the Library of Congress contains the largest, most comprehensive, single collection of published and unpublished materials in science and technology the world has ever known. Such a statement might be difficult to prove but equally difficult to disprove. It would be safe to state, though somewhat less dramatic, that the collections are this nation's largest.

More than 25 percent of the Library's total classed collection is in science, technology, and closely related areas of knowledge, or nearly two million volumes. Some 15,000 journal titles in science and technology are received currently. Nearly 300,000 technical reports and some 600,000 manuscripts related to science are included in the Library's holdings.

The size and scope of the Library's present holdings attest to the vigor with which acquisitions in these fields have been pursued. In general terms, it is the policy of the Library of Congress to collect extensively the current publications of the world in all fields of science and technology except for clinical medicine and technical agriculture. Acquisition and information service related to these latter two fields are excepted because of the extensive programs of the Library of the Department of Agriculture and the National Library of Medicine.

What has the Library done to ensure utilization of these vast and unique resources? The focal point of subject competence within the Library in all fields of science and technology is the Science and Technology Division, which has primary responsibility for reference and bibliographical services and for advising on acquisition of all pertinent scientific and technological materials. Established in 1949 with a small staff to plan and develop a science program, the division's program has matured to a point where, in many respects, it compares favorably to that of any national technical information center.

Space does not permit spelling out in detail all of the program, but some highlights may be helpful. Scientific and technical inquiries are received and answered from every state in the Union and from nearly all the principal countries in the world at an annual rate of nearly 20,000 inquiries. Exhaustive bibliographies in more than 20 scientific fields are under preparation at any given time, with the resulting publications made available to the general public. The majority of staff members responsible for the preparation of these literature surveys and for answering scientific inquiries have had graduate training in science or technology, many at the doctoral level. The division, as a technical information center, is constantly studying the application of improved and advanced documentation techniques in order to better cope with the increasing volume of information.

The latest significant development in the division's information program has come in response to many requests by industrial concerns and private researchers for broader access to government held collections of scientific and technical literature. To meet these growing demands, the Science and Technology Division in cooperation with the Office of Technical Services, U. S. Department of Commerce, in July, 1961, initiated a program designed to provide an inexpensive method by which a large segment of the public with special, often urgent, needs for research information can have almost immediate access to the science collections of the Library of Congress, as well as to the specialized holdings of the Office of Technical Services.

This new information program provides for two kinds of literature service. The first is a "current awareness" bibliography, designed to keep subscribers abreast of the latest developments in their field of interest as these developments occur, or on a periodic basis. The second is a retrospective bibliography service which provides for a literature survey of the information available at the time the request is made. Built in flexibility of the service accommodates pin-point research on individual subjects while providing at the same time for continuous, in-depth research within a broad related field. The fee for this tailor-made service is eight dollars an hour.

It is hoped that this brief report will serve to highlight the rather unique services which have come to be associated with today's technical information centers. This, together with the description of government interest and activity, particularly the program of the Science and Technology Division of the Library of Congress, should serve as an optimistic note for those interested in the management of technical information centers. Much remains to be done, for sure, but that many good things are being done is certain.

By W. C. Asbury and J. E. Moise
Esso Research and Engineering Company

6. Technical Information Services in an Industrial Organization

ENOUGH HAS ALREADY BEEN SAID here and in numerous papers at other meetings about the information crisis.[1,2] One statistical reference should suffice to provide the proper perspective for this discussion. Three hundred thousand technical articles are now being published each year in recognized periodicals, with the combined reading time for all of them in the neighborhood of 465 man years. And it is likely that this rate of publication will double in a handful of years.

As regards the general areas we propose to discuss, we will first have something to say about the need and justification for a technical information division in an industrial organization. Second, we will expain how we at Esso Research are equipped to carry out our responsibilities, including a description of the organization of our Technical Information Division, which provides technical information services. Third, we will discuss our plans for the future to maintain our effectiveness in the face of the expanding volume of information.

This discussion will be specific to our organization, whose technical information is in the field of petroleum technology. However, this does embrace quite a few disciplines, such as chemistry, physics, and mathematics, with others, such as biology, creeping in, plus the practical applications of these sciences in engineering fields.

MANAGEMENT SUPPORT

We have no magic solution to the problem of handling the flood of technical information. There is no one answer, and our system, although adequate for the moment, can stand a lot of improvement. What we can do is to assure you that the practice of science and engineering has never been more dependent on competent technical information services, and that — unless Esso Research and Engineering Company is an exception — management people will strongly support efforts to screen, process, store, and retrieve this avalanche of literature for the tailor-made benefit of the user.

Such management support doesn't always come easily, of course. Those of you who are just setting up technical information programs will certainly encounter at least a lack of enthusiasm from some quarters, if not downright resistance. There are those who state rather firmly that the technical man should read everything in his field. Mr. Howerton's paper at this meeting also emphasized the importance of management support.

One of us (Mr. Asbury) recently asked his son-in-law whether and how he managed to keep up with his professional reading. This son-in-law is an engineer working in the field of acoustics. He told Mr. Asbury that he didn't have any trouble, that he was able to rely on *Physics Abstracts* to keep abreast of what was being published. In a highly specialized field where good abstract services are available, it is quite possible for a technical man to fend for himself. In less specialized fields, the story is different. No man can do all of the reading. That's where technical information groups enter the picture, and it's on that basis that they must earn management's endorsement.

Now, to go further into why we have technical information services, let us first consider the four principal objectives of technical management in industry. The first is to maintain the company's capital and operating costs at the lowest possible effective level. Second, to help the company obtain new high quality products, efficient processes, and other technical assistance at a level that will improve or at least maintain its competitive position. Third, to provide the company with new opportunities for attractive capital investments and new markets for new and existing products. And fourth, to achieve the first three with a minimum of research expenditures, including those for technical information.

These objectives can be difficult to achieve. You can't schedule creativity or inventiveness as you can manufacturing output. There has to be a reasonable degree of investigative freedom. On the other hand, it's hardly feasible to create technology at an outlay of time and money that makes it economically useless. So management must take the attitude that industrial research is a business, to be managed as a business. And. be assured, a vigorous, well working technical information agency is essential to the businesslike conduct of industrial research and engineering.

It's management's responsibility, for example, to decide when work should begin on a research project, and when it should terminate. In most industrial laboratories, there are always far more ideas being generated than there are people to carry them out.

In all of our experience, we can't recall anyone's ever scratching his head and saying: "I wonder what we ought to do next." Technical literature is one of management's most useful guides in making the decision as to which project should get going and which should wait or be scrapped entirely.

JUSTIFICATION OF INFORMATION SERVICES

So far, we have jumped back and forth between two phases or categories of technical information which constitute its principal uses — current awareness and retrospective searching. The first of these, of course, involves keeping our research people informed of developments in their specialized fields in order to minimize the number of periodicals, patents, government reports, etc., which they would otherwise have to try to read for themselves. Current-awareness activities involve acquisition, selection, abstracting, publication of bulletins, circulation of periodicals, and

certain special information research services that we'll touch on later. Our bulletins — which generally publish abstracts within one month after the article appears in the literature or a patent copy is received — are our principal organs for achieving current awareness. This is not to say that researchers do not read magazines. Most of our researchers read certain magazines on a regular basis, but secure references to other articles of interest to them through our abstracts bulletin.

The current-awareness items of today are the retrospective searching items of tomorrow, which brings up the second phase, retrospective searching. This area involves indexing, storing and retrieving information. As you will see later, we include in searching not only storage and retrieval, but also analysis and interpretation.

Let us illustrate by example how a technical information service can help laboratory research. Our people had under consideration an exploratory program in the field of productive research; the need for it seemed beyond question. It would take a month, perhaps longer, to find the required answers, and we were about to give the go ahead when one of our information researchers came up with a document that made the whole project unnecessary. In another case, an analysis of more than 100 chemical compounds was stopped, just before starting laboratory work, when a literature search turned up the fact that someone else had already done the work.

Let us look at a quote from a talk by P. L. Saltzberg of duPont: "It might be that the term R & D is becoming a cliche and no longer means research and development. Perhaps it means 'repeat and develop' or possibly 'reconnoiter and duplicate.' What an abysmal waste of technical talent! What a dull existence."[3]

Duplication of scientific work can truly be a sinful waste of time, money, and brainpower, and no research organization that I know of has an oversupply of any of these commodities. Of the three, time is perhaps the most important. It alone is the irretrievable factor, and it takes on an added significance when the research effort is in any way tied to our national defense. In the competition between communism and the free world, the Russians are very much aware of the value of published information in scentific work.

Every Friday night, a plane leaves this country for Moscow with a cargo of technical reports and trade publications. Every day, a half dozen of our better newspapers go under the microfilm camera for transmittal to Russia. We can afford to be no less aware than they.

There are exceptions, of course. There are times when it is more practical to re-research something because of the difficulties involved in obtaining the literature, or because new techniques will provide more complete, more meaningful results. Some of the points we can consider before plunging into a project are listed below:

1. Can we determine when further extension of the literature search will cost more than the research work necessary to get the same information?

2. At what point will it become uneconomical to delay the actual initiation of a program in order to discover further pertinent literature references?

These first two points are rather specific, but what are the more general benefits from a retrospective search? They can be numerous, including such things are serendipity for a browsing exploratory worker, direct leads for further research studies, or complete abandonment of a project, as shown in an earlier example.

The evaluation of technical information on the productivity of the worker is very illusive and cannot easily be defined. Similarly, the eventual effect that the information might have as an over all benefit to the company is difficult to evaluate, but the potential benefits can be enormous.

INFORMATION SERVICE AT ESSO RESEARCH

When we speak about technical management, of course, we can speak with authority only where our own company is concerned. It might be appropriate, therefore, to tell you a little about how our technical information services are carried out.

To begin with, Esso Research and Engineering Company is the principal technical affiliate of Standard Oil Company (New Jersey) and its world-wide manufacturing and marketing affiliates. Esso Research is made up of nearly 3,000 men and women, about half of them professional people. Our main facilities are in New Jersey, in Linden and Florham Park. Our responsibilities to our affiliates include coordinated research and engineering programs concerning petroleum and petrochemical products and processes. In addition to the work of our own people, we also are responsible for related activities at affiliated research installations elsewhere in the United States, as well as in Canada, England, France, and Germany. In terms of money, this effort comes to $78 million a year.

Our company came into existence as a technical department of Jersey Standard, back in 1919. From the beginning, efforts were made

**Esso Research and Engineering Company's
Technical Information Division**

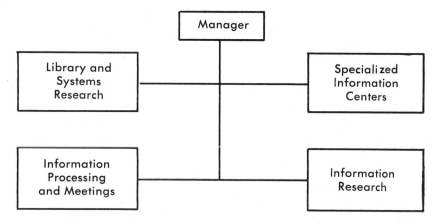

EXHIBIT 1

to support our technical people with the literature services they needed, including a well stocked library. Our abstracting services of patents and literature started in 1920, but it was not until 1957 that we expanded the scope of our information services to give this activity full-fledged divisional status. This was brought about by an internal survey of our technical people in 1956.

We are somewhat chagrined to find from this survey that our information program wasn't as effective as we'd thought. Many of our technical staff members felt that they weren't as up to date in their own fields as they could be. In some cases, our research people didn't even consider themselves adequately informed about the company's own work. The result was the creation of our Technical Information Division, five years ago, to strengthen and expand the job of gathering technical information and making it more easily available.

Exhibit 1 shows an organizational plan of the Esso Research and Engineering Company's Technical Information Division as it presently exists. As shown, the four principal areas are the library, information processing, specialized information groups, and information research.

The library includes the functions of acquisition, cataloging, reference services, and maintenance of keys to retrospective searching. The information systems research shown here involves development of improved information handling techniques for most of TID's operations, both from a cost standpoint and for obtaining satisfied customers.

Information processing includes such current-awareness activities as the publishing of five bulletins of technical abstracts and a monthly index to the company's technical reports. The abstract bulletins are given wide distribution to scientists and engineers throughout the Jersey organization. Each bulletin is tailored to meet the requirements of readers in a specific field. Carefully defined section headings, listed in tables of contents, make it easy for readers to find abstracts in their areas of special interest. Speed of reading is enhanced by use of topical-sentence-first abstracts and by "highlights" pages that discuss the most important abstracts included. In addition to the monthly index to company

reports, an annual index is prepared for reference use, and a machine based index is being developed. Other activities in this area include centralization of reports distribution to affiliates, management of technical meetings, and clearance of technical publications.

The specialized information centers include a crude oil information service which not only accumulates all assays of company interest, but also coordinates necessary action to get new assays that are needed and to distribute and interpret them. Another central activity is on physical properties, primarily of hydrocarbons; this includes deriving correlations for the prediction of physical properties.

Another new specialized center which the Technical Information Division helped to organize and staff is the Engineering Information Center, located at our facilities at Florham Park. This Engineering Information Center[4] (EIC) was set up to supply specialized needs of the Esso Engineering divisions. This center indexes in depth all correspondence and other internal documents having technical information of permanent value. The entire system is arranged around a machine based indexing system. Searches can be made manually for simple questions or through machine retrieval procedures for more complex questions. Since the indexing is done in depth, this system is felt to be capable of not only rapid but fairly complete and selective retrieval of documents.

The last area in the organization — information research — provides dynamic liaison between old and new information from all sources and current or planned research projects. This is the chief new activity of our Technical Information Division. The information research function has been discussed at length in a number of previous papers,[5,6] so we will only briefly summarize its requirements and activities:

1. Know current company interests.
2. Evaluate current technical literature in fields of interest.
3. Direct pertinent information to right people.
4. Guide abstracters in selection of material to reflect the company's current research activities.
5. Prepare comprehensive reviews of lit-

erature and internal reports in specific fields.

6. Analyze and interpret review information and suggest areas for further research studies.

Since we have now briefly described our organization, it may be fitting to present a few figures for our reports room and library holdings that show the magnitude of our operations. Company reports on file number some 10,000; our present input is about 1,500 per year. Information research reports issued by the Technical Information Division, some 50 per year, are few in comparison, but, as stated earlier, they are comprehensive reviews in specialized fields. The library's files contain some 80,000 patents, over 18,000 acquired in 1961. Books and bound volumes of periodicals number 40,000; additions are now 2,900 per year. Abstract cards are being added at the rate of 100,000 per year, with the files now holding about 2,000,000 cards representing over 500,00 abstracts. Abstracts published in our bulletins during 1961 numbered over 25,000.

About 600 journal titles are acquired, many with multiple subscriptions, and some 2,000 books are cataloged each year (gradually increasing). The circulation of these journals and books in 1961 was in answer to 43,000 requests, about half of which were based on items in our abstracts bulletins. Library reference requests totaled 2,500 during 1961.

Of course, numerous other services are provided by our library staff, and these rather broad and general type of data serve only to orient you to the scale of our operations, small compared to some, but large compared to many other information service operations.

STAFFING

From the earliest days we have followed the philosophy that technical information, being one of our major resources, warrants management's full support and attention. We staffed the new division with good technical men carefully selected from our research divisions, so that our program would be properly oriented in terms of our technical work. We had no intention of setting up a rest home for tired scientists and engineers. The men we picked were expert in their fields. Some have rotated back into research work, taking with

them a broader outlook than they had prior to their experience in the information field.

We also found that it was difficult to attract high quality scientists and engineers from experimental research into the information field, and this may be true in most countries. Listen to this complaint from the U.S.S.R.: "Regrettably, heads of industrial enterprises often staff the technical information agencies with workers made available by chance and who are difficult to employ in other divisions."[7]

We have also, of course, supplemented our staff with people having the specialized skills necessary to an effective information program, i.e., abstracters, literature searchers, information systems men, etc. Our staff in the Technical Information Division now numbers 60, over half of them technical. The budget for the operation is over one million dollars a year.

PRINCIPLES

At Esso Research, we feel there are some fairly basic principles that cannot be ignored in operating a successful technical information service:

1. The information service must dedicate itself to the active exploitation of recorded knowledge. It's not nearly enough to maintain a storehouse of learning. Information is worthwhile only if it can be put into the active stream of daily work. If this information can't be made available in the most useful and usable form — when it's needed, where it's needed, and in the amount that it's needed — then the program adds up to little or nothing.

2. The information service should not operate in an isolation booth apart from the men at the bench, but should work in close liaison with project teams from the preliminary planning stages on.

3. The information service is not an end in itself, but is a device by which its users get information to help solve their daily problems. The user isn't interested in the mechanics or details of the operation. He doesn't care how carefully the whole program has been designed and constructed. Does it work for him? That's his concern.

4. As with all services, there is need for a reasonable amount of research on new

information techniques. The evolution of office equipment has spilled over into the information service field, with punched card, punched tape, rapid copying, microfilm, and computing equipment being used in ever increasing numbers. However, the idea of a mechanical, fully automatic data handling and retrieval system has not yet been achieved. More progress can be made in this area.

5. The service ought to be measured from time to time to make certain it is fulfilling its role properly, effectively, and at reasonable cost. Those best qualified to judge the effectiveness of the service are its users.

The last two items touch on planning for the future. Some of the areas through which we hope to maintain and improve the effectiveness of our organization as the volume of technical literature, internal and external, steadily increases include:

1. The application of new procedures or techniques. As you know, numerous new techniques are constantly being proposed and developed for indexing, cataloging, storing, and retrieving information. We plan not only to work on our own ideas in this field, but also to keep in touch with others so that we can secure the best system adaptable to our needs.

2. The use of automated systems. Here, we are referring to the use of machines, whether fully automated or not. This could be considered part of the first item in applying new procedures and techniques but, since a differential can be made, we list it separately. In addition, some of the machines necessary are too expensive to justify. In our case the expensive machines are already available, and it is only a case of securing time on them.

3. Cooperative efforts with other groups. We consider these quite important, and will make a few more remarks about them directly.

4. Information systems research. Here, specifically, we are thinking of orienting our systems to the users. Our plans include additional surveys to determine user requirements and just how effective our communications systems are.

5. Evaluation of the information systems in terms of their costs, as compared to the over all benefits to the users and to the company. We should like to determine what are the real benefits of disseminated technical information, just what use the user makes of the information after he gets it. Is there a way of putting a dollars and cents figure on the value to him and to his research efforts?

ONE EVALUATION

It may be pertinent here to describe a simple exploratory study that we made to determine if we could evaluate the worth of technical information services to our research and engineering organization. An industrial research library or technical information service, unlike a public library, must result in economic benefit to the supporting organization. While there is ample evidence that scientists and engineers use technical information services,[8,9] there are no available data relating operating costs for a technical information service to the economic benefits to the organization.

This brief study was carried out to determine if a relatively simple survey technique could measure the value of reference services provided by a special technical library. Scientists and engineers who had actually used the library reference services were queried to determine the use to which the reference information had been put. Twenty reference questions from 18 different scientists and engineers were thus analyzed.

The following questions were asked:

1. Did the library provide you with an answer to your reference question?

2. If so, how did you use this information, and of what value was it to the company?

3. What would you have done if you had not obtained this information from the library and, in case you did not get the information, what did you do?

The following results were obtained:

1. Answers to reference questions:

Answered completely	12
Answered partially	3
Questions not answered by requested information	2
Answer unevaluated by requester	2
Answer not received by requester	1

2. Use of information received:

Background on R & D projects	5
Specific markets data for products	3
Specific data used in calculations, patent application, etc.	4
Information given to company customers	2
Preparation of talks, book	3

3. Consequences if information had not been provided:

Repeat previous laboratory work	6
Discuss problem with expert	2
Potentially profitable lead would not have been uncovered	3
Translation would have been ordered	1
Decision would have been more difficult	3
Existing, less efficient procedures would still be employed	2

Many interesting observations can be made, even from this limited survey, regarding the role and functioning of a technical information service in an industrial research organization. Of special interest are the 60 percent score (12/20) for complete answering of queries, the 10 percent of cases in which the questioner asked for information not germane to his problem (this percentage may represent those in our company who do not know exactly what they are looking for), and the 10 percent of cases in which the answer still lay unevaluated by the questioner.

More important for the current study are the indicated consequences if the requested information had not been provided. In 35 percent of the cases (6/17), previous laboratory work would have been repeated. It proved difficult to measure the probable costs of the laboratory work made unnecessary by the reference services. However, in one instance the research chemist estimated that two weeks of laboratory work had been saved. At current R & D costs, some one to two thousand dollars of laboratory work was avoided by a reference question costing about 15 dollars to answer. In another instance, a U. S. patent corresponding to a foreign language patent was located, thus obviating the need for a 35 dollar translation.

The results of this exploratory study indicate that a user survey to determine tangible benefits derived from specific information services may provide a satisfactory means for determining the economic justification for technical information services.

So far, we have talked mainly about what one company is trying to do. We would like to say, however, that what any one company can achieve in this whole complex field of information service will never be nearly enough. The problem is big, and it goes far beyond the borders of any single organization. Thus, we believe we have an obligation to support similar efforts by industry groups, professional societies, and the government, in any way that we can.

COOPERATION

For instance, we have been working with the American Petroleum Institute to improve and expand the abstracting and indexing programs of its Central Abstracting Service. This industry group already abstracts over 140 journals and the patents of 10 countries on an "express service" basis, providing member companies with a service which would be far more costly if each one had to produce its own. The API's output of 25,000 abstracts a year (a third of them in the petrochemical field) has for the past several years been classified on cards for later use. The number of cards gets unwieldy, and traditional methods of indexing, such as the card index now in use, have serious limitations. As a consequence the API is now setting up a machine based retrieval system which we're proud to say was derived from a system we developed at Esso Research. This is one example of our belief in the free exchange of information processing know-how. Another example, directed toward the national welfare, is the service of one of our men as chairman of the Science Information Council of the National Science Foundation. Here, the contribution is based on our know-how regarding needs and techniques.

A well organized information service, given full and continuing management support, needs one additional ingredient before it can function effectively. It needs the cooperation of its customers — the individual technical men. Unless they're willing to use your services and know-how you're in trouble. In our company, we make it a point to tell new technical people about the Technical Information Division, and to encourage them to make full use of its services.

One thing we need to do is sell the value of our services to people who can't, or won't, appreciate what can be done for them. One of the arguments that you hear over and over again in this regard, we're told, is that "nobody can do my browsing for me." This view is generally more common among people in exploratory research than it is among people in development work. The latter know just what they're looking for; the former don't know. But what information people do for the exploratory researcher is to supplement his browsing, not substitute for it. Who can tell when a relatively obscure piece of information in a remote field will catalyze the work of a man who simply doesn't have time to read everything? If you can convince your customers that you're not in business to spoon feed them, you will have gone a long way toward encouraging them to make intelligent use of your support.

INFORMATION INPUT

We also feel obliged to comment briefly on the source of the information problem today — the input aspect.

The exchange of technical information is vital to the advancement of technology, but are we publishing too much that isn't really essential to the forward momentum of science and engineering?

There is a growing suspicion that we can no longer afford the luxury of the adage, "publish or perish."

We would like to see technical organizations, including universities, set up higher standards for publication so that their people publish wisely, not wantonly. We would also like to see journals crack down more on marginal papers that don't say anything of moment, or which take six thousand words to say what could be said in the confines of a note or a letter to the editor.

We are also concerned that really worthwhile data finding its way into print often is unavoidably a year to a year and a half behind the actual state of the art. More information transfer must take the form of direct contact between those who need the information and those who are creating it. One step toward encouraging this is the newly formed Science Information Exchange at the Smithsonian Institution, where a number of government agencies are cooperating under National Science Foundation sponsorship in coordinating information as to where, and by whom, research is being conducted.

A thousand years ago, the accumulated knowledge of the world was entrusted to a small band of monks. Laboriously, they copied their previous fund of recorded intelligence so that it could be handed down to future generations.

A hundred years from now, and perhaps even sooner, your most modern methods of handling information might seem as slow and as crude. Revolutionary changes will come. They'll have to if chaos is to be avoided — if man is to avoid strangling on his own surfeit of information.

In conclusion we would like to repeat what we consider to be the responsibilities of the Technical Information Division of the Esso Research and Engineering Company from the management standpoint. Broadly, the first responsibility is to disseminate current technical information and to facilitate retrospective searching. The second responsibility is to operate effectively and efficiently. The third is to develop or procure the tools necessary to maintain a high degree of effectiveness. The fourth responsibility is to make the necessary system research studies to orient the system to meet the routine and the complex requirements of the users.

REFERENCES

[1] Walter Sullivan, *New York Times*, Articles and Editorial, December 25-27, 1961.

[2] W. T. Knox, "The Technical Information Crisis," Meeting of *Industrial Research Institute*, Pittsburgh, Pennsylvania, October 16, 1961.

[3] P. L. Saltzberg, duPont Patent Anniversary Dinner, November 14, 1961.

[4] "No Rest for Know-How," *Chemical Week*, p. 61, January 27, 1962.

[5] G. H. Cloud and W. T. Knox, "Information Research—A New Tool for the Petroleum Industry," *1959 Fifth World Petroleum Congress*.

[6] W. T. Knox, "Information, Please," 53rd Annual Meeting, *American Institute of Chemical Engineers*, Washington, D. C., December 5, 1961.

[7] Aran S. Melik-Shakhrozarov, "Technical Information in the U.S.S.R.," Moscow, 1960.

[8] S. Herner "Information-Gathering Habits of Workers in Pure and Applied Science," *Ind. Eng. Chem.*, *46*, p. 228-36, (1954).

[9] E. Tornudd, "Study of the Use of Scientific Literature and Reference Services by Scandinavian Scientists and Engineers Engaged in Research," Preprints of Papers for the International Conference on Scientific Information, Washington, D.C., November 16-21, 1958, Area I, pp. 9-66.

By DeWitt O. Myatt
Science Communications, Inc.

7. Designing an Information Center to Meet a Real-System Requirement

MY ASSIGNMENT is to address myself to the matter of the working problems that come when one attempts to translate information science into a successful information center operation. It may be termed the "engineer-designer" function. This is a presumptuous position for anybody to assume in the present state of ignorance: to link our adolescence in information science to the human user, the human institutions, and the patterns of human effort that ultimately bring to a point of actual value any particular increment of information in our recorded storehouse of knowledge.

Among the underlying reasons behind the great upsurge of concern about making more effective use of scientific knowledge are dramatic illustrations from the past fifteen or twenty years of ways this technique of science and research can be utilized for the purposes of man. Society has discovered science. Fifty years ago, most of science was a matter of interest and concern for men of intellect. Twenty or thirty years ago, through such industries as the chemical industry, it was being exploited for economic affairs and gains. Today, there is a very significant additional use that is being made of it: the use of science for social purposes. And I think that some of our current concern with it, the feeling of need to do the best we can with it, has been stimulated by this largest and grandest recent overtone associated with scientific effort.

This paper is not concerned with codes or machines, and their technology or techniques. Nor is it concerned with the library, mechanized or not, although it is a quite probable component of the information center.

In most technical fields today, the thought-ful scientist views his obligation to remain well informed with a sense of acute personal distress. Almost certainly, the annual output in his own specialty has continued to increase. But beyond that, our great triumphs in merging science at the base have unblocked new areas, previously the specialty of another, in which he can also be competent. Self interest, if nothing more, presses him to command them as well, or accept consignment to a relatively narrow and barren field.

A second major influence on the scientist has been the way our society has altered its expectations of him in the past generation. In fact, we have only to go back a few years to Sputnik I to see quite significant changes, although the historic inflection point probably should date from the OSRD activities of World War II. Before then, the scientist really lived in a comparatively simple and undemanding world. He roamed pretty much where he pleased, and the terrain of a single discipline usually proved fertile enough to keep him happy and rewarded. Society pretty much looked on his useful discoveries as windfalls. Since it had not yet grasped the full implications of creative research, it issued no socially motived directives and established no quotas for our scientists and technologists.

Today, the individual scientist usually finds himself a part of large and complex technological endeavors. These endeavors reflect the rapid industrialization of science and the scientist. And, more and more often, they are addressed to the meeting of a social desire or need, which may be the conquest of a major disease, the creation of a new tool of national defense, or the enhancement of an economic resource. The scientist and his science bear the sobering responsibilities of cultural maturity.

In this new environment, the scientist's information need cannot be dismissed as a uniquely personal concern. Increasingly it has become viewed as a responsibility his employer should share, most particularly with informational services that conserve the ever more sought talents, and ever more costly man hours, of available technical manpower. This is the shift, we believe, that has led to the appearance of the modern technical information center.

The scientist's very endorsement of the information center concept suggests strongly that new forces of actual historical magnitude have come into play. Especially significant is the scientist's philosophical acceptance of the judgment of another in sifting subject matter through a storage-retrieval mechanism that he does not ever expect to operate personally. It is true, of course, that he still is free to use other channels that give him direct contact with original material. But the fact that research scientists will even concede value to techniques requiring a third party participant indicates the magnitude of the influences they feel.

Because the information center is a young and still vulnerable institution (perhaps, in fact, the first undisputed child of an information surplus technological culture), we believe those who would design and operate them should make a real effort, however scanty the current firm knowledge, to understand underlying forces, the practical limits they imply, and the special innovations they encourage. This is the time for intellectual rigor, so far as it can be applied.

DEFINING THE TECHNICAL INFORMATION CENTER

In order to draw broad lines between what the library and information center can do and naturally tend to do, let us accept for purposes of definition that the "pure" library does not have peer competence in the technical matter dealt with. As our growing understanding of the tools of technical communication have advanced, the alert technical librarian will begin to think in terms of mechanizing the library, through the development of codes and through the choice of machinery that allows an orderly search to be made of items that have been indexed far more deeply than was considered useful or feasible previously. There is, I think, a general tendency for the librarian to assume that there is no way of knowing what kind of question is going to be thrown at him or her, and that therefore this encoding and preparation for mechanization ideally should be comprehensive, including the total input to the library and additional services that can be subscribed. In general, the picture that is evolved is one of a resource of value but one that depends upon outside request or demand for it to function effectively. There is a passive service stance if one ignores the fact that there are things like accession lists that do represent initiative on the part of the librarian. The orientation tends to be toward documents rather than toward subject matter.

In contrast, in the information center there is more of a tendency to ask, "What value is this for whom?" and to inform the scientist that here is something worthwhile and interesting. Instead of the librarian's reaction of comprehensiveness, there is an assumption or an arrogation that the information center specialist knows what the scientist wants and passes information to him on his own initiative. Rather than subscription to a service that is of interest to the using organization, although it had to be prepared to serve at least 100 other organizations to be economic, the information center staff person will make selective extractions from material as it comes in.

Any realistic definition of a technical information center must relate it to a larger functional system. This larger system contains, in addition to our center, information users and (since the use of knowledge almost invariably creates new knowledge) it contains information sources. Finally, the larger system contains a policy or managerial element. The executive element decides the users to be served and the sort of information and service the center is expected to provide.

Let us formalize an assertion from these comments:

"The proper informational mission of a technical information center is a function of the technical mission of the population it serves." (ASSERTION I)

This assertion does not differentiate the technical library from the information center. We shall contend that the staff of the information center is professionally qualified in the technical *subjects* handled, whereas the special expertise of the technical library is the management of *documents*. In any real situation, we rarely find either information centers or technical libraries whose staffs are entirely unqualified in the other's domain. But if we attempt to fix the ultimate distinction between prime competencies that lead to totally different roles within the organization, we believe the test is the presence or absence of professional capability (i.e., capacity to function as a technical expert) *in the subject matter.*

In talking hereafter of a technical information center, we mean an organization that satisfies the following definition:

"A group serving a technical organization or field by collecting and supplying pertinent and specialized information to other specified groups and individuals, and qualified and functioning in this role as a professional peer of these groups and individuals." (DEFINITION I)

The clause within this definition that reads " . . . functioning in this role as a professional peer . . . ," calls for examination of one other prime question. The question concerns the resources the center must command to collect, store, search, retrieve, and communicate at peer level. To account for them, we suggest:

"The information center's proper technical knowledgeability and subject range are determined by the technical competence of the persons being served and by the nature of the problems in which they are engaged. Its proper information processing and supply practices are determined by the knowledge patterns traditional in the special fields represented among those it is serving." (ASSERTION II)

It will be seen that a center satisfying assertion II does not require those it serves to learn anything about its information processing operations. This is possible because it has peer competence in the technical subject matter, and thus can "translate" its raw retrieval output from "information system" language to, say, colloid chemist language. In this respect, the center can make life distinctly easier for the person served than the

"pure" library we defined previously.

Assertion II also implies that working knowledge of specialized information processing techniques is not an inherent responsibility of the bench scientist. As the opposite side of the coin, it implies that there is a distinctive field of expertise pertinent to information and communication processes. (We have heard "information scientist" with increasing prevalence, so we should perhaps call it "information science" — and its applied art companion, "communication technology".) We believe that the rapidly advancing research in machine and non-machine storage-search-retrieval methods already has presented substantial justification for this very important claim. Machine data processing, for example, may be a small part of the total information art, but it is important in special areas and certainly has demanded specialized training far beyond the tolerance of the person who is not a machine specialist.

The logical consequences of this line of reasoning produce guide lines that we think are of primary importance when one actually gets down to the matter of designing or operating an information center. They include:

1. The designer should investigate the field of knowledge patterns, competency levels, personal attitudes, and working objectives of the group he proposes to serve. From these, he can derive the information service range and techniques that make connections with real customers at the other end of the line and are neither over nor under designed to serve them.

2. His information output should be purged of any characteristics imposed by the center's internal storage-retrieval techniques. (We will concede one departure from this ideal, when purging costs are greater than the combined effects of the educational costs and communication losses imposed on those he is serving.)

3. His staff must contain two professional competencies: in specified technical subjects, and in information science and communication technology. Key members of his staff must be knowledgeable in both fields.

4. He should view his staff as prime terminal vehicles for conveying information to the customer, and for accepting it initially to the center. As information carriers, face to

face discussions (or ear to ear telephone conversation) are impressively distinctive from the accession list, or even the individual memorandum. He should be most particularly aware of the novel ways in which the human can function as a component link of an information service system.

HUMANISTIC FEATURES OF THE TECHNICAL INFORMATION CENTER

When "science" and "man" are mentioned in the same breath, the first quick comparison that comes to mind — particularly to the mind of a scientist possessing the true faith — is the relative fallibility of the human when compared with the ordered beauty and reassuring reproducibility of scientific law.

Shouldn't we be doing our best to build information services that *exclude* the human, rather than making him the pivot component?

And isn't the added suggestion that the service be derived from the human interests of the group to be served really a sort of ultimate confession that there is no discipline or substance to this subject at all?

We believe neither is so.

For our first advocate of the human ingredient in the technical information service, we offer the French philosopher-scientist du Nouy. Du Nouy advances the essential argument that "science" is inherently shot through with humanism. "Science," he says, "is only that portion of nature that humans have been able to make sense of through a process of rational ordering."[2] If one follows du Nouy's basic contention to its application here, the human is the most fully compatible vessel for contending with scientific information, being its creator. Mechanisms (like index cards or computers) may aid the human but only rarely can carry value discrimination beyond the moron level. And professional scientists have only limited use for moronic services.

For our second fundamental argument in defense of the human ingredient, we offer R. E. Gibson, the scientist-executive-philosopher who heads the Applied Physics Laboratory of the Johns Hopkins University. APL originated and currently operates one of the first modern technical information centers, the Solid Propellent Information Agency. Gibson asserts:

"Knowledge, the distillate of human experience, is stored in three types of banks: (a) in the human mind and memory; (b) in the literature — periodicals, books, reports, and so forth; (c) in the products of technology and culture, commodities, tools, services, and organizations. Of these the only bank which pays interest and offers capital gains is the mind. The growth of knowledge is a function of the capacity and the number of educated minds engaged in its cultivation."[3]

So much for natural congruence of art and discipline with the human mind: what about human fallibility? To examine this question, we propose to review the conditions and consequences one might reasonably anticipate if he set up an information service.

Let us suppose you have been charged with the responsibility of designing a technical information service. Let us suppose further that a real organization, or field of interest, staffed with real scientists and engineers, with real laboratories — even real libraries and librarians — exists already, to use and be used by this service you have been asked to design.

If you subscribe, as the author does, to the belief that an optimal technical information service is a derivative of the population it serves, the logical outgrowth of your efforts should possess several gratifying characteristics:

1. Your recommended design should relate closely to the expressed interest of the population being served — which makes them happy (at least before the actual service is launched; it also helps in getting executive authorization).

2. In your design, you will find yourself virtually forced to take account of the firm data you were actually able to develop. This stricture reduces the likelihood that the "service" will really be an experimental vehicle for one person's untested theories. By no means, however, does it eliminate the opportunity for imaginative or unconventional techniques. It is more likely to stimulate innovations that have the notable added virtue of utility.

3. Even if your survey technique is creditable, there is usually enough "slop" in the returns that you can sneak a few of your pet techniques into less critical areas of the de-

sign. This usually means that the exercise leaves you happy.

So we finally get our service established, through steps we know include human fallibility. What happens then?

The normal design errors in such a system do not compound to absurdity or catastrophe like a runaway computer. For the characteristic strength of the humanistic element now comes into play. The staff members of a real technical information center, being human and able to recognize the technical shortcomings of initial operation, quite predictably will react to, compensate for, and ultimately correct the imperfections. Our basic strategy is therefore quite sound. This organic vitality of the modern technical information service, manned by professional scientists or engineers, permits—indeed, counsels—acceptance of design directives from a population that is not sophisticated in information technique *per se*. Just breathe life into the service by endowing it with a well trained, service oriented technical staff, and it will gravitate toward its optimal role. It will do more yet: it will follow the changing and evolving needs of the population it serves as the whole endeavor proceeds.

At first glance, one might conclude that an information service built on specifications laid down by the user does not allow us to make use of the more sophisticated information processing techniques. This is not so. It does, however, illuminate for us the sharp distinction that should be made between the methods used within the service group and the techniques it employs in communicating with its "clients." Internally, the search-retrieval system may be technologically formidable. Externally, the output should be delivered in a format acceptable to the recipient. The recipient (even though he is a scientist) turns out to have human fallibility, too, and woe betide the system that fails to accommodate to him.

We might have a sense of despair on reaching the conclusion that all of science is really just that slim caricature of all human experiences that we have found organizable. But we might also view the emergence of the human-centered technical information center as heartening evidence that we have at last accumulated enough science that we can no longer subject our precious hoard to the intellectual crudities of non-humanistic mass processing techniques and still retain our grip on it. Its growing richness has just begun to make demands for something better — to be specific, those store-search-retrieval schemes that employ more effectively the subtleties and discriminating powers of the human mind.

BENEFITS OF OPINION QUESTIONS IN PRE-DESIGN SURVEYS

This leads us to a justification for soliciting opinion as well as fact when one sets about designing the technical information center.

I believe we should not take too much for granted at this primitive tintype stage of technical communication and the assistance of human effort through institutional devices such as the technical information center. Therefore, I would suggest that you cannot beat the technique of going to and talking to the people who are working in the particular field the center is to serve.

If one predicates that (1) the person interviewed understands what you are asking him; (2) he is asked to answer only on behalf of himself, or a small group with which he is intimately associated; (3) he is made reasonably convinced that his personal practices, preferences, and opinions are inherently "right" answers to your questions; and (4) a sufficient sample of the population concerned is polled to eliminate statistical uncertainties; we believe that a more complete and reliable specification for the proper information service has been established than specifications one can develop through other means, and most particularly through means restricted to non-opinion measurements. We believe this because the working success of the service ("center", etc.) depends so intimately upon subjective considerations, including such "unscientific" matters as the college degrees held by the center's employees, the official name of the service, and mass attitudes of the group being served. One should make positive efforts to draw out these subjective factors, so there is some reasonable chance of dealing with them effectively in the design.

These precepts underlie the specific techniques utilized in a recent study conducted for the Office of Naval Research. A summary of the survey objectives, the approach used, and the service derived through the investigation are given.

A CASE HISTORY: DESIGN OF A TECHNICAL INFORMATION CENTER SERVING THE UPPER ATMOSPHERE TECHNICAL COMMUNITY[4]

Objectives of project

The ARIES project had the broad purpose of determining whether a technical information service would contribute to current scientific and engineering programs concerned with knowledge of the upper atmosphere (the altitude range 30 to 300 km). To accomplish this purpose, it was necessary to determine:

1. The merit of a service
2. The optimal technical coverage
3. The service techniques and staff requirements, and
4. The estimated annual operating cost.

The survey technique

The investigation method employed had to:

1. Identify the members of the population.
2. Determine the technical information usage of an adequate sample of the population.
3. Determine the most acceptable service techniques for serving it.
4. Ascertain the desire of the population for a centralized technical information service.

Depth personal interviews, coupled with "cross check" mail questionnaires on key points of the survey, were employed to obtain this information.

So far as possible, we chose persons at the "group head" level for detailed interview discussions, so a single interrogation would produce an informed appraisal of the involvement of all persons in the group with upper atmosphere data, and would yield a working-knowledge opinion of the technical information need.

Persons interviewed were asked to answer only on behalf of their own group, as we in effect synthesized a total population answer in our compilation of individual replies.

Size of population sample surveyed

The typical group head supervised three to 10 professionals. A single interview thus reflected the explicit practices and requirements

of perhaps five to 10 persons, including technicians as well as professionals.

The survey returns indicated that the following population sample was represented:

	Sent	No. Respondents	No. Professionals Represented
Interview check list	– –	38	160
Mail questionnaire	80	39	575
Total	80	77	735

In addition, relatively significant discussions were held with approximately 35 persons under circumstances not resulting in a filled-out questionnaire. (The distribution of their attitudes regarding a service appeared consistent with the more formally obtained replies.)

Analysis of returns

Statistical tests were employed to determine the significance of the replies obtained from the sample population, and to see whether sub-groups in the population varied in their information usage and their desire for an information service.

The "do you want a service" answers in the interview sample and the mail questionnaire sample were cross checked to see whether these different survey techniques indicated significantly different sample populations. (The test showed a very high probability that the populations were identical.)

To facilitate the cross correlation process, a Keysort card transcript of all mail questionnaire and interview check lists was prepared. Its model was the brief mail questionnaire. Tests of more detailed questions were made by hand compilation from the interview questionnaire.

DERIVATION OF OPTIMAL SERVICE DESIGN

Desire for an information service

The questionnaire data were analyzed to determine the desire of the technical population for an information service. The results were:

	Desire for Service, %			Desire Rating*	Statistical Significance**
	Highly	More	Less		
Interviewees (33)	55	24	21	1.67	Yes
Mail questionnaires (34)	44	44	12	1.65	Yes
Total (67)				1.66	Yes

*Composite of multiple-choice replies rating from −1 to +3.
**By X^2 test.

Subject range of the service

The data usage of the population was employed to establish the optimal subject coverage for the service. The results (10 subjects with the highest use ratings) are given, in rank order in the following table.

Inspection suggested a cut-off value of 0.8 in defining the initial subject coverage of the service.

Subject Field	Use rating*	Statistically Significant**
Density	1.84	Yes
Solar Radiation	1.4	Yes
Temperature	1.37	Yes
Winds	1.2	Yes
Pressure	1.1	
Ionization	1.05	Yes
0.8		
Water	0.63	
Oxygen	0.63	
Ozone	0.47	
Nitrogen Oxides	0.52	

*Composite of multiple-choice replies rating from −1 to +3.
**By t test.

Technical skills required

The subjects ranking above 0.8 in usage value then were inspected to determine the technical skills desirable in the service staff. They indicate principal needs for professional knowledge of:

1. Physics (especially radiation phenomena)
2. Meteorology
3. Instrumentation (electronic and mechanical)

Service techniques desired

Interview check list returns next were analyzed with respect to preferences expressed for different information service techniques. The results for the 10 service functions with the highest ratings follow, in rank order:

Technique	Desire rating*	Statistically Significant**
Loose leaf manual	2.2	Yes
Data collection-compilation	1.9	Yes
Accession list	1.5	Yes
Abstract bulletin	1.5	
Technical extract-reports	1.4	
Newsletter	1.2	
Report and document collection	1.2	
"Man Friday"	1.1	
1.0		
Language translations	0.85	
Handbooks	0.67	

*Numerical weighted average for population answering the questions.

**By t test.

Inspection of the spread of desire ratings suggested a cut-off value of 1.0.

These service preferences show a predominance of function requiring technical knowledge, and editorial rather than library skills.

The broad picture evoked by these preference rankings provides a rather explicit set of directives for the personal and information technique skills, staff activity patterns, and physical resources of a service that will satisfy the demand. They are itemized as follows:

THE SERVICE SHOULD PROVIDE:

1. A data collection-compilation activity, with the compilations disseminated in the form of "perpetual" manuals updated as appropriate with loose leaf inserts.
2. Periodic announcements of new subject knowledge sources acquired by the service. Periodic accession lists were recommended.
3. A newsletter. (We recommended that the newsletter function be provided as a "Progress Highlights" opening section of the accession list.)
4. The document collection necessary to conduct these activities.
5. Technical reportorial coverage of meetings and conferences.
6. "Man Friday" information services by staff members.
7. Technical editorial skills and personnel with the professional capacity to deal effectively on a person to person basis with project scientists and engineers.
8. An appreciable travel activity.

THE SERVICE DOES NOT NEED TO PROVIDE:

1. Conventional library services, such as document loans, book purchases, reprint ordering, etc.
2. Special correlations or mathematical services.
3. Administrative support in organizing meetings.

The operating service organization

An organization chart for an information center performing these functions is shown in Exhibit 1.

This pattern was chosen to provide a maximum assignment of specific work responsibilities to individuals, yet retain necessary flexibility for unusual work loads. Total staff includes four senior and one junior professionals (p) plus a supporting clerical-secretarial (s) force of four.

EFFECT OF CASE HISTORY SPECIFICS ON GENERAL METHOD

We suspect the ARIES case history was inherently kinder to the surveyor than many of the situations one might be called on to explore. To enumerate:

1. The sharp definition of the subject field, namely, geophysical attributes of the atmosphere and rocketsonde technology, considerably eased the conception and preparation of the "morphology list", which we feel contributed considerably in gaining professional acceptance for the interviewer and technical consistency during interview discussion.

2. The population proved quite uniform in its attitudes regarding a service, thus producing key answers possessing high statistical assurance from relatively small samples.

3. This consistency also produced substantial concordance regarding the design for certain services and subject coverages. In fact, almost no interpretive judgments by the survey group were required to reconcile the replies with a set of realistic recommendations.

4. The service desires expressed were readily accommodated in an organization of logical design and realistic size, manned by persons with conventional discipline training and career experience.

We may, of course, be leaning over backwards in this generalized judgment, in view of our introductory emphasis of the humanistic underpinnings of scientific fields. But we can readily visualize patterns of survey re-

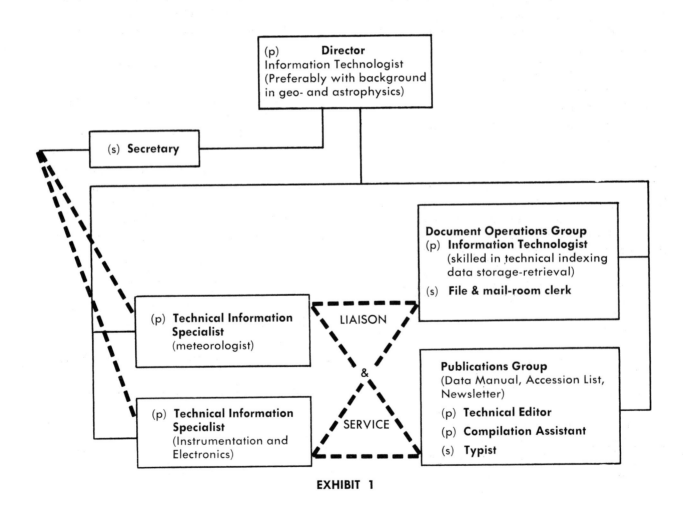

EXHIBIT 1

turns that would be much more difficult to cope with than ARIES proved to be.

Should we apply this basic survey technique to a more refractory problem, we do have available a few more tricks in our kit bag that might spell the difference between a derived design and blind guessing. For example:

1. Fields of interest might be approached by asking more than one leading member of the survey population to outline it for us, and then looking to see where their replies coincide and diverge. In some instances, a field is really a number of "schools", loosely bound together by a common purpose, perhaps, but with distinctively different technical patterns. Where such characteristics are found, some of the service functions may properly be provided to certain parts of the field, while others may serve across the board.

2. Within limits, certain statistical assurances can be obtained by increasing the survey sample size. Should an initial sample show uncertain concurrence, we can examine the return, and by risking an assumption or two, get a reasonable indication of the additional surveying needed to clarify the ambiguities.

3. At times a particular service requested is explicit and technically justified, but the specialized training required and the fractional manpower called for make it clearly uneconomic to provide a properly qualified specialist in the centralized service. In such an instance, we might recommend that part time information service duties be assigned to an appropriate specialist in the group requiring the service. In general, peer competence in the information organization facilitates practical solutions that are not strictly observant of organization chart lines.

Finally, we wish to urge this key recommendation on any person assigned the task of designing an information service: begin by just looking at the situation with the greatest perceptivity you can bring to bear. At the beginning, try to avoid any preconception as to the methods you will use to develop firm guide lines for your design. For just as certainly as a sound design study can avoid unproductive costs in the operation of an information center, the initial natural disposition of persons, attitudes, and activities usually contains hints regarding particularly apt design solutions. If you can see them, they usually suggest singularly productive approaches to data collection, and stimulate the development of imaginative and unusually well fitting designs.

REFERENCES

[1] Portions of this paper are reprinted from DeWitt O. Myatt and Thompson E. Upham, "A Quantitative Technique for Designing the Technical Information Center", *Journal of Chemical Documentation 1*, 18-24, 1961, by permission of the copyright owner, The American Chemical Society.

[2] Lecomte du Nouy, *Human Destiny*, The New American Library of World Literature, New York, N.Y., 1949.

[3] R. E. Gibson, "Impact of Government Programs on Growth of Knowledge", presented before the 134th ACS National Meeting, Sept. 9, 1958, Chicago, Ill.

[4] Project ARIES (Atmospheric Research Information Exchange Study), A Study to Determine the Merits of an Upper Atmosphere Technical Information Service. Contract 3071-00, Office of Naval Research. (Grateful acknowledgment is made to the Office of Naval Research, Code 416, for permission to utilize the results of that study for this paper. Information and opinions presented here do not necessarily carry the endorsement or represent the viewpoint of the U. S. Navy.) Check lists and questionnaire responses of this survey are available from the author on request.

By James Hillier
RCA Laboratories

8. Management's Evaluation of Information Services

MY POSITION IS AS "devil's advocate" in evaluating information services from management's point of view. I represent the manager who must pay the bill the best he can, watch out for empire builders, and separate fact from fad. We have to look at the forest instead of the trees. In giving management's view on information service, technical information, and information retrieval, perhaps I can help you in dealings with your managers on similar problems in your operations.

First, let me express a note of caution. We ought not rush ahead without giving more thought to the overall systems we are concerned about. We need to look at some of the critical problems. I am worried that, despite all the advances in this field, we may inadvertently be building limitations into the information system. These constraints may limit creativity which is so important in a research laboratory. I direct my remarks to the system as used in a research organization where, we must always remember, it is necessary to obtain results. This is an extremely complex problem; I want to re-emphasize this and to give a somewhat different perspective on the problem, from the management point of view.

There are two basic aims in a technical information system. One aim is to deal with the information explosion facing the technical staff. Management's problem here is critical: determining the optimum distribution of manpower to meet the need. The second aim is to provide management with the technical information it needs for decision making. Many decisions have to be made on technical grounds, both in government and industry. This is an unfamiliar territory for many high level managers. It, too, is related to the general problem of information services. Let us consider both aims in more detail.

TECHNICAL INFORMATION FOR THE TECHNICAL STAFF

The problem of providing technical information to the technical staff is the one most people in the field are interested in; it's the one I'm most interested in. Let us consider the parameters we deal with in this problem and how management looks at this. The basic problem in almost any research lab is trying to get productivity out of the lab, where productivity means new ideas, new developments, and progress in a scientific sense. The manager of a research lab generally has a fixed budget. Thus, optimizing the system (and information services are very obviously an exceedingly important part of the system) really means: how do you distribute this rather fixed manpower or dollars? (I shall use manpower and dollars interchangeably because in a research lab they are interchangeable.)

When you optimize, you have to have a measure. How do you measure productivity or creativity in a research lab? There are subjective judgments that are surprisingly good in measuring creativity, even though there appears to be no way to put a quantitative measure on it. If I select a group of people that several of my lab directors know very well and ask the lab directors, "Lay out in rank order the creative ability of these individuals," I will get a list from each lab director that is almost identical one to the other. There may be one or two people that are out of place by one or two marks on this ranking list. These lab directors somehow or other know how to measure creativity in an individual. Another parameter is indicated by the fact that everyone of you probably has a different idea of what is meant by "research". Perhaps it is radically different from my ideas. Here, too, we are dealing with a spectrum.

Creativity in a laboratory doing basic, exploratory research, as my own lab, needs quite a different sort of measure than might be applied to development laboratories at the other end of the spectrum, where costs and schedules, etc., are much more important.

Looking more specifically at information services, one question is, "What kind of service are you going to provide?" Again this presents a whole new spectrum of problems. One extreme is simply a traditional, limited library that does nothing but provide references on call. The middle range is information retrieval according to subject matter with all its attendant problems. The other extreme of service is provided by a highly technical group that is going to feed chosen or specified information to your bench workers. You've got to measure the situation; and then somehow or other you've got to decide within this spectrum what is the best, what is the optimum service to provide.

In the laboratories themselves there are important variables related to information services. What type of lab is it? Is it one doing very basic research, applied research, or is it the basic almost engineering type of laboratory? You have this spectrum to deal with. There is another spectrum in the technical sophistication of the group.

There are also two considerations that are quite important from the management point of view. One is the size of the lab. Obviously, the budget that might be allocated to an information service is going to depend considerably on the size of the laboratory. A second and perhaps more important variable is the homogeneity of the lab. It is possible to have a laboratory that is quite large, but in an essentially narrow discipline; that is, a lot of people doing closely related work in, say, chemistry, or a limited field within chemistry. At the other extreme is the very heterogeneous lab where there are many different disciplines. If you want to consider the limit, such a laboratory would have individual technical workers, each one doing a completely unrelated problem in different fields and different disciplines.

Thus, we have a complicated system which the mathematician would say is represented by about a five dimensional matrix. Somehow, the manager has to thread his way through that matrix and find the optimum situation for the particular laboratory he manages. This is really an operations research job made all the more difficult because, while it is fairly easy to describe these problems in qualitative terms, there are no quantitative measures for these variables. It's one thing to talk about the size of a lab, but try to put a measure on the heterogeneity of a lab. Try to define precisely in what part of the spectrum of research any particular lab exists; within the lab itself you'll find the spectrum. It's not an easy problem.

When I go into the literature on the subject of technical information services, I am concerned because I find a tendency for people to pick out only a part of the problem and make a very intensive and very intelligent study of it. There is nothing wrong with that, provided that you know that the problem studied is only a specified part of the larger problem.

When I try to find discussions of this larger problem, I don't find them very often. I have tried to resolve this overall problem; to see what the problem is, with what we are dealing, and what are some of the critical elements. The matrix approach is too complicated. However, there are some boundary conditions, some ways of describing the system, that will give an insight into what the problem really is.

I feel quite strongly that it certainly is *not* just satisfying the user's need for information. I'm not sure that the user's need for information is what the user asked for. This is quite important. In talking to my own people, I get very vague answers as to what they really need in the way of information. In many cases, they haven't analyzed what they need. Their information needs seem to be determined by tradition, by custom and by habit. I often wonder how many people have really analyzed what they need. What form would the information come in?

As has been indicated, I have the problem of trying to relate the expenditure of manpower/dollars optimally in this multidimensional matrix. I will go through the parameters already mentioned in some detail. When I place my laboratory in this multidimensional matrix, it is what I would call a worst case. In system design, worst cases are the extreme cases. I say that not because I feel particularly sorry for myself, but because it just happens to come out that way.

First, we have a very large laboratory with 450 professionals which, with all the services that go along with it, totals about 1,200 people. It is a very heterogeneous laboratory. I find that I have about 18 to 20 separate, isolated fields represented in the laboratory; this runs a span from metallurgy, to chemistry, to meteorology, and so forth, including several facets of physics which are essentially individual fields today. There are 150 clearly identifiable projects; thus, there is an average of only three people per project.

It is a very basic and exploratory laboratory. We do no development work; as soon as we establish a principle, other parts of the RCA organization do the development work. Since our 450 people represent only five or six percent of the professional staff of RCA, we in this central laboratory are a very small element of the company. Yet, the level of technical sophistication is very high. Unless you get into some very basic or nuclear physics, I doubt if there is a lab that has a higher technical level. Obviously in this environment, I'm looking for new ideas, I'm looking for new inventions — really inventions of materials or components rather than inventions of systems and apparatus. My basic criterion of evaluation has to be creativity. Of course, the decision I have to make in this environment is the magnitude and the nature of the service that I should provide to this group.

CREATIVITY AND INFORMATION

However, before this can be done I must tie creativity and information together. If you don't have an understanding of this relationship, then this paper is meaningless. For a more detailed discussion of this I would recommend a paper that I wrote which gives, I think, a rather new approach to the relationship between creativity and information flow.[1] I will now review this relationship between information and creativity, because it's quite important relative to what people should be doing in providing information services.

Let us consider the analogy between a human communication system and an engineered communication system. You're all familiar with the telephone. The system starts as a message in a brain. An encoder system then puts the message into electrical form by

means of a transmitter. The signal is transmitted over wires, radio, etc. At the other end there is another transducer that converts the electrical form back to sound waves, which the ear can appreciate. This is the receiver. The language that's used, of course, is a code. The code goes into the brain, where the message is disentangled. The expectation is that the message that was disentangled in the receiving brain was the same that was started out in the other one. Quite often it is not.

CHANNEL CAPACITY

However, the most important characteristic of any communication system is what a technical man would call signal to noise ratio. This in turn, through Shannon's theories, can be translated into the channel capacity. In other words, how much information can you put through this system? It turns out that any communication channel has a certain capacity. You can put a certain number of bits per second through that channel. The human system is no different. It has a limit, and that limit is surprisingly small. Various people measure and estimate it, and it always comes out in measures of a few tens of bits per second. Information experts tell me that in the usual presentation of a paper, allowing for the redundancy of the languages, etc., information is conveyed at the rate of only ten bits per second. The important thing is that it's a very small number. It really doesn't matter what the number is.

But if it's a small number, and there is essentially an infinity of information potentially available, obviously there must be some selection process in the information system. And selection is important when a human being can take in information at only these few tens of bits per second. There are only twenty-four hours in a day, and humans can't live in parallel; thus, everything feeds through that narrow channel. Further, that's the rate for the *total* information that he needs for living, not just for the work he's doing. Everything he does has to feed through that channel.

There are a lot of people writing, and still, when an individual reads, he's only one individual. Even though it takes longer to write than it does to read, it doesn't take long before you have more people writing than one man can read. That, in very simple terms, is the information problem.

SELECTION PROCESS

When the amount of information gets very large, there is another problem involving probability which is the key to the whole picture. There's a certain element of chance that the scientist will get certain pieces of information and not get others. Long before he became a scientist or before he became a customer of an information center, the scientist has learned through experience the most probable channels that will get information of value to him. The value of the information is usually judged on how well it satisfies his personal desires.

Remember that it is the *individual* who controls the selection process. He has learned it through his whole lifetime of experience, and he controls it. You can't do anything about changing it no matter what you try to do. If you don't provide a higher probability of value to that man, he's not going to pay any attention to you.

In response to an overload, the human or biological information system departs somewhat from the engineered system. When overloaded, the engineered system starts making mistakes and the information is garbled. The human, or biological, system is very accurate, almost on a linear scale up to and near the channel limit of the system. However, when it is overloaded, it collapses. It quits. If you were ever in an automobile accident, where information started coming too fast, you'll know what I mean by the information channel collapsing. Perhaps nervous breakdowns occur when we've exceeded the information capacity. I'm quite sure I exceed this capacity at times, and I have to get back quickly on the track and limit my input.

The important thing is that all of us at all times are controlling this input. We've learned to stay sane, if you will, by the simple process of not overloading our channel capacity. But we're always doing it by selection. This is selection on both the output channels and the input channels. You have to recognize that you're dealing with this selection whenever you start trying to provide any kind of information for an individual.

Let us return to the process of creativity.

Everybody seems to agree that a creative idea comes out of one mind only when the right pieces of information somehow coincide in time in that mind. The "flash of genius" is what the patent attorney calls it. I think any of you who have been in creative pursuits have recognized how things have been hazy, and all of a sudden the right bits of information trigger off the idea and everything falls into place. Thus, it is necessary to have the right pieces of information in the mind, and those have got to come into the mind through this selection process, keeping the channel from overloading.

This is the heart of the problem, because you've got to get the right pieces of information into this creative mind in order to get the creative act. But you don't know what the right pieces of information are; you don't know what information the man already has in his mind; you don't know at what time these will come together in the right relationship. Thus, you are back at the roulette table and dealing purely with chance.

This is very important because the management of a research laboratory is always trying to raise the level of creativity of the people in the laboratory. You have to find some means of raising the probability of a creative act, or a creative bit in that man's mind. But as you are trying to raise the probability, you do not know, *a priori*, what information is the right information, what time or how to give it to him. Somehow you've got to find ways of raising this probability, and it's not an easy problem. If you read the paper referred to, you will see a few ideas that we have been trying out which have been working quite well.

The important point is that this is a probability situation. In this type of situation, if you superimpose one probability on another the ultimate probability is always smaller. It's impossible to have a probability greater than one. This is one of the things that has bothered me about the particular type of information service which selects or feeds the so-called "right" information to the individual. I tend to look on such a service as having a probability less than one of transmitting the right information to the individual. When you superimpose that probability on his probability of getting the right channels, you have lowered the over-all probability of the situation. There still is this great mass of information potentially available and somehow you have to be able to pull together the right bits which result in creative ideas.

However, all this does not answer the problem of how to do this, and I cannot provide such an answer. It is important that the existence of this probability be kept in mind as various information systems are developed. If this is considered as the key point in the multi-dimensional matrix referred to, then there is a chance of being able to work toward a useful information service.

TYPES OF INFORMATION SERVICES

Let us return to the needs to be satisfied. I consider that there are five types of information needs in the kind of lab that we have considered. To repeat, this is a large, heterogeneous lab, doing basic exploratory work, where creativity is the important measure. These five needs will be considered in order of increasing importance.

PREVENTION OF DUPLICATION

The first is the need for avoiding excessive duplication of research, particularly in those experiments which are destined to give negative results. We don't like to waste money on projects that aren't going to go anywhere. If people would publish the negative results as well as the positive ones, we could save the country, the company and everybody a lot of time and money. This is a conventional information retrieval problem. When you have a specific project or experiment, it is a fairly straightforward information retrieval effort to find out what else has been done on this specific experiment.

We do very often have the problem of vocabulary changes. In electronics the vocabulary has been changing so fast that information gets lost because one doesn't know where to look for it. This is a familiar problem. Whether or not a specific information service is needed to handle this is a question. You certainly need the basic element, which is a reference search system. Incidentally, at our laboratory we have a good traditional library which I consider to be the reference look-up type.

SPECIFIC INFORMATION OR DATA NEED

You also need to provide specific information that the technical staff requires. The great mass of technical literature and patent data contains the specific piece of information that the man wants — it might be the thermal conductivity of some special alloy — which can usually be defined quite accurately. If it exists in literature, it should be rather a routine job to find it. If he knows it's in a certain paper, this simply requires reference look-up; if not, then conventional information retrieval may help.

CATCHING UP INFORMATION

The third most important item is "catching up" information. We have a lot of problems today in research where the individual stays current in a field for a relatively short length of time. But if he's going to stay in research, he has to catch up with something new. It may not be often — every five or 10 years, perhaps. However, when you need to do this it must be done with the maximum efficiency. Again, it seems like a fairly routine, straightforward, simple information retrieval job. It may even be simpler than the previous information retrieval jobs, because most of the time the catching up information comes in textbooks and review articles. These are useful until you get almost up to date. I do not think an information service group could help this problem unless you could build into them the skill to select exactly the right material for this indivdual who has a very specific background and very specific experience. I'm not sure this can be done.

CURRENT AWARENESS

The fourth item concerns an information service to provide an efficient means for enabling the member of the technical staff to keep current; this is the problem most people are concerned about. What is going on in the field today? What is coming out in the literature? This is one that has always presented a problem. It's one of the reasons for the abstracting services, but they, too, are becoming too voluminous and too unwieldy.

To meet this fourth need there is a possibility of having an information service which, at least in broad categories, is able to select and at least notify bench workers that certain information is available. Just how big you are willing to make this group becomes a complex problem. I have made some very coarse estimates in my own situation. If you assume that it takes maybe two or three people to be thoroughly acquainted with the field or all the literature in the field, and allowing for some overlap between fields, I estimate that I would need to add 150 people in this information service activity. This along with my staff of 450 would be 600 people. But I don't have enough money to supply 600 people, I have to stay with 450. This means I've got to cut back. Of course, I could have 115 in my information service group and only 335 on the bench in the research activity. However, let us return to this point later.

INFORMATION TO STIMULATE CREATIVITY

This fifth need gets right down to the crux of the information problem at a research activity. There is need for an information flow which will stimulate creative thought, and you must provide this flow in a way that will maximize the probability of having some creative ideas. This is the basic reason for doing true research, no matter where it is.

In a way, you could think of the four other needs as being a part of this one — but this last one is the crux of the matter. In considering my situation with 115 people in a technical information group, with 335 on the bench, but where I have 150 projects, my question is: "Is it better to separate this group out, or do I leave them where they are?" I recognize that if there is a separate group I must put highly technical people in it. They have to be just as good technically as the bench workers, otherwise this isn't going to work. On the other hand, the information group already exists in my operation; they're already in the laboratory as a part of each one of these little groups.

I conclude in my particular situation that it would be much better if I left them where they are. The reason for this is that in being closely associated with the work, the probability of their being able to add something that will make that group more creative is much higher if they were in a centralized group. This is particularly important when there is wide diversification, as in our laboratory. The

decision could be quite different in a different situation. There are information systems in other types of laboratories that differ from ours. Yet they are probably good systems for these groups. You have to look at the individual situation, and you have to think about the probabilities.

There is another consideration very pertinent to having a centralized information activity in a research laboratory. If I were to pick out certain individuals from all these different small technical groups and put them together in a technical information group, I had better be very careful how I do that or I am going to make second rate citizens out of them. When these information people are a part of the individual research groups, they are on the same status as the technical worker. If you get a research man of sufficiently high level to do this technical job, he's as good a man as the research man. But in a separate group in a service role, our social pattern is such that this information specialist may not be as acceptable as the research worker. This question of status is important, especially when you need good technical people in the information function.

SELECTIVITY OF CREATIVE PEOPLE

I picked out some of my most creative staff and had a roundtable discussion one night on this subject. I got some rather surprising results. They didn't agree with any of the points I have made but they said this is all academic, because, they said, "We don't read the literature," and, "We're so involved with the work, we know where the good work is going on."

In other words, these men have already selected their communication channels on the basis of the probable usefulness of the work of various individuals in the field. They know that one person is going to get good results, and that another won't get anywhere. So they watch the first man, and they don't bother with the second one. They watch the good one and when they see results coming, they communicate, they go to meetings, and they find out what the results are long before these results get into the literature. Even when they go into the literature, they see what the good worker has written, and they don't bother with what the other man has written. There is something to be said for this, when you have creative people, and my lab is built around the very creative people. However, I recognize that the world isn't full of such people, and you still have to provide for the people who are going to read the literature.

TECHNICAL INFORMATION FOR MANAGEMENT

When I examine the problem of technical information for management, it appears to be a separate problem from that of providing technical information to technical people. The management information problem has two aspects. First, the president of any corporation is no longer making all his judgments solely on a financial basis. He has to make a great many of these decisions on the basis of scientific data. This also applies to decisions made in the government.

However, there is an interesting conflict in this situation. The traditional system of a management hierarchy depends upon information flow. It was made possible by the consolidation of information. The sales data for a local field and local markets are consolidated; the production costs in the different shops are consolidated. Other data are consolidated piece by piece as you climb up the company management ladder. The information is thus condensed into a form that can fit into the communication channel of the manager; otherwise, if you gave him all the bits and pieces of data, you would overload his communication system. The whole system has been built up because the information was susceptible to consolidation.

But how do you consolidate technical information? At present, it just doesn't seem possible. An example will illustrate this point. Somebody goes out and finds that Joe Doakes at 58 Main St., at Podunk Hollow, doesn't like the color of the cabinet on his TV set, and he reports this to the president of the company. The president obviously can't run his business on the basis of this individual fact. The president has some national market surveys made so he knows *in general* what the population likes and dislikes in colors. He also gets from inside the company a distribution of the colors that are in inventory. If this inventory doesn't fit with the market survey, somebody down the line is not a good manager, and corrective action is taken.

Although I have simplified the situation for the example, this is basically the way the president runs his company. It does him no good at all to have the information that Joe Doakes doesn't like the color of his set. But as far as technical information is concerned, this is almost exactly what is being done. Information retrieval systems are built so that the president of the corporation can push a button and get out an individual fact. But how can he use that fact any more than he can use the fact that Joe Doakes didn't like the color of his television set? This inability to consolidate technical information in a form useful to management is a nasty problem.

There is a second aspect to this whole problem. The type of hierarchical company with which I am concerned, with its pyramid of management, is a selling-distribution system. But the national government is a concentrated customer; it works in reverse. With regard to this matter of technical decisions, I am concerned about the inverted hierarchy which seems to have developed. This is something that the information service people should give some real thought to. There is no question in my mind that a great deal of the future of this world, this country and all the companies in this country is going to depend upon major top level decisions which in the future — perhaps fifteen to twenty years from now — are going to have to be based on psychological matters and on technological facts. We have to be able to get the facts to these individuals in a consolidated form that doesn't require that they have 10 years of physics, 10 years of chemistry, or 10 years of rocketry to understand them. This is a major challenge for all of us.

REFERENCES

[1] "The Theory of Communications in a Research Laboratory," *Industrial Research Institute*, Vol. 3, No. 4, 1960, Winter ed.

By Bernard K. Dennis
General Electric Company

9. Financing a Technical Information Center

INCREASING AWARENESS OF THE technical information problem and a better understanding of the problem's nature and implications have stimulated the development of a Technical Information Center, in General Electric's Flight Propulsion Division, tailored to the needs of the business. Although originally based on traditional library methods, experience has shown that these must be improved, modified and added to in the light of newly available techniques and concepts. Also, implementing an operating philosophy of self initiated selective dissemination has required a thorough, continuing analysis of the center's functions, personnel requirements, costs and performance as related to both short and long range needs of the business.

A brief review of the center's operational philosophy, organization, personnel requirements, tools and services will help establish the perspective necessary for understanding the financial philosophy and procedures discussed in Part II of this paper.

I. THE FPD TECHNICAL INFORMATION CENTER

The Technical Information Center provides much of the technical information required by the 2,500 to 3,000 scientists, engineers and management personnel at the Evendale, Ohio plant of General Electric's Flight Propulsion Division. The center also extends its service to several hundred other G. E. personnel in other locations. Most of the center's users are engaged in applied research and development, covering many technologies related to the division's aerospace propulsion products with major emphasis on materials.

Since 1957, a continuing effort has been conducted to reorient, reorganize and restaff the Technical Information Center to assure its users more complete, efficient and reliable access into the available information pertaining to their technical activities. Efforts to establish an aggressive information program have resulted in several new information tools and services. Implementing the center's operational philosophy of self initiated selective dissemination has required the initiation of a broad range of services to meet specific needs.

AUTOMATIC INFORMATION RETRIEVAL SYSTEM

The center's Automatic Information Retrieval System (AIRS) was designed and put into operation in 1958 using an IBM 704 electronic computer and associated data processing equipment. During 1961, AIRS was transferred to an IBM 7090-1401 computer system and its programs modified to take advantage of the 7090's greater capabilities. Also, several important improvements were made to the system's programs during 1961.

The Automatic Information Retrieval System is based on an inverted coordinate index for searching, and features magnetic tape storage of abstracts with bibliographic and security data. The system can handle up to 1,300 multiterm machine questions simultaneously. Maximum asked on a single run to date is 265. There are now over 65,000 documents in the file, with approximately 1,000 new items added each month. Average depth of indexing is estimated at between 20 and 25, with about 7,000 items in the system's vocabulary. A run of 100 or more machine questions may require two to five minutes of mainframe time to perform all coordinations and deliver access numbers. Or, if desired, the system will automatically look up all abstracts with bibliographic and security data in an additional six to nine minutes of 7090 mainframe time. The relationship of machine search customer, literature searcher, machine and center is illustrated in **Exhibit 1**. Typical customer service cycle is 24 hours.

When AIRS was designed, the emphasis was on information retrieval. However, as the center learned more about its machine system's large simultaneous search capacity, it became apparent that selective dissemination would be its primary role, with retrospective searching a by-product.

CURRENT AWARENESS SERVICE

A current awareness program conducted by the center attempts to keep specific individuals abreast of world-wide technology in subject areas of immediate importance to them. Other participants in the program are attempting to keep informed on a broader, longer range basis. The Current Awareness Service principle is illustrated in **Exhibit 2**. The Technical Information Center's monthly input of potentially useful information is estimated to be between 15,000 and 20,000 items in the form of reports, books, memoranda, technical society papers, journal articles, patents, abstracts, etc. This input is in more than 20 broad subject areas, such as

physical sciences, fluid mechanics, mathematics and computation, propulsion systems, management and administration, and materials and processes.

At the center's present level of operation, about 5,000 of these items are reviewed, and out of these, 1,000 are selected and indexed into the Automatic Information Retrieval System for dissemination and retrieval. By defining an individual's information needs and setting up his interest profile expressed in the retrieval system's language (key words), he is periodically given a very selective look at the center's indexed input of 1,000 documents per month, and automatically receives abstracts of new material entered into the file since he was last contacted.

Thus, in less than an hour's reading time per month, a Current Awareness Service client, in effect, scans 5,000 new documents of potential value to him, carefully reviews the contents of 1,000 of them and then focuses his attention on only a few for detailed study.

AEROSPACE MATERIALS INFORMATION PROJECT

At the beginning of 1961, through close cooperation with the division's materials groups,

Exhibit 1

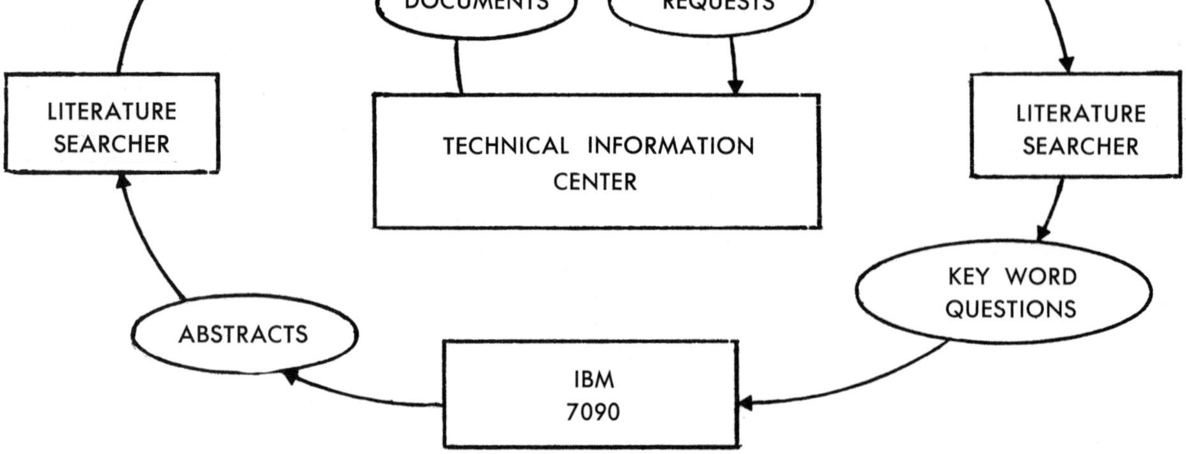

INFORMATION OUTPUT

the Aerospace Materials Information Project was established within the center to better meet the information needs of more than 125 materials scientists and engineers in six materials laboratory groups in the Evendale complex. The AMI project was staffed with an experienced metallurgical engineer and a chemical assistant. The project's functions are illustrated in **Exhibit 3**. To accomplish its purposes, the project serves as a continuing technical liaison between its materials clients and the center. The AMI project has brought to the center a far better understanding of the division's materials information needs than ever before possible. This is resulting in a significant upgrading of the center's acquisition, indexing, dissemination and retrieval of materials information.

Two major dissemination programs have been conducted by the Aerospace Materials Information Project for the past year. One of these is a continuing alkali metals technology survey conducted by a local consulting chemist under the AMI project engineer's direction. Results of the survey are indexed and selectively disseminated by the project to several interested scientists and engineers in the division.

The other continuing dissemination effort conducted by the Aerospace Materials Information Project involves both the American Society for Metals information searching service and the Technical Information Center's Automatic Information Retrieval System as seen in **Exhibit 4**. By correlating the major information needs of its clients, the AMI project has established a bi-weekly input of abstracts from ASM. As they are received, the ASM abstracts are screened and distributed to appropriate materials clients. On a monthly basis, the Automatic Information Retrieval System is used to selectively disseminate its current input in the same subject areas to the same materials clients.

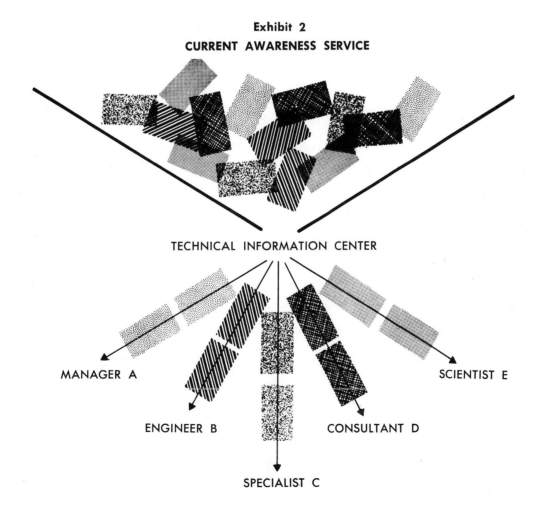

Exhibit 2
CURRENT AWARENESS SERVICE

TECHNICAL INFORMATION CENTER

MANAGER A

ENGINEER B

SPECIALIST C

CONSULTANT D

SCIENTIST E

Exhibit 3

AEROSPACE MATERIALS INFORMATION PROJECT

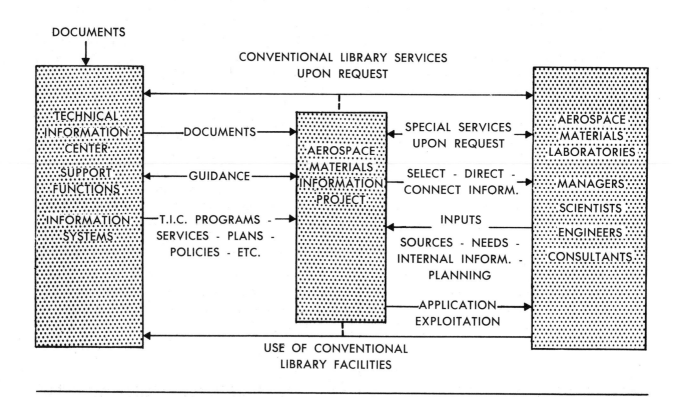

DOCUMENTS

CONVENTIONAL LIBRARY SERVICES
UPON REQUEST

TECHNICAL INFORMATION CENTER

SUPPORT FUNCTIONS

INFORMATION SYSTEMS

DOCUMENTS

GUIDANCE

T.I.C. PROGRAMS - SERVICES - PLANS - POLICIES - ETC.

AEROSPACE MATERIALS INFORMATION PROJECT

SPECIAL SERVICES UPON REQUEST

SELECT - DIRECT - CONNECT INFORM.

INPUTS

SOURCES - NEEDS - INTERNAL INFORM. - PLANNING

APPLICATION EXPLOITATION

AEROSPACE MATERIALS LABORATORIES

MANAGERS

SCIENTISTS

ENGINEERS

CONSULTANTS

USE OF CONVENTIONAL
LIBRARY FACILITIES

Exhibit 4

AEROSPACE MATERIALS INFORMATION PROJECT

SELECT — DIRECT — CONNECT

T.I.C. INDEXED INPUT 1000 DOC./MO.

HOT ITEMS

AIRS

300 ABSTRACTS PER MONTH

AMI PROJECT

COMPOSITE INTEREST PROFILES

Ⓐ   Ⓑ   Ⓒ   Ⓓ   Ⓔ

200 ABSTRACTS PER MONTH

ASM INFORMATION SEARCHING SERVICE

Ⓐ   Ⓑ   Ⓒ   Ⓓ   Ⓔ   Ⓕ

CUSTOMER GROUPS

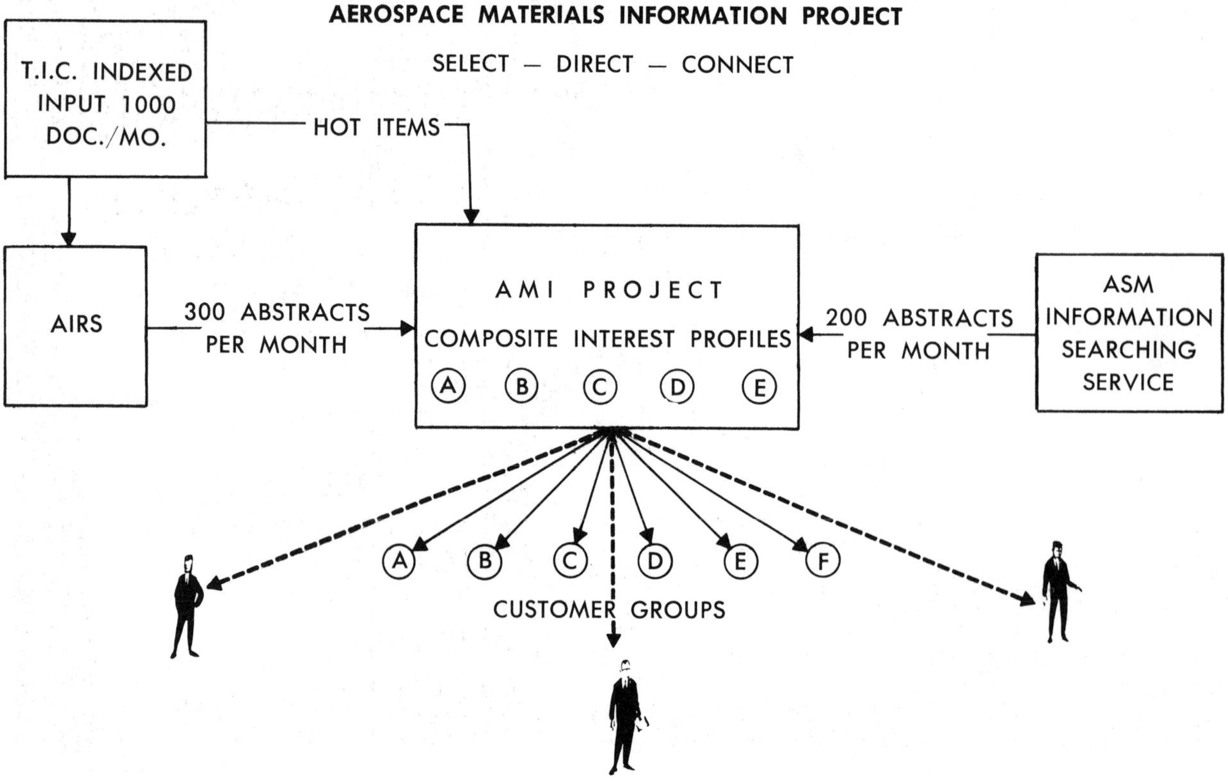

OTHER MAJOR SERVICES

1. *Conventional library services*

The center maintains two libraries in Evendale, with appropriate self service literature research facilities including manual uniterm coordinate indexes, conventional card catalogs, and 30 indexing and abstracting services. The center's technical report collections contain over 100,000 reports, with security classification through secret R.D. The center subscribes to 375 technical periodicals and its book collection numbers over 20,000. The center's collections also include technical society papers, U. S. and foreign patents and translations.

2. *Auxiliary document service*

Several supporting services are provided by the center to make its documents more available to requestors and potential users. For example, through use of Xerox and microfilm reproducing equipment, prompt, low cost, appropriate photoduplication service is provided. Other auxiliary services include coordi-

nation and maintenance of the division's internal report system, translations, and special acquisitions.

3. *Announcement bulletin*

TIPS, the center's weekly bulletin, is distributed on a subscription basis. Issued 50 times each year for the past five years, TIPS has consistently appeared at its subscribers' desks on schedule. TIPS announces over 200 new items per week and accounts for 75 percent of the requests for specific documents handled by the center's libraries.

As shown in **Exhibit 5**, *TIPS* is one of four products obtained from the same punched cards. This integrated approach to automation has improved accuracy and has speeded the publication of TIPS. In addition to substantial cost savings, clerical time is freed for other documentation work.

4. *Special purpose retrieval systems*

The Technical Information Center develops and maintains small scale information retrieval systems to meet special needs. These

Exhibit 5

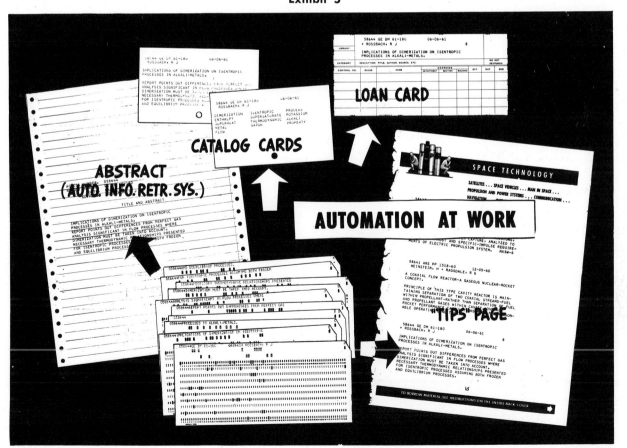

systems are physically located in the immediate areas of their users, along with the special collections into which the systems provide access. Since documents indexed into the small scale systems are also input for AIRS, they are thereby available to all Technical Information Center clients.

5. *Information searching*

Although the Automatic Information Retrieval System is the center's major IR tool, it provides reasonably complete coverage of only the division's internal reports. For more exhaustive, comprehensive searches, AIRS serves as the first step. Information searching is provided by the center's two engineers who specialize in this field. Both specialists have been in the division for 10 years in various engineering activities and, as a consequence, are well acquainted with the division's products and key technical personnel.

6. *FIND-X*

A manual version of the Automatic Information Information Retrieval System, FIND-X is presently contained in four large "search" books and 25 abstract binders. This manual search tool gives immediate but limited access into the more than 65,000 documents now contained in AIRS. For those questions too complex or time consuming to handle satisfactorily manually, a machine run can be made. With FIND-X already in use in the Small Aircraft Engine Department's library in Lynn, Massachusetts, we expect to install FIND-X in several other G.E. locations.

7. *AutoCom*

An experimental technical information dissemination tool under development by the center has been dubbed "AutoCom", for automatic communication. The system utilizes an electronic telephone answering device to collect input for the Automatic Information Retrieval System. By using his phone (as shown in **Exhibit 6**) — inside or away from the plant; day or night — a scientist or engineer may call in information he thinks may be of interest to others, or that he may wish to refer to at some future date. In response to instructions he receives over the phone, the information contributor identifies himself and gives bibliographic data, an abstract and his choice of index terms for each item he calls in.

The key to Automatic Communication lies in the fact that when information is fed into the retrieval system, the contributor's identity

Exhibit 6

HOW AUTOCOM WORKS

FROM OFFICE . . .

OR HOME . . .

INPUT

ELECTRONIC SECRETARY

FPD TECHNICAL INFORMATION CENTER

is maintained in association with his contribution. Thus, when that information appears as machine output during either a retrospective search or a current awareness run, the recipient of that particular abstract bearing the contributor's name, title and extension may be led to a person of related interest and experience or, perhaps, to one who even is actively engaged in related or overlapping research. Hence, AutoCom may correlate people as well as recorded information. Not to be overlooked is the information selection function served by such a device. With several hundred scientists and engineers using Auto-Com, the Technical Information Center's normal acquisition efforts may be greatly extended.

PERSONNEL REQUIREMENTS

To provide the wide coverage of services reviewed above, we have found that three different types of capability are essential. First, to provide conventional library and auxiliary services requires personnel trained in the handling of technical documents. Next, to select useful information and to process it requires personnel with competence in the subject content being handled. Third, personnel trained in documentation and information

system work are needed to operate the center's systems and to perform research and development to advance the state of the information handling art for the center. A more detailed view of the three capabilities required by the center is given in **Exhibit 7**.

ORGANIZATION

The Technical Information Center's relationship to its primary user groups is seen in **Exhibit 8**. By being administratively part of the Applied Research Operation, the center maintains close and continuing contact with the longer range, more sophisticated information requirements of the division.

How the center has organized its functions is seen in **Exhibit 9**. Ratio of professional to supporting personnel is approximately one to one.

An information group with the nature and scope of the one just described requires a considerably higher level of financial support by the user organization than that usually accorded a traditional technical library providing passive, non-specialized technical document services. In Part II of this paper, the FPD Technical Information Center's approach to achieving financial support is presented.

Exhibit 7

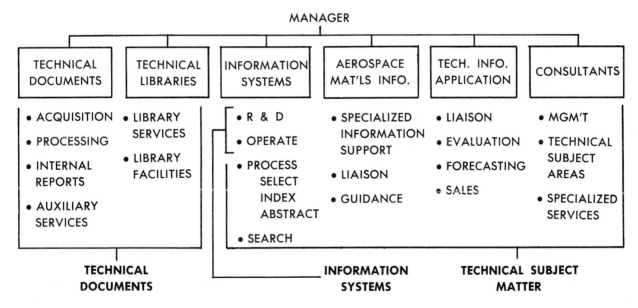

FPD TECHNICAL INFORMATION CENTER

3 CAPABILITY AREAS

II. FINANCING THE FPD TECHNICAL INFORMATION CENTER

Over the past four years, the Technical Information Center of General Electric's Flight Propulsion Division has attempted to develop a method for maintaining a level of operation realistically related to the information needs of its users, the expanding parameters of the technical information explosion and the needs of the business. Even though a permanent long range funding plan has not yet been fully defined, certain basic indications have begun to emerge.

The first and most significant indication is that the level of funding which can be expected as a direct charge against general overhead or administrative costs is not likely to exceed the requirements for a bare minimum of basic library services. Therefore, in the long run, the more refined and specialized technical information services must in some way be supported by a direct charge against the specific using group, whether or not the using group is part of the local organization. In other words, customers must pay for the services.

This means, of course, that the Technical Information Center must act to a certain extent as a business entity, complete with continuing problems of customer satisfaction, sales volume and seeking out of new markets. It is obvious that the financial as well as the technical success of the center depends upon its consistently "delivering the goods".

BALANCE OF SOURCES

In its efforts to achieve a more secure financial basis upon which to operate, the Technical Information Center has attempted to develop three major sources of income. We believe that by distributing our "risk" across a broader base, a greater degree of stability should ensue. Whether an optimum balance (**Exhibit 10**) among the sources may exist, is not clear. If so, we have not yet found a magic rule for achieving it.

However, in view of the continuing technical information explosion, with all of its ramifications and implications, and the increasing complexity of the division's aerospace propulsion systems products, it seems reasonable to expect that the center's users

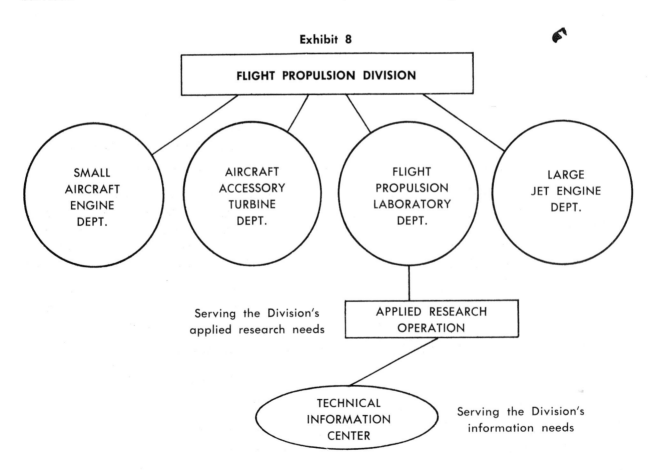

Exhibit 8

FLIGHT PROPULSION DIVISION

SMALL AIRCRAFT ENGINE DEPT.

AIRCRAFT ACCESSORY TURBINE DEPT.

FLIGHT PROPULSION LABORATORY DEPT.

LARGE JET ENGINE DEPT.

Serving the Division's applied research needs

APPLIED RESEARCH OPERATION

TECHNICAL INFORMATION CENTER

Serving the Division's information needs

should provide the largest share of its support in the form of direct payment for specialized information services. This may tend to offset short range fluctuations in that part of the center's income from general overhead, thereby enabling the center to maintain a longer range, higher level of technical effectiveness during local business recessions.

Sources among which the Technical Information Center is attempting to achieve a balanced support are:

1. *Management subsidy*

This old, traditional support for technical information services is, to whatever extent it may exist, usually a secure base since management generally feels the need for some sort of library or technical information service. However, with only this single source of support, the Technical Information Center is subject to the individual views of a relatively few people who, generally speaking, are directly benefited by the center to a far lesser extent than the scientists and engineers at the technical work level. Thus, when funded solely as a direct charge to overhead, the center may be particularly vulnerable during short term business fluctuations, with the immediate need to reduce overhead taking precedence over the longer range benefits of an effective technical information service.

Because of the intangible or unmeasurable nature of the center's influence on the profit making capability of those it serves, it becomes an early target in a management drive toward overhead reduction. This is, at least in part, due to the fact that a scientist or engineer will get as much information as he can — one way or another — with or without the assistance of an information group.

Unfortunately, immediately increased costs and longer range penalties in duplicated effort and reduced productivity incurred in so doing are usually not apparent, particularly in a large, complex organization. Therefore, reducing the center's level of operation may not produce any immediate, clearly discernible ill effects.

With management subsidy as its sole source of support, the center is handicapped in its efforts to keep pace with the increasing scope and complexity of the technical information service problem. It may be virtually impos-

Exhibit 9

FPD TECHNICAL INFORMATION CENTER

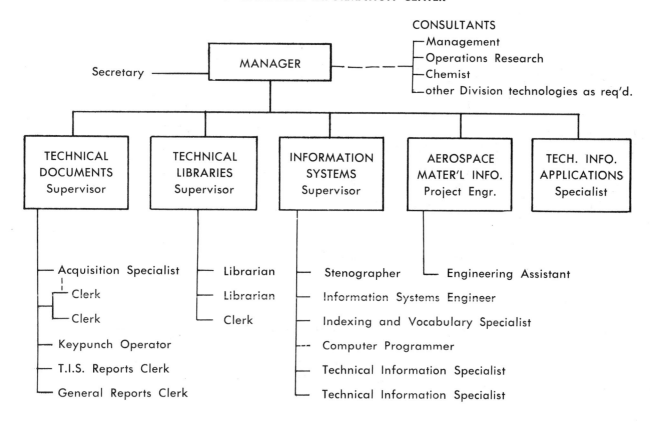

sible to negotiate the funding required for advancing the state of the art in tools and services. This is because of the severely limiting traditional ratio of information service expenditures to all activities of the business components it serves.

Thus, although management subsidy is generally a secure source of financial support in that it is seldom completely withdrawn, it can also be widely fluctuating and severely restrictive.

2. *Direct sales — internal*

We have attempted to initiate the more refined and specialized information services on a "will it sell?" basis. This means that once a new service has been launched, it must provide visible value compatible with cost in terms of specific results to the buyer.

There are distinct disadvantages to selling technical information service. For example, more effort is required to provide service on a direct sales basis. There is a fragmentation of effort, since effort which might have been spent in providing the service is expended on selling, billing and customer relations. Also, funding is piecemeal and not guaranteed. This generates a certain element of uncertainty in planning manpower and expense budgets.

As might be expected, making a direct charge for a specific service reduces its utilization. This may be economically desirable, since level of the service will more likely be a function of real need or benefits. However, this means that the center will need to provide a greater range of services and that it must be prepared to adjust quickly to keep its services more nearly tailored to the requirements of its users.

Exhibit 10
FINANCIAL SUPPORT

SOURCES:	Managem't Subsidy		Internal Sales		External Sales	
1.	33⅓	—	33⅓	—	33⅓	?
2.	50	—	25	—	25	?
3.	60	—	30	—	10	?
4.	?	—	?	—	?	

BALANCE { 1. 2. 3. 4.

DISTRIBUTE RISK — — INCREASE STABILITY

There is a major advantage to providing information services on a direct sales basis. By broadening the center's market — if the services sell — a more balanced income is attained. The center has a hedge against economic fluctuations since it is unlikely that all components buying its services will drastically reduce their purchases at the same time.

3. *Direct sales — external*

A third source of revenue available to the Technical Information Center is the sale of services or work to entities, industrial or non-industrial, outside General Electric. Although the center is primarily an "in house" engineering service, it may provide certain services and development work for others to the extent that in so doing, it strengthens its capabilities (or at least does not diminish them) to perform its internal mission.

Contracts with organizations outside General Electric may involve the development, installation and operation of information handling systems, information systems studies and experiments, and routine services such as information searching or current awareness.

Due to several factors, there is a relatively limited external market available to the Technical Information Center. Geography may tend to restrict the center's activities to a significant extent, since only a small portion of the aerospace or related industries are within a reasonable service radius. Problems associated with handling proprietary and security classified information also tend to restrict the center's freedom to operate in an external market. And, of course, our first consideration is to General Electric. This has not yet been a deterrent factor in external efforts, but in certain instances it could become one.

A natural hazard in developing an external market is the probability of major fluctuations in demand. This confronts the center with problems related to building up for a large contract and letting down after its completion.

Our progress toward achieving a broader funding base is indicated in **Exhibit 11**. We believe our rate of development has been slower than it should have been. Yet, we have made significant progress. Barring unforeseen occurrences over which the center has little or no control, we expect to make more rapid progress toward our goal of financial stability.

Exhibit 11

INCOME DISTRIBUTION TREND

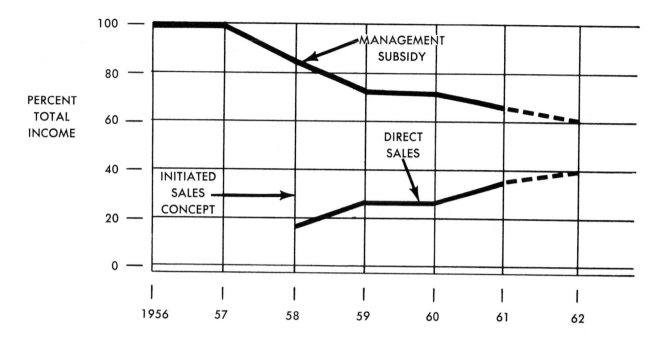

OPERATING COSTS

In arriving at its annual operating expense forecast, the Technical Information Center attempts to determine what is needed to operate in terms of its current workload. In arriving at a distribution of costs, full consideration is given to the "axiom" that people without tools are hardly more useful than tools without people. Thus, every attempt is made to arrive at the most reasonable fund allocation in the center's budget (**Exhibit 12**).

How to achieve balance in activities as well as a stable financial base is an extension of the balance problem. In other words, how can the center expend the effort and funds necessary to advance the information handling art in ways that will prove useful to our customers, while providing services only to the extent that they are self supporting? It is the old "which came first — the chicken or the egg?" story.

There is no predetermined formula to achieve balance in either support or activities. At its present stage of development, the FPD Technical Information Center has not yet achieved the established status which would permit a high degree of administrative, long range planning. In lieu of this, the modus operandi which appears nearest to being effective consists of keeping fully aware of all of the above factors, coupled with a good degree of flexibility and rapid response to meet short term requirements and to take advantage of opportunities as they are recognized. This does not prevent us from having long range goals as to professional standards in the technical information field in keeping with economic justification.

Exhibit 12
Technical Information Center
OPERATING COST BREAKDOWN — 1961

SALARIES (INCL. BENEFITS)	55.7%	
ACQUISITIONS	5.6	
DATA PROCESSING	11.5	
OFFICE SERVICES	3.6	
PRODUCT INFORMATION	1.5	PERCENT OF TOTAL COST
TRAVEL, LIVING	1.2	
TELEPHONE, TELEGRAPH	1.1	
ALL OTHER VARIABLE	5.8	
RENT, DEPR., AMORT.	12.2	

Establishing a budget and securing its acceptance by higher management are two different things. We have found no secret path to successful budget negotiations. To the contrary, as shown in **Exhibit 13**, we have followed a rocky road in our efforts to finance the center. We have learned to accept unexpected and sometimes drastic deviations in support as a normal operating hazard of a Technical Information Center serving a defense contractor — particularly when a disproportionately large share of the center's income is in the form of management subsidy.

The center's continued progress toward a higher level of operation is due mainly to two factors. First, customers have proved willing to pay for information services, thereby providing the center with income to help offset drops in management subsidy. Second, exploitation of automation has raised the center's capabilities to provide more specialized services for a larger market. In fact, the center is now headed toward the point where it would be impossible to provide its services manually without adding people.

The trend in automation expense incurred by the center is shown in **Exhibit 14**. It should be noted that 1961's increase was due primarily to a heavy programming effort required to transfer the center's Automatic Information Retrieval System from an IBM 704 to an IBM 7090-1401 computer system, and to modify its programs to take advantage of the 7090's greater capabilities. Also, several significant improvements were programmed into the system. Effects of these improvements are reflected in the lower 1962 computer expense forecast. In spite of the rapidly growing AIRS file and increased use of the system, 1962 total computations expense is expected to be 10 percent or less of the center's total expenditures.

A major financial problem faced by the Technical Information Center is how to finance advancements while operating on a tight budget. The implications of this with respect to management subsidy are obvious. If management doesn't see the need for advancing the state of the art of information handling, then development of systems is definitely

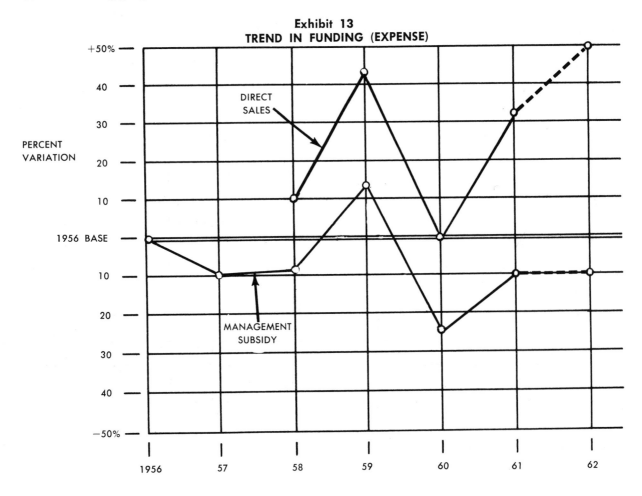

Exhibit 13
TREND IN FUNDING (EXPENSE)

slowed. Individual users are unwilling to gamble on the development of new services. They are only interested in paying for ones already established and proven.

INCOME

Thus far, the Technical Information Center has achieved only limited success in its efforts to establish a broader financial base. In order to achieve what we believe to be a more stable balance, two major jobs need to be done:

1. We need to secure more outside business, both of a development nature and services.

2. We need to increase internal direct sales, primarily in the more advanced or specialized service areas.

The center's direct sales of services in 1961, as shown in **Exhibit 15**, were substantial but below target in most areas. There were several mitigating factors, the chief one being an 11 percent reduction in management subsidy, at the end of the first quarter, which was necessitated by certain defense contract reductions. Because of reduced funding and a highly unstable internal market during 1961, the center held up staffing at 20 instead of moving ahead to a forecast manpower level of 24. This, of course, restricted services to some extent.

During the latter half of 1961, the center began actively seeking business outside General Electric. We believe we have a unique and marketable situation consisting of an experienced, well staffed Technical Information Center productively operating in a live, industrial R & D environment, using a large general purpose computing system as a major information handling tool and with its well developed Automatic Information Retrieval System in practical operation. We see this as a practical development and proving ground for technical information systems. It is our plan to develop outside markets for both development effort and services. How rapidly we can accomplish this — we wish we knew!

SELLING AND PROMOTION

Thus far, we have spent insufficient effort on selling. We have been mainly occupied with building up the center's staff, and with developing our tools and services while gaining sufficient acceptance by management to move ahead. We have done considerable selling, but not enough.

In selling our technical information capabilities and services, we have attempted to develop sales and promotional plans much as is done for any business, except for two major

Exhibit 14

AUTOMATION EXPENSE TREND

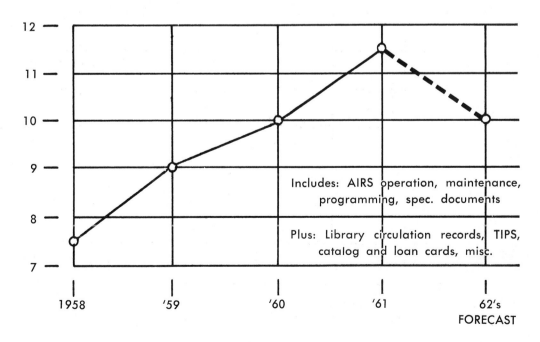

PERCENT OF TOTAL T.I.C. EXPENSE

Includes: AIRS operation, maintenance, programming, spec. documents

Plus: Library circulation records, TIPS, catalog and loan cards, misc.

1958   '59   '60   '61   62's FORECAST

distinctions. First, the unusual nature of our merchandise, technical information, must be kept in mind. Unlike a hard goods product, benefits usually cannot be readily identified or measured. Need for and use of the product, technical information, is a very personal matter which may make clear recognition of benefits impossible.

Also to be kept in mind are the peculiar professional inhibitions of our technical customers. They do not like a lot of ballyhoo or a hard sell approach in our promotion or sales efforts. Generally speaking, they are not susceptible to normal forms of advertising and promotion. Our product has no utility to them as persons outside their work. Their attitude is such that to gain their respect and acceptance, we must prove to them that information handling has the stature of a profession. They traditionally look down upon a library as being a non-technical activity which can be helpful when asked to do so and if given careful guidance. The concept of a Technical Information Center staffed with technical people and aggressively selling technical

services is new to them. Thus, in attempting to promote itself and its services, the center is bucking many obstacles — not the least of which is tradition.

III. FUTURE

A number of implications for the Technical Information Center's financial future have emerged from our experiences thus far. First, it is to be expected that information services and methods for providing these services will require continuing review and adjustment if the center is to adequately cope with the technical information explosion and the changing needs of its customers. The center's work will become increasingly technical, requiring a corresponding increase in the capabilities of its technical staff.

This gradual upgrading of the center's staff and services means an increase in operating expense which, of course, will intensify the support problem. It is extremely probable that maintaining an adequate level of management subsidy will always be a problem, since in the final analysis, internal sales are an operating

Exhibit 15

1961 DIRECT SALES	% OF TOTAL SALES		% DEVIATION
	*GOAL	**ACTUAL	
SERVICES:	28	24	14
AEROSPACE MATERIALS INFO.	22	17	23
INFORMATION SEARCHING	25	24	4
INTERNAL REPORTS	12	11	8
SPECIAL ACQUISITIONS	5	4	20
TIPS	3	2	33
PHOTOREPRODUCTION	1	1	0
INDEX CARDS	4	4	0
PENALTIES (Mat'l Lost, Overdue)			
	100	87	13

*Forecast based on T.I.C. staff of 24
**Accomplished with a staff of 20

expense to the business. The solution lies in achieving and maintaining a high level of management understanding and acceptance, so that its level of support will be more closely related to the information needs of the business and less affected by opinion as to what the business can afford to pay.

Another implication for the center's future is concerned with changes in the requirements for personnel working in the technical information service field. Today, most information workers fall into two extremes. At one end is the theoretician and at the other is the conventional library functionary. Both are essential to the field. In addition, however, we need people in between, who might be called "information engineers" and "information technicians", who can develop the skills required in the practical application of information handling technology.

A fourth implication for the center's future operation concerns planning. Due to the nature of the Flight Propulsion Division's business, financial planning in the Technical Information Center is of necessity short term, usually one year or less. This means that management subsidy must be negotiated, and challenging but attainable goals for direct sales must be established, on an annual basis.

The only long range planning that can be done by the center is concerned with the achievement of a state of readiness to take advantage of opportunities. This infers that the center's planning must aim toward:

1. More sophisticated and flexible systems which are proven and ready for expansion.

2. High caliber personnel trained in both information systems and subject content areas.

3. Acquiring a detailed knowledge of the information requirements of present and potential customers.

4. Keeping fully informed of the professional resources in applicable portions of the information field — services, people, technology and equipment.

IV. CONCLUSIONS

Operating an industrial Technical Information Center is both a special profession and a business function, and has to be treated as both at once. To plan and direct the center's programs and activities, one must be a professional in the technical information handling field and a business manager at the same time.

We have found no magic formula for relating the many variables pertinent to the operation of the Technical Information Center. The situation is complicated more than may be generally realized, with many "new" problems peculiar to information handling and information services in addition to the "old" administrative type problems common to most businesses.

However, the center's most crucial problem is how to maintain a stable level of support, realistically geared to the needs of the business and obtained from a balanced variety of sources. Progress toward solution of its many other problems is, in one way or another, a function of how well the center finds long range solutions to its financial problems.

By **Helen L. Brownson**
National Science Foundation

10. Documentation Needs of Scientists[1]

I SHOULD LIKE TO BEGIN by explaining briefly why I agreed to consider the documentation needs of scientists. I feel that an explanation is in order because I am not a scientist and can say nothing, therefore, about the subject on the basis of any personal experience. Nor can I say much at all about documentation needs as such, for we have very little precise, objective knowledge about them. It is because of this lack of knowledge that I welcomed the opportunity to discuss the importance of learning more about scientists' documentation needs.

Since "documentation" is a word that means different things to different people, it may be helpful if I explain that I use the word broadly to include all the processes involved in preserving, disseminating, and gaining access to recorded information. By "documentation needs" I mean the needs of scientists with respect to effective use of recorded scientific information. Scientists have other information needs, of course, that are met, and perhaps could only be met, by conferences, visits, and other means of direct communication. We have yet to determine the actual significance of documentation in the total communication process in the sciences. Undoubtedly we would all agree that, since science is a cumulative endeavor, access to recorded information is vital to scientific advance. But for a number of reasons we must work toward a deeper understanding of the whole research process, of the role of documentation in that process, and of the real documentation needs of scientists:

1. We need a more rational basis for reaching decisions as to the relative importance and utility of different types of existing and proposed services, for choices must be made from time to time — in the Federal government, in the scientific societies, and elsewhere — concerning the expenditure of available funds and skilled manpower on information services.

2. We need a more rational basis also for choosing the most productive areas for experimentation, in order to try to improve the flow and accessibility of information.

3. We need to be able to assess the results of an experiment with a new information service or system in terms of the needs of its users.

4. We need much more precise knowledge about needs, in order to design improved retrieval systems that will meet those needs.

I do not mean for a moment to argue that we must fully understand documentation needs before we try to improve existing services or to design or try out new services. On the contrary, one of the best ways to learn more about needs may be to experiment with new or modified services, such as a new means of disseminating research results, a new type of index, or a new searching service, in order to find out if they do, in fact, meet a need and prove to be truly useful.

I plan to summarize briefly the growing interest in the problem of information needs as exemplified in three conferences. I shall then discuss the studies that have been made of the way scientists now communicate and use information. Finally, I shall mention some relevant studies now in progress or being planned.

CONFERENCES

The first conference that was concerned with the information needs of scientists and the uses they make of information, was the Royal Society's Scientific Information Conference in London in 1948.[2] In preparation for that conference, some studies of the use of scientific information were made; and one of the conference recommendations invited the Royal Society to consider the initiation of further research into the uses of scientific literature. I am not aware that this recommendation directly stimulated any subsequent studies in the United Kingdom following the conference, but both the recommendation and the studies prior to the conference stimulated interest in the United States in further studies of the use of information.

The second major conference concerned with this problem was held a decade later in 1958, namely the International Conference on Scientific Information in Washington, sponsored by the National Academy of Sciences-National Research Council, the National Science Foundation, and the American Documentation Institute.[3] One session of it was devoted to the "literature and reference needs of scientists". The papers discussed in this area of the conference were representative of the types of studies that had been made during the decade since the Royal Society Conference.

They included studies of the time devoted by chemists to communication activities, the use of scientific literature and reference services in Scandinavia, the use of information in an atomic energy establishment, the use of technical literature by industrial technologists, the information gathering habits of medical scientists, the use of scientific periodicals, the planned and unplanned communication activities of scientists in several disciplines, the ways in which scientists learn of work important to them, and the determination of information requirements from reference questions asked of scientific libraries. All but one of these studies were of information activities and uses, not of needs. From a careful analysis of their results, one might hope to come up with inferences or hypotheses about needs; but these should be tested experimentally before they are accepted as valid. The only study dealing specifically with requirements was the analysis of reference questions asked of libraries. From such a study, however, one learns about needs as they are made known to libraries and not necessarily the real needs, for it is quite likely that scientists tailor such requests to fit what they think the libraries can do for them.

In the conference discussions there appeared to be tacit agreement that the needs of users and the uses to which they put the information should determine the design of scientific information systems and services, and that we must learn more about needs and about factors affecting the efficiency of scientific communication. It was admitted that study of the information requirements of scientists is difficult, for the communication of scientific information is extremely complex. Needs vary with the subject field, the type of research, the availability of information services and source materials, geographical situation, and differences in human abilities. In fact, the needs of a single individual may vary from time to time, depending on his current interests and activities. Furthermore, the real needs of scientists and their conscious or expressed needs may be quite different.

It was suggested that all completed studies of information use be carefully reviewed, evaluated, and compared. This suggestion was acted upon and a review was prepared. We will return to this review later in this paper.

A number of suggestions were made concerning future studies of information uses and needs — namely, that effort be made in the future to obtain qualitative judgments as to the value of information, in addition to quantitative data on the use of it; that psychologists be consulted in planning future work because their knowledge of human perception, motivation, capabilities and limitations is relevant to the whole communication problem; and that oral and informal means of communication be studied in order to make meetings more effective.

The third conference was a small meeting late in 1960, devoted exclusively to the subject of information needs in the field of psychopharmacology.[4] Some 30 specialists in psychology, psychiatry and pharmacology were called together to discuss informally their own information needs. A few documentation experts were also invited to take part in order to discuss technical advances in the field of documentation and to learn at first hand about the needs in psychopharmacology. According to my notes, at one time or another the scientists mentioned the following needs — it is a long list but it indicates the variety of needs this particular group was concerned about. These are not in order of importance, for no priorities were mentioned:

 Current information about who is doing
 what

 Directories of various kinds about people
 in the field

 Information about meetings scheduled

 A centralized collection of transcriptions
 of the proceedings of meetings

 Higher editorial standards for primary
 journals

 Better access to government reports

 Better access to the patent literature

 Access to information on negative results,
 provided they are obtained under proper
 conditions

 Prompt information about new books and
 about reviews of them

 Specialized bibliographies adequately
 indexed

 A central source of reprints or photocopies
 of journal papers

 More and better critical reviews

 Up to date information about reviews in
 preparation

 More up to date textbooks

 Exhaustive handbooks of data

 Better correlation and interpretation of
 data

 A central service for preparing translations
 on request and furnishing translators and
 interpreters for international conferences

 Greater specialization of libraries so that
 particular libraries can build up comprehensive collections in their special fields

 More trained library scientists to help researchers

 A searching service to identify all publications and documents relevant to any
 particular question or topic.

I feel certain that this informal discussion of needs was helpful to the persons concerned with planning and providing information services for psychopharmacology. It seems to me, however, that in order to determine the actual needs in any area it is essential to consider each need and each information service as a part of the whole and to reach some conclusions about the relative import-ance of each with respect to the others. I cannot imagine that there will ever be enough money and skilled manpower to provide all the information services that might be desir-able if there were no limit to our resources; so I think we shall always be faced with the necessity of making choices.

During this discussion, as in many others in recent years, the scientists frequently ex-pressed the hope that machines could be used to advantage to handle information. But gen-erally speaking, scientists do not seem to feel any responsibility for helping to outline in some detail precisely what a mechanized information system would be expected to do for them. To design a system that would meet their needs, the designers should know the sorts of questions the scientists would put to the system, as well as, the types of responses wanted. It is not enough to say, as they often do, that they will want everything relevant to any stated question without specifying the probable types of questions.

Moreover, as the volume of recorded infor-mation grows larger, one wonders if scientists really will want everything relevant to a question. It may be that they will find the results of a mechanized searching system helpful only if some way can be found of insuring that the system does not burden them with a lot of material that may be "relevant" but of little value. In a recent paper on the state of the art of information retrieval,[5] Don Swanson states: "Clearly in a situation in which the volume of informa-tion exceeds the individual scientist's digestive capacity, some method of assisting him to discriminate between the important and the unimportant literature can be counted among the most crucial of requirements."

STUDIES OF INFORMATION USE
AND PRACTICES

I want to discuss briefly the studies that have been made of scientists' information gathering behavior and their present com-munication practices. It is extremely difficult to summarize what has been learned thus far from these studies. Some of them have been conducted within individual organizations, or for the purpose of learning about the use of a particular publication or service. These studies have usually produced results that served as a basis for decisions about informa-tion services within the organization or about the future of the particular publication.

For example, the study of physics abstracting in 1950 was a survey of a large number of U. S. physicists to learn more about their use of the journal, *Physics Abstracts*.[6] Its findings resulted in some recommendations regarding coverage and indexing, and in certain decisions about American financial support of this journal which is prepared and published in England. It led both to the increased use of author abstracts in American physics journals and to the acceptance by the editors of these journals of responsibility for the adequacy of the abstracts. These changes helped to speed up publication of the abstracts in the abstract journal.

Because it was restricted to a single type of information service, however, this study did not shed any light on the relative importance of abstracts in the whole complex of existing and potential information services in physics. An example of a study within an organization was the study of scientists' use of library materials in the United Kingdom Atomic Energy Authority in 1957, which resulted in a number of recommendations concerning the library services available to scientists within that organization.[7]

Some of the studies, however, have had the broader purpose of gaining insight into scientists' present information practices and problems. All the studies supported thus far by the National Science Foundation fall into this category, and they have all had the principal objective of experimentation with a particular methodology. One study, conducted by the Department of Agriculture, employed a diary technique.[8] Its results indicated that this technique, as it was used in this study at least, may not produce the complete record of information activities one would hope for, probably because it places too great a burden on the participating scientists who must keep detailed diaries.

A study at Columbia University, in which faculty members of three scientific departments participated, made use of extensive interviews in depth covering use of the literature and informal means of communication as well.[9] An attempt was made to learn about specific instances of failure to locate existing information that would have been useful, and about the circumstances surrounding the receipt of unlooked-for pieces of useful information. The principal result of this study was a long list of questions or topics that are believed to require systematic investigation.

Still another study, conducted by an operations research group at Case Institute of Technology, experimented with the use of observational techniques for determining how chemists spent their time and the use made of publications by chemists and physicists.[10] The results indicated that the average chemist working in industry spends more time in scientific communication (that is, in reading, writing, listening, and talking about scientific matters) than in all the rest of his activities directly concerned with science. Of a total of 32.4 hours per week, both during and after working hours, devoted to scientific activities, 16.5 hours (just over 50 percent) were spent in scientific communication.

Such findings have reinforced our belief that it is important to try to find ways of making scientific communication more efficient. It appears that an observational technique such as employed in this study produces reliable data on what scientists do, but it must be admitted that this method alone tells us nothing about why they now do what they do, or what they would do under other circumstances. The logical next step is to develop hypotheses as to the services that might enable scientists to spend more productively the time they devote to communication activities, and then to undertake controlled experiments to test these hypotheses.

A review of the studies in this field, some 20 of them, was prepared for the National Science Foundation by Herbert Menzel of Columbia University in 1959.[11] It displays the diversity of approaches that have been used in studies of the behavior, habits, experiences, and expressed needs of scientists with respect to scientific information. It also serves to suggest the very large variety of topics that can be studied. By and large, the results of the different studies made in different places and for a variety of purposes were simply not comparable for a number of reasons: the populations studied were diverse; the units of observation or recording were different; communication media and channels were classified differently; and few studies included careful analysis and interpretation of the collected data.

The reviewer stated that he believed the time had come to devise new research strategies, and he suggested some neglected approaches that seemed to him to be both feasible and promising, such as studies focusing attention on the functions of the scientific communication system and the ways in which each is being met.

There is not sufficient time to go into the details of the comparative results of the different studies brought out in Dr. Menzel's review. I shall give one illustration to show what such a comparison produces. In five diary studies and two interview studies, scientists were asked how they learned about the publications they read or found useful.[12] The results appear to add up to an indication that routine perusal of the literature and pure chance accounted for the largest percentage of materials read, ranging from 14 to 70 percent, an average of 38 percent for these seven studies. Citations in other publications was the next highest category, averaging 11 percent. Personal recommendations averaged 10 percent; previous use of memory averaged nine percent; abstracts or indexes, six percent; initiative of the library, five percent and result of a search, six percent. This last category includes the use of a library catalog, personal index, bibliography, or other reference work, and may overlap the "abstract or index" category.

Although I have figured these averages to show how one would thereby rank the various sources calling items of information to scientists' attention, I do not believe that any conclusion should be drawn from such averages. Some of the studies covered all materials read and others covered only materials found to be useful or significant. Some of the studies were restricted to different subject fields. Some were of senior scientists only, and one was of technologists only. So to draw any conclusions from their composite results, it would be essential to consider the findings with all the obstacles to comparability in mind.

At this point, you may very well be asking if studies of information use are worth while. Dr. J. D. Bernal, in his paper for the 1958 conference,[3] stated succinctly both the reason for and the limitations of such studies. He said, " . . . enquiries as to present uses of scientific information services, though a necessary background, can by themselves tell us little of use for improving the service. They tell us what people do with an admittedly very imperfect service, not what they would do with a better one (which would naturally include proper training for its users)." I would agree that such studies, if they produce reliable data on the use and lack of use of existing services, are a necessary background, making it possible to determine later how much the situation has been changed, and hopefully improved, by new or modified services.

With respect to the lack of use of existing services, perhaps some of you have seen "Mooers' Law", which was formulated by Calvin Mooers, a documentation specialist.[13] He pointed out that as we furnish users with more and better retrieval systems, we cannot be assured that they will make greater use of them. He phrased his "law" this way: "An information retrieval system will tend *not* to be used whenever it is more painful and troublesome for a customer to have information than for him not to have it."

He went on to justify his assertion as follows: "Having information *is* painful and troublesome . . . If you have information, you must first read it, which is not always easy. You must then try to understand it. To do this, you may have to think about it. The information may require that you make decisions about it . . . The decisions may require action in the way of a troublesome program of work, or trips, or painful interviews. Understanding the information may show that your work was wrong, or . . . needless. Having information, you must be careful not to lose it. If nothing else, information piles up on your desk — unread . . . Finally, if you do try to use the information properly, you may be accused of puttering instead of working. Then in the end, the incorporation of the information into the work you do often may not be noticed or appreciated. Work saved is seldom recognized. Work done — even in duplication — is well paid and rewarded." Perhaps we should also try to develop an understanding of the effect of this so-called "law", which, it seems to me, is only partly facetious.

CURRENT STUDIES

As for current studies in this field, I shall mention only those of fairly general interest and of broader scope than "use" studies alone. The major trend at present seems to be toward broad studies of communication within major scientific disciplines, in which studies of information use are only a part. The American Institute of Physics for the past two years or so has been studying a number of publication problems and the utility of various types of indexes in physics. At present, they are devising techniques for determining some of the parameters of an efficient information retrieval system for physicists. More specifically, they are planning an extensive survey to accumulate information about questions physicists would put to an idealized information retrieval system for physics.

The American Psychological Association is undertaking a broad analysis of communication in the field of psychology, in order to learn more about the conduct of psychological research and the behavior of the researcher, especially as it relates to needs for information services. They are planning a number of separate but related studies of psychologists' use of information; of the cost, readership and other aspects of psychological journals; of the adequacy of abstracting and indexing services in the field; and of effectiveness of communication at meetings and conferences.

The American Institute of Biological Sciences has established a biological sciences communications project to study and improve the flow of information in the biological sciences. As a part of this project, plans are being made for an intensive study of the research process, and of the role of information exchange in that process, in a number of biological laboratories.

The National Science Foundation is supporting all these current studies I have mentioned, and is encouraging other scientific societies and groups of related societies to take a fresh, and a critical, look at their present communication practices and information needs.

One other study we have supported recently should be mentioned here. The Stanford Research Institute, in the course of an exploratory study of criteria for evaluating the performance of information systems, has developed and tested an interview guide for determining more specifically than has been done heretofore, the requirements of users of a retrieval system. A "critical incident" technique was used in which specific questions were asked about the latest search the indi-

vidual had made or had had made for him — questions about the length of time he could have waited for the relevant references, the need for current or quite recent documents, the preferred form in which information about relevant documents could be supplied, and the amount of time he is willing to spend weeding out irrelevant material. The results indicated that a wide array of requirements would be of some importance to the performance of a retrieval system serving the population studied.

IMPORTANCE OF DETERMINING DOCUMENTATION NEEDS

Even though we have as yet barely scratched the surface in gaining real insight into the process of communication in the sciences and the documentation needs of scientists, it is encouraging that a number of scientific societies are now engaged in studies that should add to our understanding, and encouraging also that recognition of the need for such understanding is growing.

In a recent, extensive survey of the "state of the library art", Margaret Bryant, the author of the portion on bibliographies, abstarcts and indexes,[14] stated, "We can say without fear of contradiction that we know a good deal more about our techniques than we do about our objectives." She urged that research to determine objectives and the needs of users be given the highest priority.

Don Swanson, in his paper on the state of the art of information retrieval,[5] pointed out that the studies of scientists' communication habits have thus far been "descriptive rather than diagnostic", and that there have apparently been no reports of "controlled experiments which exert a perturbing influence on the scientific community." He went on to say that "It is premature to attempt to translate a description of present behavior into future requirements; to discern any relationship between the two requires considerable further study." He indicated that he thought emphasis should possibly now be shifted to experimental studies subject to greater control.

In a recent book entitled *Science Since Babylon*,[15] Derek Price, a historian of science, devoted a chapter to the "diseases of science", — its superabundance of literature, its manpower shortages, its increasing specialization, and its tendency to deteriorate in quality. These so-called "diseases" all stem from the exponential rate of growth of scientific activities and publications, a growth which, he says, is "very much more active, much vaster in its problems, than any other sort of growth happening in the world today." Price argues that "there should be much scope for scientific attack on science's own internal problems, yet curiously enough," he goes on to say, "any attack is regarded with much skepticism, and the men of science prefer, for the most part, to talk as unskilled laymen about the general organizational problems with which science is currently beset." I imagine Price would regard the current studies of communication I have mentioned as encouraging signs that scientists in some fields are concerned with one of science's internal problems, namely that of management of scientific information.

In closing, I should like simply to emphasize that the problem area I have discussed, that of determining scientists' documentation needs, is wide open for new approaches and for soundly conceived research and experimentation.

REFERENCES

[1] Most of this paper was presented previously at the International Conference on Scientific Information in the Field of Crystallography and Solid State Physics, Nishinomiya, Japan, October 3, 1961, and appears in the proceedings of that conference.

[2] *The Royal Society Scientific Information Conference, June 21 - July 2, 1948: Report and Papers Submitted*, The Royal Society, London, 1948.

[3] *Proceedings of the International Conference on Scientific Information, Washington, D.C., November 16-21, 1958*, National Academy of Sciences-National Research Council, Washington, 1959 (two volumes)

[4] *Information Service in Psychopharmacology: Proceedings of the Conference on Scientists' Needs for Information*, November 25-26, 1960. Prepared by Psychological Research Associates, June 1961, for the Scientific Information Unit, Psychopharmacology Service Center, National Institute of Mental Health, Washington 25, D.C.

[5] Don R. Swanson, Ramo-Wooldridge Division, Thompson-Ramo-Wooldridge, Inc., Canoga Park, California), *"Information Retrieval: State of the Art"*, Presented at the Western Joint Computer Conference, May 9-11, 1961.

[6] Dwight E. Gray, *"Physics Abstracting"*, American Journal of Physics, vol. 18, October 1950, p. 417.

[7] I. H. Hogg and J. Roland Smith, *"Information and Literature Use in a Research and Development Organization"*, Proceedings of the International Conference on Scientific Information (reference 3) pp. 131-162.

[8] Ralph R. Shaw, *"Pilot Study on the Use of Scientific Literature by Scientists"*. Mimeographed report to the National Science Foundation, 1956.

[9] *The Flow of Information Among Scientists: Problems, Opportunities and Research Questions*. Submitted to the National Science Foundation by the Columbia University Bureau of Applied Social Research, May 1958.

[10] *An Operations Research Study of the Scientific Activity of Chemists, November 1958. An Operations Research Study of the Dissemination and Use of Recorded Scientific Information: I - Journal Reading by Physicists and Chemists; II - The Cost of Journal Publication; and III - The Effect of Condensation on Comprehension of Journal Articles*, December 1960. Both submitted to the National Science Foundation by the Operations Research Group, Case Institute of Technology.

[11] *Review of Studies in the Flow of Information Among Scientists*. Submitted to the National Science Foundation by the Bureau of Applied Social Research, Columbia University, January 1960.

[12] *Ibid.*, Table F-20.

[13] *"Mooers' Law, or Why Some Retrieval Systems Are Used and Others Are Not"*, American Documentation, vol. 11, no. 3, July 1960.

[14] Margaret S. Bryant, *"Bibliographies, Abstracts, and Indexes"*, volume 2, part 2 of the series, The State of the Library Art, Rutgers University Press, New Brunswick, N.J., 1960.

[15] Derek J. de Solla Price, *"Science Since Babylon"*. Yale University Press, New Haven, 1961.

By William B. Kehl
University of Pittsburgh

11. Communication Between Computer and User in Information Searching

THIS IS A REPORT of an educational experiment at the University of Pittsburgh Computing Center. I believe it may offer several suggestions to large organizations which have a centralized large scale computing center, on how to take advantage of the availability of such a facility.

We have a tape oriented IBM 7070/1401 system at the center. The tape oriented configuration determines the flow of activity, as shown in **Exhibit 1**.

The IBM 1401 computer is used only to transfer information from cards to magnetic tape and, at the completion of the task, from tape to printer. Not even editing is done on the 1401. All computation is carried out on the IBM 7070 system proper. Such a system pro-

vides very high efficiency of operation since the 7070, which serves as the central processor, is never "waiting" to read cards or to print results.

Such an operation is typical of most large computing centers. The question that immediately arises is, how does the user communicate with such a system? This problem is solved in general by the use of a monitor system computer program. We refer to our monitor, somewhat facetiously, as PEST, Pitt Executive System for Tapes. It controls the sequencing of programs, one after the other, automatically, allowing a mixture of student homework, graduate theses, faculty research, and production type runs without interruption. Some of the runs use a compiler language

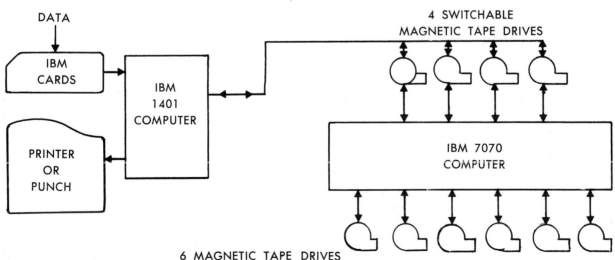

Exhibit 1

Flow of Data in Tape Oriented Configuration

like Fortran, some are in machine code or an assembly language, and some are just the execution of a program in our computer program library. Approximately 150 different runs are executed each day.

One expects a scientist or an engineer to adapt to such a technique of operation. But we also wanted our computer to be used by schools other than the natural sciences. We wanted to allow the professor of education to be able to analyze the vocabulary of first grade readers, the student of Middle English to use computer aids, and the lawyer to make similar use of a computer.

It was in this latter area that our programming received the greatest impetus. We have transferred to magnetic tape over 10,000,000 words of statutory materials from selected states. This material was prepared by Mr. John Horty, Director of the Health Law Center, at the university. Free or natural text was typed using Friden Flexowriters to prepare paper tape, which was then converted to punched cards. There are about 10 words on each card. There are no deletions. The sentences average approximately 18 words long. All material was punched as complete sentences. Each statutory section was treated as

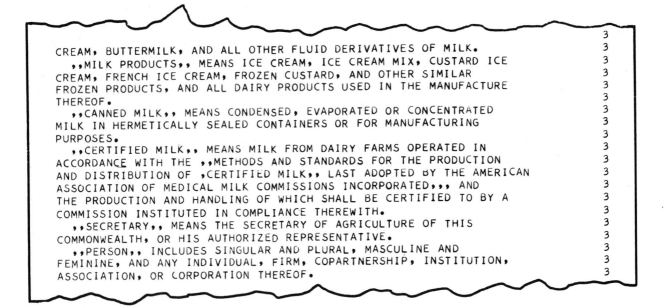

Exhibit 2

Sample Input Text

Exhibit 3

Vocabulary

a separate document, and the documents were assigned numerically increasing document numbers. The documents average 200 words in length.

Since we knew that the user might wish to identify a word within a sentence within a document, we assigned a numerical identification to each word. **Exhibit 2** shows the text of a typical document as stored on magnetic tape. This document was entered as document number 1. **Exhibit 3** shows that the word, ACCORDANCE, appears in document number 1, line 15, sentence 7, word 10, matching the reference in **Exhibit 2**. A computer program to prepare a vocabulary tape containing such a concordance listing was written by the center. Thus, for each of approximately 20 states there is a *text tape* and a *vocabulary tape*. While the text tape is complete, common words of no interest have been eliminated from the vocabulary tape. These account for about half of all the occurrences of words.

But let us return to the topic of primary interest. How does an English teacher, lawyer, or professor of education communicate with the computer to use such text data? Suppose he wants to find the documents dealing with "food poisoning". Does he have to learn the intricacies of computer coding?

The usual answer to this is that he has to depend on some expert. He may hire a computer programmer, or he may even go further and seek the help of a professional library scientist skilled in all the devices of indexing. In the spirit of a university atmosphere, we felt there should be another answer for him. He should be given aids so that he could communicate with the computer directly himself. In this way he would be able to do his *own* study and not be dependent on "experts".

For this reason, a *User Oriented Search Language* was developed. One example will serve to illustrate its use. Suppose I were interested in the regulations concerning food

Exhibit 4
Search Request on Food Poisoning

REGULATION	+	REGULATIONS	
	+	PENALTY	
	+	PENALTIES	
	+	FINES	
	+	SUSPENSION	
	+	SUSPENSIONS	JJ
FOOD	+	FOODS	
	+	FOODSTUFFS	
	+	FISH	
	+	MEAT	
	+	SEAFOOD	
	+	SEAFOODS	AA
POISON	+	POISONING	
	+	POISONOUS	BB
ILL	+	ILLNESS	
	+	SICK	
	+	SICK	
	+	SICKNESS	CC
SPOILED	+	SPOILING	
		SPOILATION	
	+	DECAYED	EE
HOTEL	+	HOTELS	
	+	RESTAURANT	
	+	RESTAURANTS	GG
AA	D	EE	MM
AA	D	BB	
	+	MM	
	IFD+0+10		+6
	D	CC	CITE
	IFD+0+10		+4
	D	JJ	CITE
	IFD+0+10		+2
	D	GG	
			PRINT

poisoning. Several concepts come to mind. These can be identified by actual words that appear in the texts.

AA   The concept of food *or* fish *or* meat *or* seafood as represented if one of these words appears in a document.

BB   The concept of poison *or* poisonous.

EE   The concept of spoil *or* decayed.

GG   The concept of a hotel *or* restaurant.

JJ   The concept of regulations *or* penalties *or* suspension (of a license).

MM   The combination of the concept labeled AA, above, and the concept labeled EE, above, in the same document would insure that we were interested in spoilage of food. To provide this, we wish to require that the document to be retrieved would contain at least one word in group AA and at least one word in group EE. We let MM serve as a label for this group of documents. Now if there were less than, say, 10 documents dealing with the concept MM of spoiled food, we would like to print them out. If there were more than 10 such documents, we might wish to insist that there be a reference to concept CC (sickness) in the same document and we would like a citation to these.

Exhibit 4 shows how such a search request is prepared by a user — namely, the lawyer, himself.

+ is used for *or*

D is used for "*and* in the same document".

IF D+0+10 +6 means, "if the number of documents in the list collected up to this point is between 0 and 10, then skip 6 lines to the line which has the word PRINT and execute that command".

Cards are punched just as shown in **Exhibit 4**, one card per line. A header card identifying the program to be used is also added, and this small batch of 35 cards is fed into the system shown in the flow chart in **Exhibit 1**. Preceding this problem in the card input stack may be an engineering problem, and following it may be a business school inventory model study. The output is shown in **Exhibit 5a** through **5e**.

A few comments will complete our report:

1. Notice the use of the IF statement provides a means for the user to control his answers, conditionally dependent on some intermediate results. This is a necessary and really a *key factor* in communication between the user and the computer. It avoids the necessity of his returning many different times, dissatisfied with getting either too many irrelevant documents or having restricted his search by the excessive use of the D or "and" command and getting no output.

2. Because the search language is trivial to learn, every user may phrase his own search. His satisfaction is infinitely higher. Personal participation means much to him compared with dependency on an "expert".

3. His learning curve on his own work goes up very fast. He is quick to perceive his own successes and failures. He comes to understand his own use of language and the language of his subject much quicker.

Many other computer programs for analysis of natural text have been developed by our center. Some of these are described in the *Communications of the Association for Computing Machinery,* September, 1961, issue. But the one idea I feel is an original contribution to the area of information retrieval has been in the introduction of a User Oriented Search Language and the communication link it provides a user with the computer.

The programs described in this paper were written by Charles R. T. Bacon of the computing center staff, and have been made available through the GUIDE library by contacting the IBM Program Librarian, IBM, White Plains, New York. Mr. Bacon's work has been a significant contribution to the use of our center in new areas beyond the usual scientific applications.

The legal retrieval applications research under the direction of Mr. John Horty is supported by the Council on Library Resources, the National Institutes of Health, the U. S. Office of Education, and the Ford Foundation.

Exhibit 5a

```
NO LIST - SPOILATION
NO LIST - SPOILING
REGULATION                    +        REGULATIONS
                              +        PENALTY
                              +        PENALTIES
                              +        FINES
                              +        SUSPENSION
                              +        SUSPENSIONS              JJ
FOOD                          +        FOODS
                              +        FOODSTUFFS
                              +        FISH
                              +        MEAT
                              +        SEAFOOD
                              +        SEAFOODS                 AA
POISON                        +        POISONING
                              +        POISONOUS                BB
ILL                           +        ILLNESS
                              +        SICK
                              +        SICK
                              +        SICKNESS                 CC
SPOILED                       +        SPOILING
                              +        SPOILATION
                              +        DECAYED                  EE
HOTEL                         +        HOTELS
                              +        RESTAURANT
                              +        RESTAURANTS              GG
AA                            D        EE                       MM
AA                            D        BB
                              +        MM
                              IFD+0+10                         +6
                                                              PRINT
MD. CODE ANN. ART. 27, SEC. 451                                486
SEC. 451.   POISONING OR CONTAMINATING WATER, DRINK, FOOD OR
            FOOD PRODUCTS
   EVERY PERSON, HIS AIDERS AND ABETTORS, WHO KNOWINGLY AND WILFULLY
POISONS, DEFILES OR IN ANY WAY CORRUPTS OR CONTAMINATES THE WATERS OF
ANY WELL, SPRING, BROOK, LAKE, POND, STREAM, RIVER, RESERVOIR OR OTHER
SOURCE OF WATER SUPPLY, OR ANY TRIBUTARY THEREOF, USED OR USABLE FOR
DRINKING OR DOMESTIC PURPOSES, BY MEANS OF DISEASE GERMS OR BACTERIA
OR THE INSERTION OF ANY OTHER POISON OR POISONOUS MATTER THEREIN,
OR ATTEMPTS SO TO DO, OR CONSPIRES OR CONNIVES THEREAT, AND EVERY PERSON,
HIS AIDERS AND ABETTORS, WHO, BY LIKE MEANS, KNOWINGLY AND WILFULLY
POISONS, DEFILES OR IN ANY WAY CORRUPTS OR CONTAMINATES ANY DRINK, FOOD
OR FOOD PRODUCTS OR SUPPLY, OR ATTEMPTS SO TO DO, OR CONSPIRES OR
CONNIVES THEREAT, SHALL BE GUILTY OF A FELONY, AND UPON CONVICTION THEREOF
SHALL BE SUBJECT TO IMPRISONMENT IN THE PENITENTIARY FOR NOT MORE THAN
TWENTY YEARS, IN THE DISCRETION OF THE COURT.
ATTEMPTING TO POISON ACT
MD. CODE ANN. ART. 43, SEC. 175                                838
SEC. 175.   SALE OF DISEASED, CORRUPTED OR UNWHOLESOME FOOD
   IF ANY PERSON SHALL SELL OR OFFER FOR SALE ANY KIND OF DISEASED,
CORRUPTED OR UNWHOLESOME PROVISIONS SUCH AS POULTRY, GAME, FLESH,
OR PREPARATIONS OF FLESH, FRUITS, VEGETABLES, BREAD, FLOUR, MEAL,
MILK OR OTHER THINGS INTENDED TO BE USED FOR HUMAN FOOD, HE SHALL
BE PUNISHED BY IMPRISONMENT IN THE COUNTY JAIL NOT MORE THAN ONE
YEAR, OR BE FINED NOT EXCEEDING FIVE HUNDRED DOLLARS, OR BE BOTH
FINED AND IMPRISONED IN THE DISCRETION OF THE COURT HAVING
JURISDICTION, AND THE UNWHOLESOME PROVISIONS OFFERED OR
EXPOSED FOR SALE SHALL BE FORFEITED AND DESTROYED OR SO DISPOSED
OF AS TO PREVENT THEIR BEING USED FOR FOOD., PROVIDED, THAT
```

NOTHING IN THIS SECTION SHALL APPLY TO THE SHIPPERS OR CONSIGNORS
OF GREEN FRUITS OR VEGETABLES THAT MAY BE SPOILED IN TRANSITU.
ADULTERATION OF FOOD AND DRINK ACT--- MISCELLANEOUS PROVISIONS
MD. CODE ANN. ART. 43, SEC. 189   852
SEC. 189. WHAT DRUGS, FOOD AND WATER DEEMED ADULTERATED
   DRUGS.--- FOR THE PURPOSE OF SECTIONS 187 TO 197 AN ARTICLE SHALL
BE DEEMED ADULTERATED IN CASE OF DRUGS.*
   FIRST. IF WHEN A DRUG IS SOLD UNDER OR BY A NAME RECOGNIZED IN
THE UNITED STATES PHARMACOPOEIA OR NATIONAL FORMULARY, IT DIFFERS
FROM THE STANDARD OF STRENGTH, QUALITY OR PURITY AS DETERMINED
BY THE TEST OR TESTS LAID DOWN IN THE UNITED STATES PHARMACOPOEIA
OR NATIONAL FORMULARY., PROVIDED, THAT NO DRUG DEFINED IN THE
UNITED STATES PHARMACOPOEIA OR NATIONAL FORMULARY, EXCEPT
PREPARATIONS OF OPIUM, SHALL BE DEEMED TO BE ADULTERATED UNDER
THIS PROVISION IF THE STANDARD OF STRENGTH, QUALITY OR PURITY BE
PLAINLY STATED UPON THE BOTTLE, BOX OR OTHER CONTAINER THEREOF,
ALTHOUGH THE STANDARD MAY DIFFER FROM THAT DETERMINED BY THE
TEST OR TESTS LAID DOWN IN THE UNITED STATES PHARMACOPOEIA OR
NATIONAL FORMULARY.
   SECOND. IF ITS STRENGTH OR PURITY FALL BELOW THE PROFESSED
STANDARD OR QUALITY UNDER WHICH IT IS SOLD.
   THIRD. IF USED IN THE COMPOUNDING OF A MEDICINE OR MEDICINES
INTENDED FOR THE CURE, MITIGATION OR PREVENTION OF DISEASE IN MAN
OR ANIMAL, IT SHALL NOT BE OF THE STANDARD OF STRENGTH, QUALITY
OR PURITY AS DETERMINED BY THE TEST OR TESTS LAID DOWN IN THE
UNITED STATES PHARMACOPOEIA OR NATIONAL FORMULARY., PROVIDED,
THAT MANUFACTURING CHEMISTS IN COMPOUNDING MEDICINES MAY USE,
WHEN NECESSARY, DRUGS OTHER THAN OF STANDARD STRENGTH IF THE
FINISHED PRODUCT OBTAINED FULLY MEETS THE REQUIREMENTS OF THE
UNITED STATES PHARMACOPOEIA OR NATIONAL FORMULARY.* IN THE CASE
OF CONFECTIONERY, IF IT CONTAINS TERRA ALBA, BARYTES, TALC,
CHROME YELLOW OR OTHER MINERAL SUBSTANCE, EXCEPT SALT, OR
POISONOUS COLOR OR FLAVOR, OR OTHER INGREDIENT DELETERIOUS OR
DETRIMENTAL TO HEALTH, OR ANY VINOUS, MALT OR SPIRITUOUS
LIQUORS OR COMPOUND, OR NARCOTIC DRUG.
   FOOD.--- IN THE CASE OF FOOD.*
   FIRST. IF ANY SUBSTANCE HAS BEEN MIXED OR PACKED WITH IT SO AS
TO REDUCE OR LOWER OR INJURIOUSLY AFFECT ITS QUALITY, STRENGTH OR
PURITY.
   SECOND. IF ANY SUBSTANCE HAS BEEN SUBSTITUTED WHOLLY OR IN PART
FOR THE ARTICLE.
   THIRD. IF ANY VALUABLE CONSTITUENT OF THE ARTICLE HAS BEEN
WHOLLY OR IN PART ABSTRACTED, OR IF THE PRODUCT BE BELOW THAT
STANDARD OF QUALITY, STRENGTH OR PURITY REPRESENTED TO THE
PURCHASER OR CONSUMER.
   FOURTH. IF IT BE MIXED, COLORED OR CHANGED IN COLOR, POWDER
COATED, STAINED OR BLEACHED, IN A MANNER WHEREBY DAMAGE OR
INFERIORITY IS CONCEALED.
   FIFTH. IF IT CONTAIN ANY ADDED POISONOUS OR OTHER ADDED
DELETERIOUS INGREDIENTS WHICH MAY RENDER SUCH ARTICLE INJURIOUS TO
HEALTH., PROVIDED, THAT WHEN IN THE PREPARATION OF FOOD PRODUCTS
FOR SHIPMENT THEY ARE PRESERVED BY AN EXTERNAL APPLICATION
APPLIED IN SUCH MANNER THAT THE PRESERVATIVE IS NECESSARILY
REMOVED MECHANICALLY OR BY MACERATION IN WATER OR OTHERWISE, AND
DIRECTIONS FOR THE REMOVAL OF SAID PRESERVATIVE SHALL BE PRINTED
ON THE COVERING OF THE PACKAGE., THE PROVISIONS OF SECTIONS 187
TO 197 SHALL BE CONSTRUED AS APPLYING ONLY WHEN SAID PRODUCTS ARE
READY FOR CONSUMPTION.
   SIXTH. IF IT CONSISTS IN WHOLE OR IN PART OF A FILTHY,
CONTAMINATED, DECOMPOSED OR PUTRID ANIMAL OR VEGETABLE SUBSTANCE

OR ANY PORTION OF A SUBSTANCE UNFIT FOR FOOD, WHETHER
MANUFACTURED OR NOT, OR ANY ANIMAL OR VEGETABLE SUBSTANCE
PRODUCED, STORED, TRANSFERRED OR KEPT IN A CONDITION WHICH WOULD
RENDER THE ARTICLE DISEASED, CONTAMINATED OR UNWHOLESOME, OR IF IT
IS THE PRODUCT OF A DISEASED ANIMAL OR ONE THAT HAS DIED OTHERWISE
THAN BY SLAUGHTER, OR THAT HAS BEEN FED UPON THE OFFAL FROM A
SLUAUGHTERHOUSE, OR IF IT IS THE MILK FROM AN ANIMAL FED UPON
SUBSTANCES UNFIT FOR FOOD FOR DAIRY ANIMALS, OR FROM AN ANIMAL
KEPT AND MILKED IN A FILTHY OR CONTAMINATED STABLE, OR IN
SURROUNDINGS THAT WOULD RENDER THE MILK CONTAMINATED.
     WATER.--- IN THE CASE OF WATER.*
     FIRST.   IF MANUFACTURED FOR SALE, PRODUCED FOR SALE, EXPOSED FOR
SALE OR ADVERTISED FOR SALE, AS A SPRING, WELL OR MINERAL
WATER, OR IF SERVED IN A PUBLIC PLACE AS A SPRING, WELL OR MINERAL
WATER, IT BE FOUND UPON ANALYSIS TO DIFFER IN COMPOSITION OR
CONSTITUENTS FROM THE COMPOSITION OR CONSTITUENTS OF THE WATER
TAKEN FROM THE SPRING, WELL OR OTHER ORIGINAL SOURCE, OR ALLEGED
ORIGINAL SOURCE, FROM WHICH SUCH WATER IS OBTAINED OR ALLEGED TO
BE OBTAINED, UNLESS THE CHANGES THEREIN OR ADDITIONS THERETO BE
PLAINLY INDICATED UPON THE LABEL., PROVIDED, THAT IN THE CASE OF
WATERS MANUFACTURED TO RESEMBLE NATURAL MINERAL WATERS, SUCH
WATERS MUST BE LABELED IN A CONSPICUOUS MANNER ,,ARTIFICIAL,, .,
AND PROVIDED FURTHER, THAT WHEN SUCH WATERS ARE SOLD OR SERVED AS
MINERAL WATERS, THEY MUST CONTAIN ONE OR MORE MINERAL CONSTITUENTS
IN SUFFICIENT QUANTITIES TO HAVE A THERAPEUTIC EFFECT FROM
THESE CONSTITUENTS WHEN A REASONABLE QUANTITY OF THE WATER IS
CONSUMED.
     SECOND.   IF WHEN ADVERTISED AND SOLD AS A PURE DRINKING WATER,
SPRING, WELL OR MINERAL WATER, IT SHOWS CONTAMINATION.
ADULTERATION OF FOOD AND DRINK ACT--- FOOD AND DRUG LAW
MD. CODE ANN. ART. 43, SEC. 190   853
SEC. 190.   WHAT DRUGS, FOOD, WATER AND DISINFECTANT DEEMED
            MISBRANDED
     THE TERM MISBRANDED, AS USED HEREIN, SHALL APPLY TO ALL DRUGS OR
ARTICLES OF FOOD OR ARTICLES WHICH ENTER INTO THE COMPOSITION OF
FOOD THE PACKAGE OR LABEL OF WHICH SHALL BEAR ANY STATEMENT, DESIGN
OR DEVICE REGARDING SUCH ARTICLE OR THE INGREDIENTS OR SUBSTANCES
CONTAINED THEREIN, WHICH SHALL BE FALSE OR MISLEADING IN ANY
PARTICULAR, AND TO ANY FOOD OR DRUG PRODUCT WHICH IS FALSELY
BRANDED AS TO THE STATE, TERRITORY, PLACE OR COUNTRY IN WHICH IT
IS MANUFACTURED OR PRODUCED., THAT FOR THE PURPOSE OF SECTIONS 187
TO 197, AN ARTICLE SHALL ALSO BE DEEMED TO BE MISBRANDED.*
     DRUGS.--- IN THE CASE OF DRUGS.*
     FIRST.   IF IT BE AN IMITATION OF OR OFFERED FOR SALE UNDER THE NAME
OF ANOTHER ARTICLE.
     SECOND.   IF THE CONTENTS OF THE PACKAGE AS ORIGINALLY PUT UP SHALL
HAVE BEEN REMOVED IN WHOLE OR IN PART AND OTHER CONTENTS SHALL HAVE
BEEN PLACED IN SUCH PACKAGE.
     THIRD.   IF IT BE LABELED OR BRANDED SO AS TO DECEIVE OR MISLEAD
THE PURCHASER, OR PURPORTS TO BE A FOREIGN PRODUCT WHEN NOT SO.
     THIRD A.   IF ITS PACKAGE OR LABEL SHALL BEAR OR CONTAIN ANY
STATEMENT, DESIGN OR DEVICE REGARDING THE CURATIVE OR THERAPEUTIC
EFFECT OF SUCH ARTICLE OR ANY OF THE INGREDIENTS OR SUBSTANCES
CONTAINED THEREIN, WHICH IS FALSE OR MISLEADING IN ANY PARTICULAR.
ANY REPRESENTATION CONCERNING THE CURATIVE OR THERAPEUTIC EFFECT
OF ANY DRUG SHALL BE DEEMED FALSE IF SUCH REPRESENTATION IS NOT
SUPPORTED BY SUBSTANTIAL MEDICAL OPINION OR DEMONSTRABLE SCIENTIFIC
FACTS.
     FOURTH.   IF THE PACKAGE FAILS TO BEAR A STATEMENT ON THE LABEL OF
THE QUANTITY OR PROPORTION OF ANY ALCOHOL, OPIUM, MORPHINE,

DIACETYL MORPHINE, HEROIN, COCAINE, HOLOCAINE, ALPHA OR BETA EUCAINE,
NOVOCAINE, ALYPIN, CHLOROFORM, CANNABIS, INDICA, CHLORAL HYDRATE,
CODEINE, ACETANILID, ANTIFEBRIN, ACETPHENETIDIN, PHENACETINE,
ANTIPYRIN, OR ANY DERIVATIVE OR PREPARATION OF ANY SUCH
SUBSTANCES CONTAINED THEREIN.. PROVIDED, THAT NOTHING IN THIS
PARAGRAPH SHALL BE CONSTRUED TO APPLY TO THE DISPENSING OF
PRESCRIPTIONS OF REGULARLY LICENSED PHYSICIANS, VETERINARIANS
AND DENTISTS, INTENDED FOR IMMEDIATE OR TEMPORARY USE, AND KEPT
ON FILE BY THE DISPENSING PHARMACISTS., AND PROVIDED FURTHER, THAT
NOTHING IN THIS PARAGRAPH SHALL BE CONSTRUED TO APPLY TO SUCH
DRUGS OR MEDICINES AS ARE PERSONALLY DISPENSED BY REGULARLY
LICENSED PRACTICING PHYSICIANS, DENTISTS AND VETERINARIANS IN THE
COURSE OF THEIR PRACTICE. PHYSICIANS CONDUCTING DRUG STORES SHALL
BE SUBJECT TO ALL THE LAWS, RULES AND REGULATIONS GOVERNING
PHARMACISTS.
   FOODS.--- IN THE CASE OF FOODS.*
   FIRST. IF IT BE AN IMITATION OF OR OFFERED FOR SALE UNDER THE
DISTINCTIVE NAME OF ANOTHER ARTICLE.
   SECOND. IF IT BE LABELED OR BRANDED SO AS TO DECEIVE OR MISLEAD
THE PURCHASER, OR PURPORT TO BE A FOREIGN PRODUCT WHEN NOT SO,
OR IF THE CONTENTS OF THE PACKAGE AS ORIGINALLY PUT UP SHALL HAVE
BEEN REMOVED IN WHOLE OR IN PART AND OTHER CONTENTS SHALL HAVE
BEEN PLACED IN SUCH PACKAGE, OR IF IT FAIL TO BEAR A STATEMENT
ON THE LABEL OF THE QUANTITY OR PROPORTION OF ANY OPIUM, MORPHINE,
DIACETYL MORPHINE, HEROIN, COCAINE, HOLOCAINE, ALPHA OR BETA
EUCAINE, NOVOCAINE, ALYPIN, CHLOROFORM, CANNABIS INDICA, CHLORAL
HYDRATE, ACETANILID, ANTIFEBRIN, ACETYPHENETIDIN, PHENACETINE,
ANTIPYRIN OR ANY DERIVATIVE OR PREPARATION OR ANY SUCH SUBSTANCE
CONTAINED THEREIN.
   THIRD. IF IN PACKAGE FORM, THE QUANTITY OF THE CONTENTS BE
NOT PLAINLY AND CONSPICUOUSLY MARKED ON THE OUTSIDE OF THE PACKAGE
IN TERMS OF WEIGHT, MEASURE OR NUMERICAL COUNT., PROVIDED,
HOWEVER, THAT REASONABLE VARIATIONS SHALL BE PERMITTED AND
TOLERANCES AND ALSO EXEMPTIONS AS TO SMALL PACKAGES SHALL BE
ESTABLISHED BY RULES AND REGULATIONS MADE IN ACCORDANCE WITH THE
PROVISIONS OF SECTION 194.
   FOURTH. IF THE PACKAGE CONTAINING IT, OR ITS LABEL, SHALL BEAR
ANY STATEMENT, DESIGN OR DEVICE REGARDING THE INGREDIENTS OR THE
SUBSTANCES CONTAINED THEREIN WHICH STATEMENT, DESIGN OR DEVICE SHALL
BE FALSE OR MISLEADING IN ANY PARTICULAR., PROVIDED, THAT AN ARTICLE
OF FOOD WHICH DOES NOT CONTAIN ANY ADDED POISONOUS OR DELETERIOUS
INGREDIENTS SHALL NOT BE DEEMED TO BE ADULTERATED OR MISBRANDED
IN THE FOLLOWING CASES.*
   /1ST/ IN THE CASE OF MIXTURES OR COMPOUNDS WHICH MAY BE NOW OR
FROM TIME TO TIME HEREAFTER KNOWN AS ARTICLES OF FOOD UNDER
THEIR OWN DISTINCTIVE NAMES AND NOT AN IMITATION OF OR OFFERED
FOR SALE UNDER THE DISTINCTIVE NAME OF ANOTHER ARTICLE, IF THE
NAME BE ACCOMPANIED ON THE SAME LABEL OR BRAND WITH A STATEMENT OF
THE PLACE WHERE SAID ARTICLES HAVE BEEN MANUFACTURED OR PRODUCED.
   /2ND/ IN THE CASE OF ARTICLES LABELED, BRANDED OR TAGGED SO
AS TO PLAINLY INDICATE THAT THEY ARE COMPOUNDS, IMITATIONS OR
BLENDS, AND THE WORD ,,COMPOUND,, OR ,,BLEND,, AS THE CASE MAY
BE, IS PLAINLY STATED ON THE PACKAGE IN WHICH IT IS OFFERED FOR
SALE., PROVIDED, THAT THE TERM BLEND AS USED HEREIN SHALL BE
CONSTRUED TO MEAN A MIXTURE OF LIKE SUBSTANCES, NOT EXCLUDING
HARMLESS COLORING OR FLAVORING INGREDIENTS USED FOR THE PURPOSE
OF COLORING AND FLAVORING ONLY.
   WATER.--- IN THE CASE OF WATER.*
   FIRST. IN CASE OF MINERAL WATERS LABELED ,,ARTIFICIAL, ,, IN
CONFORMITY WITH THE PROVISIONS OF SECTIONS 187 TO 197, THE LABEL

BEAR ANY DESIGN OR DEVICE WHICH WOULD LEAD THE CONSUMER TO
BELIEVE THAT THE WATER IS A NATURAL ONE.
  SECOND. OR IF CHARACTERIZED BY A GEOGRAPHICAL NAME WHICH GIVES
A FALSE OR MISLEADING IDEA IN REGARD TO COMPOSITION OF SAID WATER.
  DISINFECTANTS.--- AS TO DISINFECTANTS.*
  IF IN THE CASE OF DISINFECTANTS MANUFACTURED OR SOLD IN THIS
STATE THE MANUFACTURERS, SALES AGENTS OR DEALERS FAIL TO SHOW ON
THE LABELS THE CARBOLIC ACID COEFFICIENT OR RELATIVE GERMICIDAL
STRENGTH OF SUCH DISINFECTANTS AS COMPARED WITH PURE CARBOLIC ACID.,
PROVIDED, HOWEVER, THAT DEODORANTS AND ANTISEPTICS HAVING NO
GERMICIDAL STRENGTH MUST BE PLAINLY LABELED AND SOLD AS SUCH AND
SUCH PREPARATIONS AS HAVE NO SUCH GERMICIDAL STRENGTH, SHALL NOT
BE LABELED ,,DISINFECTANTS. ,,
ADULTERATION OF FOOD AND DRINK ACT--- FOOD AND DRUG LAW
MD. CODE ANN. ART. 43, SEC. 194   857
SEC. 194. ENFORCEMENT BY STATE BOARD
  THE STATE BOARD OF HEALTH SHALL ENFORCE THE PROVISIONS OF SECTIONS
187 TO 197, AND SHALL HAVE THE POWER TO ADOPT FROM TIME TO TIME,
PROMULGATE AND PUBLISH BY CIRCULAR OR OTHERWISE, SUCH GENERAL RULES
AND REGULATIONS FOR THE ENFORCEMENT THEREOF AND FOR THE GOVERNMENT OF
THE ANALYSTS, CHEMISTS, INSPECTORS AND EMPLOYEES APPOINTED BY THE SAID
BOARD AS IT MAY DEEM PROPER., AND SAID BOARD MAY ADOPT THE RULES AND
REGULATIONS LAWFULLY ADOPTED FROM TIME TO TIME BY THE SECRETARY OF THE
UNITED STATES DEPARTMENT OF AGRICULTURE, SO FAR AS SUCH RULES AND
REGULATIONS MAY BE APPLICABLE TO THE DUTIES OF SAID BOARD UNDER AND
TO THE PURPOSES OF SECTIONS 187 TO 197. THE STATE BOARD OF HEALTH
SHALL HAVE COPIES OF SECTIONS 187 TO 197 PRINTED AND SHALL ISSUE THEM
AS FAR AS POSSIBLE TO PERSONS, FIRMS OR CORPORATIONS MANUFACTURING OR
SELLING, AT WHOLESALE OR RETAIL, ARTICLES OF FOOD OR DRUGS, AND SHALL
FURNISH THE SAME TO ALL PERSONS, FIRMS OR CORPORATIONS REQUESTING THEM.
THE STATE BOARD OF HEALTH SHALL ALSO ENFORCE THE PROVISIONS OF SECTIONS
315 TO 318, INCLUSIVE, OF ARTICLE 27 OF THE ANNOTATED CODE OF PUBLIC
GENERAL LAWS, TITLE ,,CRIMES AND PUNISHMENTS, ,, SUBTITLE ,,HEALTH---
BICHLORIDE OF MERCURY, ,, AND SECTIONS 456 AND 457 OF SAID ARTICLE 27
/1924 ED./, SUBTITLE ,,POISON, ,, AND SECTIONS 249, 250, 264 AND 265
OF THIS ARTICLE, SUBTITLE ,,COMMISSIONERS OF PHARMACY. ,,
ADULTERATION OF FOOD AND DRINK ACT--- FOOD AND DRUG LAW
MD. CODE ANN. ART. 48. SEC. 149   1468
SEC. 149. LABEL REQUIREMENTS
  EACH CONTAINER OF TREATED AGRICULTURAL, VEGETABLE, FLOWER, AND TREE
OR SHRUB SEEDS WHICH IS SOLD, OFFERED FOR SALE, OR EXPOSED FOR SALE,
OR TRANSPORTED WITHIN THIS STATE FOR SOWING PURPOSES SHALL BEAR THEREON
OR HAVE ATTACHED THERETO IN A CONSPICUOUS PLACE A PLAINLY WRITTEN OR
PRINTED LABEL OR TAG IN THE ENGLISH LANGUAGE, GIVING THE FOLLOWING
INFORMATION, WHICH STATEMENT SHALL NOT BE MODIFIED OR DENIED IN THE
LABELING OR ON ANOTHER LABEL ATTACHED TO THE CONTAINER. FOR ALL
SEEDS NAMED AND TREATED AS DEFINED IN THIS SUBTITLE /FOR WHICH
A SEPARATE LABEL MAY BE USED/.*
  /1/ THE WORD OR STATEMENT INDICATING THAT THE SEED HAS BEEN TREATED.
  /2/ THE COMMONLY ACCEPTED, COINED, CHEMICAL, OR ABBREVIATED
CHEMICAL /GENERIC/ NAME OF THE APPLIED SUBSTANCE.
  /3/ IF THE SUBSTANCE IN THE AMOUNT PRESENT WITH THE SEED IS HARMFUL
TO HUMAN OR OTHER VERTEBRATE ANIMALS A CAUTION STATEMENT SUCH
AS ,,DO NOT USE FOR FOOD OR FEED OR OIL PURPOSES. ,, THE CAUTION FOR
MERCURIALS AND SIMILARLY TOXIC SUBSTANCES SHALL BE A POISON STATEMENT
OR SYMBOL.
SEED ACT

By H. P. Luhn
Consultant

12. Automated Intelligence Systems[1]

WHEREVER A GROUP OF PEOPLE is engaged in an effort toward a common goal, their success depends to a significant degree on the facility with which they are able to communicate. Not only need information be exchanged within the group but it is essential that access be had to past and current external information that may have a bearing on the activity of such a group. The quality of performance of the group will furthermore depend on the speed with which information is able to flow through their communication network or can be summoned from likely sources.

Presently the amount of information being generated and accumulated is growing at an alarming rate and this is bound to continue. Specialization in all areas of human endeavor has increased, while at the same time the conventional boundaries of disciplines in science and technology have vanished. Everybody needs to have access to knowledge relating to his interests, no matter where it might exist. It appears doubtful whether sufficient competent manpower will be available in the future to perform the intellectual tasks required to organize and channel this information adequately and effectively. If one accepts this prediction, the question arises whether the principles of automation may be effectively applied to this area, as they have been to the area of manufacturing.

In the following discussion, an answer to this question will be sought by investigating some of the problems that will be encountered, by delineating a comprehensive intelligence system, and by establishing some of the prerequisites for the solution of the intellectual problems involved.

A COMPREHENSIVE INTELLIGENCE SYSTEM

The information needed within an organization to carry on its business is manifold in character and substance. Certain units of information are generated to be utilized at other points of an organization. At times a message is directed to a very specific point while at other times it is directed to substantial sections of an organization. Still other elements of information enter an organization from external sources and information generated within an organization is directed to external destinations. Information is stored within an organization for future reference and access is desired to this store at any time to answer questions that come up in the course of doing business. All these functions constitute a business intelligence system[2] which is the more complex, the larger the organization. The difficulty of adequate communication within an organization arises because of incomplete knowledge of one point of the organization as to the information requirements of any other point of the organization. This is particularly true where communication is desired horizontally across a vertically oriented hierarchical organization chart. An effective communication system should permit free flow of information between any two points of an organization. A model which will substantially perform this type of communication is shown in diagrammatic form in **Exhibit 1** and will be described in brief.

A first objective of the system is that of selective dissemination of new information.[3] In order to accomplish this, an interest profile is created and stored for each action point of a system. Such a profile consists of the description, in some appropriate language, of the current sphere of interest or activity of the action point. A document entering the system, irrespective of its having been generated internally or externally, and despite the fact that it might have been addressed specifically to an action point, is characterized with respect to its information content in a language similar to that used for the action point profile. This document profile is then compared with all of the action point profiles in store and wherever a predetermined degree of similarity between the profiles is detected, the affected action point is made aware of the information involved. If, upon receipt of this notification, the action point desires to have the complete information, the whole document will be made available. Acceptance of this information in one way or another will be noted by the system and be used to update the action point profile so that it may reflect actual current interests.

The second function of the system is that of information retrieval. By storing all document profiles and the documents characterized by them, a library is built up for future reference. If an action point wishes to obtain information which might be contained in the library, it composes a synthetic document profile characterizing the information needed in the language used for creating the document profile. By comparing this query profile with all of the profiles of the library documents and by establishing the degree of similarity wanted, the inquiring action point may then be notified of those documents which appear to be pertinent to the query.

The third function of the system is that of interest or activity matching (skill matching). If an action point wishes to find out which action point concerns itself with a given subject, it may synthesize the action point profile characteristic of the subject in question and charge the system with comparing this synthetic profile with all of the action point profiles and to announce the identity of those of the action profiles which match the synthetic profile to a given degree. This function will aid in discovering who is knowledgeable or skilled in certain areas or where to send inquiries of problems which cannot be resolved by an action point contacted originally.

The fourth function of the system is that of matching, as a matter of course, any new profile with any part or all of the profiles in store. This function serves to uncover duplications, to various degrees, between new activities and current activities, whether within the organization or between the organization and the outside world.

It is easily recognized that the exhibit model comprises most of the information and communication activities conventionally performed in any organization today. The present objective is to automate this system, that is, to perform the various functions to the high-

Exhibit 1

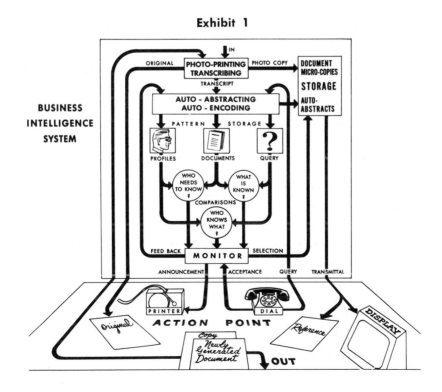

est possible extent with the aid of machines. Some of the problems that arise in replacing intellectual and manual effort by automatic procedures will be reviewed subsequently.

DIFFERENT TYPES OF SYSTEMS

So far the intelligence system has been described in general terms, covering its basic functions. It is important to realize at this point that in practice such systems will necessarily vary considerably in accordance with the particular situation they are to serve. Also, while the system has been treated as a comprehensive one covering all phases of an organization, there are many good reasons why specific phases of an operation should be treated individually in order to achieve utmost efficiency. However, such specialization must not prevent a special purpose system from being an integral part of the comprehensive system.

It is beyond the purpose of this paper to enumerate the many variables that enter into the design of a special system but, instead, to create an awareness of the fact that these variables range wide and far. Without such realization it becomes difficult to interpret generalities and determine the degree to which they apply to a given situation.

In order to illustrate the range of diversity, two tables are shown in **Exhibit 2,** based on four arbitrarily chosen variables. One table relates three degrees of access time to an information store to three degrees of activity in terms of inquiries per day. The other table relates three degrees of complexity of indexing a document to three sizes of document collection. Because of the lack of any standard of measurement at this time, an arbitrary index of difficulty has been placed at the intersection of the variables in question, such index being a relative value of rank. According to these tables

Exhibit 2

SOME CHARACTERISTICS OF IR SYSTEMS

Access Time	Queries Per Day		
	10	100	1000
1 day	1*	2	4
1 hour	3	5	7
real time	6	8	9

Indexing Effort	Items in Store		
	10 thousand	100 thousand	1 million
low	1	2	4
medium	3	5	7
high	6	8	9

* Arbitrary index of difficulty

one may, for instance, characterize the information retrieval system of a medium size chemical laboratory by index number 1 in the inquiry table and 6 in the storage table, while an information retrieval activity of an airline reservations system might be characterized by indexes 9 in the inquiry table and 2 in the storage table.

Typically all such systems involve the storage of items of information in such a manner that certain ones of these may be recalled in answer to a given inquiry. There is, however, a great difference of format of the items manipulated by various systems, bringing with it varying degrees of difficulty in characterizing the items so that they may be recognized. The process of characterizing stored items is generally referred to as indexing. This process, as currently performed, ranges from ordering factual data by unique identifications such as names of persons or things, to the categorization of descriptive articles and books by the assignment of classifications or subject headings. We shall concern ourselves here with only the more difficult tasks of characterizing extensive texts as would be typical of technical papers.

AUTOMATIC INDEXING

The problems that arise when contemplating the automation of intelligence systems lie in two distinct areas, namely, the operations concerning the meaning carried by documents and the processing of all physical aspects of documents. In making this distinction it is realized that meaning per se is not negotiable for purposes of communication, except by means of arbitrary physical tokens such as the spoken or the written word. While present day technology provides many ways for processing or manipulating such physical manifestations, meaning comes into existence only at the moment a human, familiar with the tokens used, interprets them.

Since automation is the objective here and since the intellectual effort in organizing and processing information is the critical area, machine methods must be found which will characterize documents in a manner that will produce results similar to those obtained by intellectual effort. This reduces to the question of whether some physical characteristics may be discovered in the make-up of documents which to a satisfactory degree are typical of

a given meaning content. The result hoped for is that if two documents display similar physical characteristics, the probability is high that upon human interpretation the two documents will disclose similar ideas. There is no need that the patterns by which such analogies may be constructed and recorded by a machine, be meaningful in themselves.

A first approach to the solution of this problem is the performance of a statistical analysis of the physical word pattern of a document. This would result in a vocabulary, including the frequency of occurrence for each word which would constitute the profile of that document. By comparing such vocabularies of various documents with each other, an indication may be obtained as to the extent that similarity of the vocabularies signifies similarity of meaning contents. Preliminary tests of this method have produced promising results.[4] During these tests it was also found that the vocabularies may be reduced substantially by disregarding certain classes of words. Even when such vocabularies were reduced to twenty to thirty top ranking words, adequate results were obtained for discovering similarity of subject matter for the purpose of selective dissemination of information.[5] In this latter case apparently high ranking (significant) words were manually extracted from the document, a procedure which anticipates the eventual extraction of keywords by machine.

The method just described is generally referred to as keyword indexing. While this method has simplicity to its credit, considerable experience is required before the limits of its effectiveness will have been established. This method disregards any specific relationship that an author might have established between the words of the vocabulary. The assumption here is that within the framework of a coherent presentation of a subject, there are few ways in which the words of a vocabulary can be meaningfully associated or related.[6]

A refinement of keyword indexing consists of indicating a first degree of physical relationship between words by denoting word pairs. The improvement that is expected here is that such words usually modify each other and therefore become more specific. A simple method is based on the notion that if two words occur in the same sentence and are not more than three or four words apart, there is a high probability that the meanings of these two words have been directly related.[7] Again, no specific relationship is indicated, relying upon probability as to meaningfulness among all possible combinations.

Exhibit 3

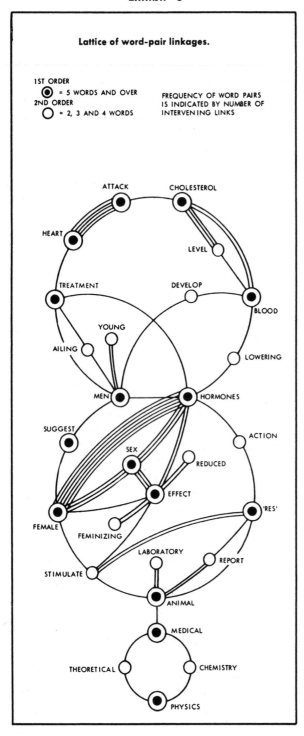

Lattice of word-pair linkages.

Even though this particular scheme has not yet been evaluated on the basis of sufficiently large samples, an impression of practicability may be derived from **Exhibit 3**. This figure represents a lattice of word-pair linkages constructed from a list of word pairs automatically derived from a short report on scientific research,[8] by the method just described. By tracing various paths interconnecting the less than 30 words, intelligent statements may be synthesized which have a high probability of matching those of the author.

As long as such keyword indexing methods have not been proven to be impractical, it appears to be premature to consider methods of higher complexity, such as would involve the determination of parts of speech, for instance. There appears to be a point of diminishing returns in that the more specific an indexing term becomes, the lower is the probability that it will match an equally specific term in a searching procedure.

Assuming for a moment that auto-indexing of the types just described will effectively serve to characterize information contents of documents for the purpose of comparison, it is of interest to point out that this method differs significantly from manually applied indexing methods in current use. Such current methods rely on the judgment of the indexer based on his understanding, at least in general terms, the message carried by a document and that he is thereby enabled to assign to a document as many class designations or subject headings as have been provided for by a preestablished classification structure or subject heading list. Depending on which of several indexers perform this job and under which conditions, such assignments will vary appreciably. No matter how detailed the rules might be to govern the indexer in doing his job, the interpretation of such rules again will vary. It is furthermore the job of the indexer to predict the point of view that a future inquirer might assume in his search for past knowledge. It is obvious that the decisions an indexer is capable of making to categorize a new document, can only be based on past experiences and that his predictions can at best be subjective and incomplete. The philosophy underlying this method assumes a low rate of change of point of view of the inquirers the system is to serve. In the area under discussion this is contrary to experience in recent years and it is doubtful therefore whether classification and subject heading systems can survive here, even if their systematic updating is accelerated.

In the case of auto-indexing, the characterization of the document is "derived" by extracting certain physical elements from the original text in accordance with some standard rule. As long as the same rule is applied, the product is the same, no matter by whom, where and when the extraction is performed. Since only the physical make-up of the text is the basis of this operation, it can be performed by machine, provided the full text is available in machine readable form. Except for the effects of contraction, no bias has been exerted on whatever meaning might have been expressed by the tokens extracted. The document remains unclassified in the conventional sense, although it might be said that classification has been exercised on the primitive level of words. No intellectual effort needs to be expended in this indexing operation.

At the instant of searching for information relating to a given topic, through the intermediary of index terms, the respective procedures for the two systems differ as follows: In the conventional system, classes or subject headings have to be identified which most appropriately delineate the topic of the query. In the automatically indexed system an appropriate class or subject heading is created to order for the occasion, so to speak, by synthesizing the vocabulary of keywords or word pairs embracing the subject matter as if it too had been stated in the form of a document. In the first case the inquirer has to adjust himself to the point of view that an indexer might have taken in the past, while in the second case he has complete freedom in reflecting his own viewpoint of the present.

As far as intellectual effort is concerned, it will be seen that in the conventional system it had to be expended on indexing each new document entering the system, even though only a fraction of documents of a collection is usually ever referred to again. In the auto-indexed system, on the other hand, intellectual effort is spent at the instant of search. The techniques of search will necessarily be different and in the case of auto-indexed documents, additional effort is required to overcome differences of word usage and problems of semantics, as discussed further on. In those functions of an automatic system where auto-indexed profiles are matched to each other, no intellectual intervention is required.

REORIENTATION OF PROFESSIONAL SKILLS

The procedures dictated by automation call for a major readjustment of professional talent presently engaged in the information services. For the present the idea of having the average user of an information system push buttons appears impractical since such procedure presupposes complete familiarity with all aspects of the system, attainable only through extensive training. Communication with the system should instead be carried out through the intermediary of an information specialist.

Constant awareness of users' demands and of the capabilities of the system will enable the specialist to negotiate and amplify inquiries so as to produce optimum results. To this end the properties of mechanically transformed and condensed texts need to be well understood. It is essential that statistical data are collected regarding word usage in both the indexing operation and retrieval operation. Cumulative dictionaries must therefore be compiled and subjected to periodic analysis. These latter operations would of course be performed mechanically as a by-product of indexing, abstracting and retrieval processes. The information thus obtained will assist the specialist in formulating inquiries more effectively and to adjust his procedures to the peculiarities of the information stored. It will furthermore enable him to develop thesauri and check lists denoting synonyms or near-synonyms and associated words which need to be included in certain search patterns to home in on pertinent information.

There are many other schemes which may have to be evolved to cope with the dynamic requirements of the users of information systems. It is up to the experience and resourcefulness of the specialist as to the extent to which automated information services may become useful and effective. Even when users are enabled to communicate directly with automated information systems, it will be because of machine routines developed by information specialists for guiding and supervising an inquirer in his searching operations. There is, therefore, a new challenge to the profession of documentalists, information specialists and librarians. Education and training directed at these new requirements should be an early concern of universities and library schools.

AUTOMATIC ABSTRACTING

Another intellectual operation which is presently performed to facilitate communication is that of preparing abstracts. Abstracting is a highly developed art which differentiates between many forms of abstracts depending on the purpose they are to serve. The common objective is to characterize the content of a document by deriving from it such fractions as will convey the essentials of the author's message.

A mechanical approximation to this process would depend, as was the case in automatic indexing, on the assumption that certain physical patterns of texts coincide with desired patterns of meaning. Thus it may be argued that the frequency with which certain words have been used by an author is a measure of significance and that the greater the concentration of such significant words is within a sentence, as compared with other sentences, the more significant is such a sentence as a conveyor of information characteristic of the contents of the related document. By selecting from a document an appropriate number of these highest ranking sentences and by reproducing them verbatim in the order of occurrence, an extract is derived which may approach the usefulness of conventional abstracts.[9]

While the mechanical solution to the procedure just described does not offer any difficulties it has been hard so far to evaluate the results.[10] Fully automatic abstracting of articles contained on punched tape created in conjunction with conventional typesetting methods was demonstrated for the first time at the International Conference on Scientific Information, Washington, D. C., October, 1958.[11] Subsequent experimental operations have indicated the usefulness of such "Auto-Abstracts" where great masses of documents are involved and where prompt availability is essential.

The perfection of automatic abstracting methods is an important step toward the reali-zation of automation. Further research and development in this area is in progress.

AVAILABILITY OF MACHINE READABLE TEXTS

In order that machines may perform the various processes referred to above, written material must be available in machine readable form, such as punched cards, punched or magnetic tape, or other storage media. While the printed or written page may eventually join the ranks of such media, there will always be an advantage in accommodating the machine, where possible, by providing it with input of the most suitable format. This facility therefore becomes a major requirement in automation.

Many miles of punched tape are produced daily through the use of teletype and typesetting equipment. Such tape has so far been regarded as a means to an end and has not as yet found its way into the processing phase of individual intelligence systems. The amount of manual recopying of textual material and the attendant proof reading that is being done today is staggering. Yet there must be a lack of awareness of this fact since improvements of this situation are so slow in coming, even though the development of remedies is well advanced.

Ideally there should be but one single manual effort of creating an original record or document. This effort should be applied in such a form and with the aid of such tools as will eliminate all further human intervention in processing for purposes of printing, indexing, abstracting, storing, disseminating, retrieving or transmitting. A reasonable control of the format of such original records or documents is desirable and will contribute to their negotiability wherever information is exchanged in the public domain.

Since a substantial portion of the input to automated intelligence systems would consist of published information, the transcriptions of such material into machine readable form would entail an undue manual effort and expense for each individual system. It will therefore be another prerequisite that such material becomes generally available in machine readable form. This may be accomplished through cooperative arrangements among organizations of similar areas of interest. The text of current material may be made available in machine readable form by the respective publishers on a subscription basis. In the remaining cases professional societies and commercial or governmental service agencies may be expected to perform the task of transcribing needed texts into machine readable form and storing them appropriately at machine text centers.

The service of such centers would include the furnishing of machine texts of current literature relating to a prescribed area, on a subscription basis, and the furnishing on demand of specific items, new or old. A further service would consist of delivering this material in a specified format dictated by the requirements of the user's system. This would require that the centers are equipped to transform or reduce the machine texts to order, relieving the user of this step and limiting the transmittal of material to only that portion or degree of information which is actually needed.

A further requirement is that machine texts are available promptly. Since machine texts are already in the very (digital) form needed for electrical transmission, existing communication networks are capable of relaying such information from center to user or exchanging it between centers or individual systems. Eventually, by means of direct communication between electronic information processing machines, the interrogation of machine text centers or associated systems may be carried out entirely automatically.

ACCESSIBILITY OF THE PICTORIAL ASPECTS OF DOCUMENTS

As was mentioned earlier, the problems connected with the automation of intelligence systems consist of those concerning the manipulation of meaning and those concerning the manipulation of the mere physical appearance of documents. Automatic approaches to the solution of the former have been dealt with in some detail. It should be pointed out, however, that a special case has so far been made for texts and that the many other tokens of meaning, such as may be contained in pictorials of all kinds, have not been gone into. The reason for this is that the degree of difficulty in the art of automatic recognition and characterization of pictorials appears to be of a much

higher order than that encountered with texts and that proposed solutions are as yet in the early stages of experimentation. However as desirable and necessary as such refinement may be in the future, it is felt that significant progress can be achieved at this time without this capability.

Dealing then with the purely physical aspects of documents including pictorials, the processing requirements which arise are usually referred to as document storage and retrieval. Since the performance of these functions does not involve intellectual processes per se but is instead the consequence of such processes, this phase of the system will not be elaborated on as being outside the topic of this paper.

In the foregoing some of the problems in mastering the intellectual aspects of intelligence systems have been presented and possible mechanical solutions for them have been reviewed. The approaches indicated in detail are considered to be realizable in the very near future. No attempt was made to speculate on the feasibility of mechanizing intellectual problems of higher order. The position here taken is that it is entirely practical to start automatic systems today, provided that they permit step by step growth and adjustment to changed and new conditions as well as to technological advances for their implementation. In fact, this adjustability must be a primary design objective so as to parallel the dynamics of modern life. The availability of information processing equipment will have a particular bearing on this aspect in that once a basic machine readable record has been created, suitable transformations or extractions may be derived from it to meet changing systems requirements as time goes on.

REFERENCES

[1] This article first appeared in *The Clarification, Unification, and Integration of Information Storage and Retrieval* and is reprinted with the permission of the copyright owners, Management Dynamics, P.O. Box 2864, Grand Central Station, New York 17, N.Y.

[2] H. P. Luhn, "A Business Intelligence System", *IBM Journal of Research and Development*, New York, N.Y., October, 1958.

[3] H. P. Luhn, "Selective Dissemination of New Scientific Information With the Aid of Electronic Processing Equipment", *American Documentation*, April, 1961.

[4] S. Stiassny, "Coefficients of Similarity Between Documents", IBM Advanced Systems Development Division, Yorktown Heights, N.Y., September, 1959.

[5] A Selective Dissemination of Information System utilizing profiles made up of 25 or less keywords has been satisfactorily serving 450 professionals and technical people at the ASDD Laboratory of IBM in Yorktown Heights, N.Y., since the Fall of 1959.

[6] An information retrieval system based on automatically derived keywords is operating experimentally at the Health Law Center, University of Pittsburgh, Pa. So far over five million words of machine readable texts have been processed and stored.

[7] H. P. Luhn, "Auto-Encoding of Documents for Information Retrieval Systems", IBM Monograph, *IBM Journal of Research and Development*, New York, N.Y., April, 1958.

[8] Plumb, R. K. "Experiments Suggest a New Approach to the Treatment of Heart Attacks", *New York Times*, September 22, 1957.

[9] H. P. Luhn, "The Automatic Creation of Literature Abstracts", *IBM Journal of Research and Development*, New York, N.Y., April, 1958.

[10] J. Rath, A. Resnick, T. Savage, "Comparisons of Four Types of Lexical Indicators of Content", *American Documentation*, April, 1961.

[11] Papers for this conference were distributed to participants two months ahead for study. By arrangement with the Columbia University Press the Monotype tapes used in publishing these preprints were made available for experimentation. At the conference exhibit, IBM researchers demonstrated the automatic transcription of these Monotype tapes to magnetic tape via punched cards and thence the automatic creation and print out of abstracts by means of electronic data processing equipment at the Space Systems Center in Washington, D.C. All this was done without any human intervention, except for the handling of the input and output records. Also, preprinted Auto-Abstracts of Papers of Area 5 of the conference were made available to participants at the beginning of the conference. See: "An Experiment in Auto-Abstracting", Progress Report, IBM Research Center, Yorktown Heights, N.Y., November, 1958.

By C. D. Gull
General Electric Company

13. Guidelines to Mechanizing Information Systems

AS MY AUDIENCE, you may represent one of many different operating information systems. If you don't have such systems actively under your own control, you have these systems nearby in your organizations. We can assume that most of these systems are manual, and that you are aware that there is a trend away from manual systems to a variety of mechanized systems. Some of you may be using edge notched cards or the fully punched cards which are used with electric accounting machines. A few of you may be using electronic digital computers and devices which are peripheral to computers. A few information systems have been put through the gamut of changes in the past ten years from manual methods to edge notched or fully punched cards and on to the use of computers.

You can check these trends for yourself by studying the material about several companies in the article in *Fortune* by Francis Bello,[1] in the articles on information retrieval in the *Chemical and Engineering News* of last July,[2] and in the latest publications in two of the National Science Foundation's series, *Current Research and Development in Scientific Documentation,*[3] and *Non-conventional Technical Information Systems in Current Use.*[4] The trends are discernible in General Electric, Du Pont, Eastman Kodak, Smith, Kline and French, and in Charles Pfizer and Company, for example. The examples in these firms include several different combinations and types of equipment, but the trend is very definitely evident.

You want to be able to answer these questions about your own information handling needs:

Should we get on the bandwagon and join the trend to mechanized information systems?

Should we give up our manual system in favor of a machine system?

Why should we undertake the transition from a manual system to a machine system?

How do we accomplish this transition?

Is a change to a machine system desirable in itself?

Will a machine system produce the required results?

Many detailed questions are given in the following paragraphs for you to answer before you can draw conclusions to answer the above questions, particularly the last two.

The notable characteristic of this analysis is that I am asking you a set of questions. They are rhetorical only in the sense that you will not be expected to answer them immediately. They are designed to enable you to find out your own position on the questions which are asked. The reason for asking questions is that it is virtually impossible to give guidelines that would fit all situations. Each of you has a different problem, and the potential solution that may seem reasonable to you is probably different in many specific details from the solutions that your fellows will adopt in answer to their problems. You will have to derive the guidelines for yourself by answering the questions.

It is desirable to emphasize at this point that information systems process information as their commodity. This attribute makes them different from other control systems where information is used to control the processing of some other commodity. The information handled in manufacturing processes is really secondary to the commodity manufactured, but in the business of handling information, it is desirable to understand that information is the primary commodity. Even so, you may discover that the systems which you have are hybrids because you are handling physically discrete objects as well as information. You have to put these objects away, serve them out, get them back, and serve them out again to new customers. You are dealing with commodities, these physical entities, and you are also dealing with the contents, the information therein. Another way of phrasing this is the familiar question:

Are you indexing documents or are you indexing information?

YOUR ORGANIZATION'S CAPABILITIES FOR CHANGE

What are you own organization's capabilities for change?

Do you have sufficient competence in management to contemplate a change from a manual to a mechanized system?

Do you have adequate communication with management?

Dr. James Hillier has given a very informative and penetrating analysis of how he approached the managerial problem of what to do about information services in a research laboratory doing basic research work.[5] Essentially, he reached the conclusion that he should not do anything at the present time, because RCA maintains a conventional special library and Dr. Hillier has assigned the information handling duties for each research project to at least one member of every project team in his laboratory. He concluded, "That a centralized information service probably is impractical and uneconomical and could even have a detrimental effect on the creativity level of the laboratory. That a rapid and efficient information retrieval system for specific references is essential". In response to a question, Dr. Hillier said that he had not asked his special librarians to participate in his evaluation. He talked his evaluation over with his creative people, who stated that the provision of information services is academic because they don't read the literature. They communicate only with their peers and productive colleagues. I believe that Dr. Hillier's special librarians, if consulted, could have demonstrated that creative research men cannot provide a rapid and efficient information retrieval system for specific references, and that it is not possible at this time to provide

such a system for a laboratory without centralizing the activities. It appears that Dr. Hillier reached contradictory conclusions because of inadequate communication with the personnel assigned full time to information handling problems. He recognized this lack, because he also concluded, "That there is an urgent need for effective means of condensing and consolidating technical information for management's use". This conclusion needs to be applied to information handling services as much as to any other activities of an organization.

The experience of the Battelle Memorial Institute provides a contrasting example. A number of years ago it was decided to institute a high level information system and Battelle has followed that decision since. Battelle had a fine traditional special library and put great emphasis on its research and development personnel to serve as outstanding information specialists in their own projects, but Battelle also added a high level manual information activity to fill the gap which they determined existed between the library's service and reliance upon laboratory and technical personnel.[6]

Bernard K. Dennis of General Electric, has described a different managerial environment,[7] one in which he is permitted, as manager of the technical information center, to develop and carry out an aggressive program to provide information services. I believe a similar situation has prevailed for Christopher G. Stevenson in managing the technical information center at the Hanford Atomic Products Operation, General Electric, Richland, Washington. Both men introduced computers for information retrieval early in the history of this application. Bernard Dennis has added another computer application, the current dissemination of information, and finds that it represents the greater load and is more useful than retrospective retrieval by computer. Stevenson has given up retrieval by computer on finding that the number of requests did not warrant the service, but he has placed his serial and periodical order and accounting processes onto a computer.

Another management situation is seen in the Bell Telephone Laboratories, where W. O. Baker, vice president in charge of research, has actively supported the information activities. W. K. Lowry has put computers to regular use there as part of the extensive information services provided to personnel of Bell Laboratories.

These examples show that, when you begin to look at mechanization of your information system, you need to investigate very early the various questions about the competence, openmindedness, and support of management.

A number of questions can be asked about the new man and machine relationships:

Will you be able to prepare for the new man and machine relationships?

Are your own personnel adequately flexible for this purpose?

Are they openminded; are they adaptable to change; are they willing to vary their routines to accomplish the objective of making your information system more productive?

Do you have within your own organization capabilities of undertaking a preliminary analysis?

There is a useful bulletin from the Bureau of the Budget in the Executive Office of the President. Its title is *Automatic Data Processing (ADP) Program of the Executive Branch: Studies Preceding the Acquisition of ADP Equipment.* Just to give you the flavor of this useful analysis, I quote from section IV, *Preliminary Analysis,* substituting the phrase, "Information System", instead of "ADP", where "ADP" occurs in the text.

"An 'Information System' study can be a lengthy, complex, and costly undertaking. For these reasons, a preliminary analysis or 'feasibility study' should be made to determine the overall soundness of applying the 'Information System' to the operation of an organization.

"1. Informational Requirements. Establish an inventory of 'Information System' processing by major functional areas . . . Additionally, it is necessary to secure or develop a distribution of man-hour effort and other significant cost elements to be used in identifying costs by major operation, function and/or organization".

Bernard Dennis gave that kind of information in his paper.[7]

"2. Analysis. The analysis of data developed should be undertaken in a logical sequence. Several starting points are suggested, namely, unmanageable backlogs, those operations which are the most costly, take the most time, or are presently mechanized".

There are several more points listed. I am skipping them to go on to —

"3. Determination of the Impact. The end product of the preliminary analysis should include determinations regarding the areas susceptible to immediate or ultimate application, the size and cost range of equipment, the extent of the conversion problem, the sufficiency of available resources to support the 'Information System', the expected economies and benefits, and the overall effect of computer use on the personnel procedures, and organization. The preliminary analysis should identify the organizational units that might be affected by the possible utilization of the 'Information System' and make adequate provision for participation by staff representatives of such units in the subsequent studies.

"4. Decision. If the preliminary analysis shows that application of the 'Information System' is generally justified, further and more definitive plans are in order to proceed with a full study".[8]

These quotations give you some idea how useful this bulletin is for your needs.

SYSTEMS DESIGN COMPETENCE

Can you detach a task force of your own people for a preliminary analysis or an actual design?

Where the manpower exists within your information activity, can you detach it?

To cite an example, when we studied the Undergraduate Division Library of the University of Illinois at Chicago, the Council on Library Resources insisted that people from the library staff be put full time on the study. Two people were detached from the staff for one year. Their task did not interfere with the library's daily operations, nor did they need to feel any responsibility for current operations of the library. Their only job was to look forward.

COMPETENCE TO EVALUATE STUDIES AND RECOMMENDATIONS

Will you be able to evaluate the study

which you prepare or which someone else prepares for you?

This isn't an easy question to answer. There are several publications to study in order to prepare yourself to answer this difficult question. The book called *System Engineering,* by Goode and Machol,[9] is the classic in system engineering textbooks. The third volume of the *Handbook on Automation and Systems Engineering,* edited by Grabbe, Ramo and Wooldridge,[10] is just published and also useful for this purpose.

ASTIA has published a number of reports on their automation effort. The first was on their preliminary design and what they intended to accomplish.[11] They subsequently issued reports on what they have done with their computer and how it has affected the services which they perform for the Government and for Government research and development contractors.[12,13] They are now undertaking to improve the thesaurus of descriptors which is used in their indexing and retrieval operations. These reports provide a case history of the installation of a machine system.

The Western Reserve University (WRU) experience is an example of the development of a mechanized information system for which you cannot find guidelines. They had an intuitive feeling that machinery was needed and that machinery required the use of a very detailed analytical indexing method. Following their intuitive assumptions the WRU personnel built a combination of certain aspects of subject heading indexing and of hierarchical classification into the telegraphic abstracting method. They built a paper tape prototype of a searching selector. After trying for a magnetic tape searching selector, WRU began to use a general purpose computer to accomplish retrieval and current dissemination for the metallurgical Documentation Service of the American Society for Metals.

But note that the WRU personnel are undertaking the tests after the information system has been put into operation. By contrast, if you haven't already moved in the direction of mechanization, you can try to get some answers to the guideline questions which are in this paper before you design your system.

There is also another paper by Charles Bourne and Douglas C. Engelbart who wrote on the aspects of the technical information problem.[14] Many of their questions and points are related to the problem of a national centralized information system, but they are useful and you can cut back from the national aspect to your own applications.

THE PRESENT STATE OF YOUR MANUAL INFORMATION SYSTEM

Eva Lou Fisher has prepared *A Checklist for the Organization, Operation, and Evaluation of a Company Library.*[15] The first fifteen pages provide a number of questions which will enable you to evaluate an existing manual system which is oriented toward a special library rather than toward an information system. It gives a starting point in print from which to begin to answer these questions:

Is our present system satisfactory?

What does our system fail to provide now?

A careful examination of the present system must be made before you decide to explore the desirability of a mechanized system.

Let us examine the current performance of your information activity.

Has your activity reached the point where human decisions in handling information need to be supplemented by machine decisions?

Actually, this situation occurs when you begin to employ machines. You are relying on machines to give you some of the answers, perhaps all of them, when you ask a retrieval question or when you disseminate information.

Do you even know what these human decisions are?

From the standpoint of your people, could you stretch their capabilities and their present performance to reach a satisfactory level in your own manual system now?

This is a managerial problem. Its solution will require ingenuity on your part. There is always the possibility that you can achieve this better operational level without adopting machines. Mr. Luhn's paper covered the point of this next question very fully.[16]

Do you have a communication problem in your information handling activity?

He answered it positively,

> But have you looked at it as a communications problem?
>
> Have you identified what this communication is — how it flows?
>
> Do you require an optimal system?

Other than the form of the words,

> Do you understand what an optimal system implies?

There is an engineering meaning to this question, and it needs to be investigated.

One of the valuable points brought out at the second of American University's Institutes on Information Retrieval was the recognition by Dr. Robert M. Hayes, as a mathematician and data handler viewing libraries, that in many ways the present manual systems are fairly close to being optimal. It has required perhaps a century to develop the optimal state of a manual operation of a library.

> Is it realistic to ask for optimal performance within three months after the installation of your machine system?

Whether you are going to be the operators of the system or whether you are going to hire machine oriented experts to be the operators,

> Do you understand the operator's responsibilities in making the optimal system work?
>
> Do you already possess the quantitative data and a qualitative evaluation of your present performance?

Certainly attempts to answer this question will uncover major deficiencies in many places. Most of the systems with which I have come into contact do not possess the type of information which Bernard Dennis has illustrated.[7] The traditional library will know how many books it cataloged last year, it will know how much money was expended for books, and perhaps how many cards were filed in the catalogs. However, it will be unable to identify the unit operations and the hours spent on each operation, and consequently it will not know the manpower costs on each of these operations. These are facts you must obtain before you can change from one system to another.

In summary, here are some questions which are useful to ask before proceeding to the next phase of your investigation.

> Can you actually define your problem?
>
> Can you define the performance of your system?
>
> Can you now define what you want to advance to?
>
> Have you properly stated the basic question to yourself?

LOGICAL FLOW CHARTS

One of the contributions of the computer industry to system engineering is a method of analysis called logical flow charting. There is a small and humorous example in **Exhibit 1** to illustrate the product of flow charting. The operation of making a logical flow chart need not be a particularly difficult task. It is a form of writing as well as a form of analysis and a great deal depends upon the choice of words within the boxes of this type of diagram.

> Can you make a logical flow chart of your existing system?

After the flow charts are made, the person responsible for the administration of a certain set of operations can often spot difficulties in the system, such as unnecessary operations, bad timing, and interruptions in the smooth flow of the operations. Immediate action can be taken to correct the situation administratively, and better performance can be provided within a manual system.

> After you have flow charted your existing system, can you make a logical flow chart to show how you wish to have the new system operate?
>
> Can you make a block diagram of the new system?

Oftentimes the block diagrams are made first, because they are more generalized and they do not have to have the specific yes-no character of the flow diagram. If you implement a system with a computer, the logical flow diagram will be required by the computer programmers.

FUTURE REQUIREMENTS
AND EXPECTATIONS

We need to watch our tendency to wish for too much too soon.

> What are your expectations?
>
> Have you identified the basic requirements which your system must fulfill and

"How to Get to Work in the Morning." Original source unknown.

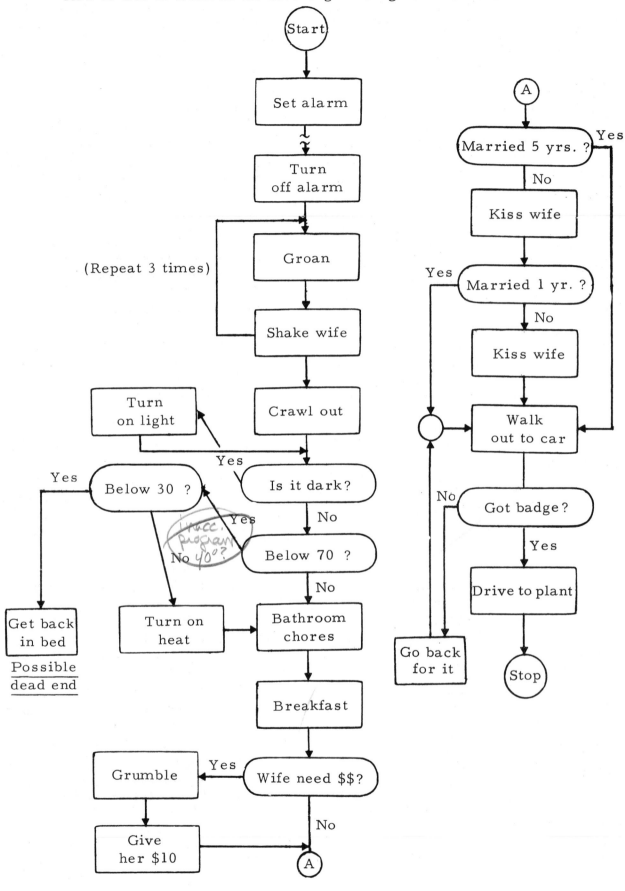

eliminated your desires and wishes about the performance of the new system?

If you are going to require that all your wishes and desires be fulfilled in these systems, certainly you will find them costly to implement.

Perhaps you can separate requirements and wishes by considering the information operation for which computers were first used: to search for answers to questions.

> Do you want a machine system for information retrieval?

> Do you require speed in retrieval, or exhaustiveness in retrieval?

It seems to be generally understood now that the speed of retrieval for one person's single question search is not improved by using a computer, as compared to the time that a person spends in consulting a card catalog, for example. You must spend time to code the question in a form that the computer will accept and you have to take your turn on a computer with the other people who use it, with the result that it may take longer in elapsed time to get an answer from the computer than it does to search manually in a card catalog or in an abstracting and indexing service.

As to exhaustiveness of retrieval, not only is it costly to put information into a form that permits retrieval, but also there will remain a lot of material outside of the computer facility which will have to be searched manually.

> Do you have such a large volume of retrieval questions that you cannot handle the searches with your present staff?

If yes, computerized retrieval offers the advantage of batching many questions for one machine retrieval operation. This capability offers a dramatic reduction in cost per question but offers no reduction in elapsed time per question per person. This capability has introduced a new problem, too, of overcapacity in retrieval services, or underconsumption, depending on your point of view.

Most of the installations which are performing computerized retrieval are operating considerably under their capacity for answering batched questions. For example, Bernard Dennis indicated he could batch 1,300 questions in one search; in actual practice, he batched 250 questions for one search.[7] It is more common to batch 5 to 40 questions per search. There is a two-way communications channel which his people are not loading to capacity. He has difficulty in getting his 3,000 potential customers to realize that the system has a capability which they ought to use. Thus, you acquire an education problem when you increase your retrieval capacity.

The retrieval situation is in better balance at ASTIA, which has a large, daily question load, derived from Government agencies and some 1,500 contractors (3,200 contracts), to be searched on a small computer with an uncomplicated program in contrast to Bernard Dennis' situation of a small daily load to be searched on a large computer with a sophisticated program.[7]

There are other activities you might consider:

> Do you wish to accomplish the input processing activities in your information activity or can you obtain the desired results elsewhere?

> Do you want to undertake automatic indexing to replace human efforts?

H. P. Luhn indicated that he questions the effectiveness of automatic indexing.[16] Don Swanson has reported in *Science* magazine, however, on the results of one experiment which indicates that perhaps machine indexing is actually more effective than human indexing.[17]

One of the basic problems is:

> Do you want to sort, that is to reorder or rearrange, the indexed information?

The material comes in chronologically (or serially) and whatever indexing you accomplish acquires that same attribute. Yet you may have to reorder the index so that you can use it with a manual system.

> Do you want to use electronic devices to accomplish this rearrangement?

Computers can be programmed to sort text into new arrangements more economically than by having the same work done by people. The rapid adoption of the new technique to prepare key-word-in-context (KWIC) indexes or permuted title indexes for publication is evidence of this advantage. This technique is being used to prepare all varieties of catalogs, indexes and bibliographies and furnish them with author, title, subject, and numerical index sections as required. Publication of the computer's work enables users to consult the new arrangements without resorting to the computer for search and retrieval.

Do you wish to add a new service, selective dissemination of current information, to your information system?

This service is prohibitively expensive in a manual system, but you can consider it with a mechanized system. The computer matches the results of current indexing against the customer's questions collected and stored over a period of weeks or months, and prints out notices to individuals telling them that new publications have been received which satisfy their stored questions. The individuals return marked cards to the information center, requesting publications for themselves or to be forwarded to others, or requesting modification of their stored questions. The center tells local authors who asked for their works. Altogether, the selective dissemination of current information is one of the most significant advances in service in recent years.

Do you fully appreciate that selective dissemination of current information is the converse of retrospective retrieval when you are using a mechanized system?

If you select equipment and procedures to provide one of these services, you may have the other service also. For example, in retrospective retrieval you match a small number of questions against a massive index store; in selective dissemination you match a small index store to a large collection of stored questions; and in each case you may print the results in question order, index order, or document-number order.

ROUTINE OPERATIONS

Do you want to use these mechanized devices for routine operations in your library?

If you circulate materials, circulation records may be necessary.

Do you want to mechanize circulation records?

Do you want to keep your serial checking records with the aid of a computer?

Do you want all your acquisitions work, the financial and detailed record keeping of your purchases, or gifts, or exchanges to go through the computer?

Do you want your binding records incorporated also?

Do you want to handle payroll and personnel records as well?

The large scale capabilities of the devices we are talking about argue that you do want to mechanize all of these operations, so that you can load the machine adequately to achieve low unit cost and maximum efficiency. Plan to take as much of the workload off your staff as possible and place it on the machine, leaving your personnel free to help your customers.

One question that calls for very serious consideration is:

Do you want to put all of these operations together and start out with a large jump; that is, put every operation you can think of onto the computer and its related devices?

Or will you put the several operations together one after another in a gradual fashion?

Probably the organization which elects to synthesize the system and start all the operations together will be the outstanding pioneer, if it is successful in accomplishing the change in one large effort, but there is still a real challenge in changing one operation at a time.

Are you seeking improved performance in your information activity; e.g., improved coverage, improved timeliness, lowered cost?

Do you desire to free the staff to serve the users?

These are questions that will aid you in paring down the original question and separating your desires from the practical accomplishments which are required.

CAPABILITIES OF MACHINE SYSTEMS

Some of the things that cannot be overlooked are:

Do you understand what can actually be done by machines?

Have you an idea of the relative effectiveness you can attain from a manual system, edge notched cards, or an electronic accounting machine complex?

What are the advantages of adding computers as a more sophisticated system than the punched card and paper tape systems?

The great amount of literature in this field provides very little information and insight into the answers to these questions.

SYSTEMS DESIGN FOR A MECHANIZED INFORMATION SYSTEM

Let us assume that you have considered all the preceding questions and that you wish to undertake the transition from a manual system to some form of a mechanized system. The transition involves system design.

Who will design this system for you? There are various methods of determining system design. For example, the government sends out invitations to bid on its requirements. The resulting proposals are then carefully analyzed and a contractor is selected to do the work. Private institutions and private corporations can investigate the field of potential contractors by inquiry and select an organization to do their systems design. It is also possible to elect to do the systems design within your own organization. However, very few organizations have such capabilities in their total structure. It is very unusual to find an organization within the library and information business which can undertake the design of its own system. It is usually necessary to call in specialized assistance from outside the organization altogether.

SYSTEM DESIGN DIFFICULTIES

How difficult is your systems design problem?

Do you have any good information on the boundaries of the system?

What will your performance criteria be?

Will you have a queuing problem; that is, too much of any one operation on the system at one time?

Is it possible for you to evaluate and predict how successful your information system design is going to be?

Is this something that you can undertake?

Are you going to use analytical or simulation techniques?

What kind of equipment difficulties are you facing?

Are you aware of the various instructions that can be given to a computer?

Are you aware of the problems of computer programming?

Do you have any concept of the time it takes to do the programming?

Can you borrow computer programs which have already been written and have been proven satisfactory in similar situations?

Can you use them without change; can you modify them?

Can you use available sub-programs which can be combined to produce full programs?

The programming problem is certainly a serious one; you may find its costs range anywhere from $5,000 to $100,000 for certain types of information retrieval programs.

If you are actually going from one existing machine system into another one,

What problems of conversion are you going to have?

Is there enough information in the existing system already in a form compatible with a new system that conversion will be worthwhile?

Are you going to have to undertake a major conversion of existing information?

Since universal print readers do not exist yet, how much more key punching will be required?

If you are in the area of the larger information systems,

Have your architectural and engineering requirements been fully considered?

Also, there is the paramount problem of costs:

Do you know what your costs were in the past?

What are they now?

What do you expect they will be after you have implemented a new system?

Who is going to do your implementation work?

Is this going to be a different group than the one who did your systems design, or will you use the same group?

Who is going to retrain your personnel?

Are you going to do this internally, or are you going to use specialized outside help for retraining?

CHECKLIST OF RECOMMENDATIONS

As the closing paragraph, I shall quote

again from the Bureau of the Budget Bulletin 60-6, to provide a checklist of things you want to be sure you are covering:

"Items to be included in the Information Systems study recommendations. A carefully documented Information Systems study would normally include the following:

"a. Definitive indications of the benefits that are expected to accrue from the proposed system that cannot otherwise be attained, and justification for these benefits in terms of economic gains or improved management effectiveness.

"b. A general description of the data processing needs of the activity in relation to the basic mission of the activity.

"c. Workload and employment statistics describing the magnitude of the activity's problem.

"d. A chart depicting the organizational effect of 'The Information System' on the activity as well as showing the location of the proposed data processing function.

"e. Flow charts supplemented by clear and precise narrative indications of the nature and scope of each application. There should be included for each application the following:

  (1) A description of the contents and purpose of proposed outputs.

  (2) A description of the content and source of all input data.

  (3) Record lengths and number of records.

  (4) Processing frequencies.

"f. Narrative descriptions of those present systems which correspond to the proposed application.

"g. Detailed comparative cost data for the proposed system and the present system, adjusted by improvements developed in the course of the study.

"h. Indication of personnel implications in terms of reduced or augmented staffing needs.

"i. Indications of the availability of and expected costs of site preparations.

"j. Projected schedule should be provided covering plans for equipment selection, detailed application development, personnel training and orientation site preparation, installation, transition and attainment of normal operations.

"k. Indications that consideration was given to locating or obtaining equipment which could be shared with other bureaus in your agency, or with other agencies.

"l. All factors which might have a bearing upon top management's decision, including problems or disadvantages."[8]

REFERENCES

[1] Francis Bello, "How to Cope with Information", *Fortune*, Vol. 62, Sept., 1960, pp. 162-168.

[2] "Information Retrieval", *Chemical and Engineering News*, Vol. 39, July 17, 1961, pp. 103-112; July 24, 1961, pp. 90-98.

[3] *Current Research and Development in Scientific Documentation*, No. 9, National Science Foundation, Washington, D.C., Nov., 1961.

[4] *Non-Conventional Technical Information Systems in Current Use*, No. 2, National Science Foundation, Washington, D.C., Sept., 1959, and its Supplement, March, 1960.

[5] James Hillier, "Management's Evaluation of Information Services", *Information Retrieval Management*, Data Processing Library Series, American Data Processing, Inc., Detroit, Mich., 1962, Chap. 8.

[6] G. S. Simpson, Jr. and J. W. Murdock, "Qualitative Approach to Scientific Information Problems", *Battelle Technical Review*, Nov., 1960, pp. 3-7.

[7] Bernard K. Dennis, "Financing a Technical Information Center", *Information Retrieval Management*, Data Processing Library Series, American Data Processing, Inc., Detroit, Mich., 1962, Chap. 9.

[8] *Automatic Data Processing (ADP) Program of the Executive Branch: Studies Preceding the Acquisition of ADP Equipment*, Bureau of the Budget, Bulletin 60-6, March 18, 1960, pp. 2-3.

[9] Harry H. Goode and Robert E. Machol, *System Engineering*, McGraw-Hill Book Company, Inc., New York, N.Y., 1957.

[10] E. M. Grabbe, Simon Ramo, and Dean Wooldridge (eds.), *Handbook of Automation, Computation, and Control, Volume 3*, John Wiley & Sons, Inc., New York, N.Y., 1961.

[11] *Automation of ASTIA — A Preliminary Report*, Armed Services Technical Information Agency, Dec., 1960, AD 227000.

[12] *Automation of ASTIA-1960*, Armed Services Technical Information Agency, Dec., 1960, AD 247000.

[13] *Evolution of the ASTIA Automated Search and Retrieval System*, Armed Services Technical Information Agency, Jan., 1961, AD 252000.

[14] Charles P. Bourne and Douglas C. Engelbart, "Facets of the Technical Information Problem", *Stanford Research Institute Journal*, vol. 2, no. 1, 1958, pp. 2-8. Also in *Datamation*, Sept.-Oct., 1958, pp. 6-12.

[15] Eva Lou Fisher, *A Checklist for the Organization, Operation, and Evaluation of a Company Library*, New York Special Libraries Association, 1960.

[16] H. P. Luhn, "Automated Intelligence Systems," *Information Retrieval Management*, Data Processing Library Series, American Data Processing, Inc., Detroit, Mich., 1962, Chap. 12.

[17] D. R. Swanson, "Searching Natural Language Text by Computer", *Science*, 132, Oct. 21, 1960, pp. 1099-1104.

By Hattie T. Anderson
W. R. Grace & Co.

14. Compatibility of Information and Data Systems within a Company

RECENTLY, I ASKED FOUR PERSONS knowledgeable in the field what "compatible" systems meant to them. One replied that any systems which work are compatible. The second stated that compatibility doesn't matter; we will simply have a separate program for each system. The third thought of the capability for hooking together various pieces of equipment. The fourth related compatibility to universal language.

The literature today abounds with references to "compatible", "integrated", "convertible", "coordinated", "mergible", "company wide", "universal", "centralized", "unified", "flexible", and above all, "machine processable" information and data systems. Singly, these loosely used and ill defined terms may mean something different to each one of us, depending upon our orientation within the field and the problems we are trying to solve. Cited together, however, they suggest a definite, overall management approach for handling information problems.

The purpose here is to examine such an approach against a company background and to ask ourselves whether, in spite of the opinion of one of the above quoted experts, compatibility between systems does matter. Can management and should management try to build compatible, integrated, company wide information and data systems? If so, how?

To lend feasibility to our investigation, we will first note some of the information problems which result from the characteristic structure of a large, technology based company. Secondly, we will try to determine what types of compatibility could be attempted between scattered company information centers to alleviate the problems noted. Thirdly, we will look at the more complex types of compatibility and search for factors which are basic to their achievement. Finally, we will mention a few of the difficulties which would be encountered in the development of a grandiose, corporate information network.

A CORPORATE PICTURE — JUSTIFICATION FOR COMPANY WIDE SYSTEMS

A large, technology based company typically consists of a number of decentralized divisions, affiliates, or subsidiaries, some having many laboratories, plants, or offices of their own. These are scattered throughout the world. Intradivisional liaison is difficult enough to maintain, not to speak of interdivisional liaison. Activities of the units that require technical information range through basic and applied research covering many fields and scientific disciplines, patent work, applications and product development, process engineering, economic evaluation, commercial intelligence, plant engineering and operations, technical services, sales, management, etc. A moment's thought tells us that there will be measurable overlap in interests, activities, and information needs between many parts of the corporation, no matter whether these parts are organized along product, functional, or geographical lines. The overlap may vary in type, extent, and frequency, but there can be little doubt that it exists.

There are very likely those within our company model who suspect that duplication and waste are rampant, but some rationalize it as a healthy thing. Some, through fear of leak of proprietary information or through divisional and professional jealousies, may wish to keep it that way. Others think the whole information problem is hopeless anyway, so why worry.

There is a high probability that our company is thus characterized by excessive costs resulting from repetition of work, frequent lack of information needed for stimulation or decision making, inadequate cross-fertilization of ideas, loss of time advantage, and waste of professional talents. Yet today, anything short of maximum possible flow of information between the parts of a single competitive entity has become intolerable in the face of keen rivalry between companies and national economic systems. Indeed, we can theorize that our company will be noncompetitive with organizations that do succeed in breaking the communication barriers.

Looking more deeply into the situation, we find within the corporation numerous libraries and information services operating with staffs that are quite diverse in number and qualifications, ranging all the way from secretaries through formally trained librarians, self trained scientific librarians, literature scientists, information specialists, analysts, systems engineers, programmers, consultants, and the like. Services begin with simply ordering books and shelving them by some homemade scheme and extend to experimental study of information storage and retrieval problems. One unit may feel lucky to have bookcases and a reading table, while another takes computers and mechanization for granted. Collections vary from a few text and reference books to comprehensive and very costly subscriptions to published or custom searching and current awareness services.

It is important to note that a one to one relationship between the need for information and financial support for services does not always exist. There are some laboratories that are too small to pay for expensive collections and information services. Others cannot convince management of their importance. Conversely, Mooers' Law has taken over in still others. Adequate means for equalizing the dissemination and use of information based on need are lacking.

A startling discovery might be the amount of inefficiency and duplication that exists between the very libraries or information centers which are the hope for reducing much of the duplication elsewhere within the company.

Examples of inefficiency may be seen in staff situations. With trained personnel difficult to find and keep, we often see novices independently struggling to rediscover even the most elementary library procedures. With each turnover in staff, especially in the small library, there may be a total loss of familiarity with sources of information and disastrous lack of continuity and consistency in maintaining catalogs and retrieval systems. Cross-fertilization of ideas and sharing of knowledge is just as lacking among information personnel as among other professionals within the company.

Inefficiency is further seen in the failure of company libraries to use their resources additively, even though each one differs in its subject orientation and in the familiarity of its staff with unusual or local sources of information. The latter is especially pertinent in the case of overseas units, since it is often difficult to identify, at home, foreign sources of information.

Examples of duplication are found in acquisitions of very expensive reference materials and in services provided, the costs of which continue to rise at a rate which should be a matter of serious concern and analysis by any company. The same documents may be indexed and even translated several times. Patent and literature searches may be repeated at great costs. Each unit spends many man hours developing authority lists of terms, some good, some poor — none compatible.

External to the corporation there are also circumstances which bear on the feasibility of compatible, integrated, company systems. These, I think, are of three types.

One is the phenomenal development of the technology for processing, communicating, and disseminating large volumes of information, even at long distances. Remote collections can now be exploited where they could not before. It may soon become negligence for a large company to ignore new capabilities for handling information.

The second is the origin of new sources of scientific information and data, some of which we cannot purchase and store on our shelves, or if we can purchase something for searching within the organization, it may be tapes or punched cards. I am speaking of the several hundred (427 is the latest figure I have seen)[1] scientific information and data centers which have cropped up everywhere with very little apparent coordination. The small, ill-funded, and ill-staffed company library cannot hope to keep up with these developments. The larger information center may even find difficulty justifying the use of some of the expensive equipment, techniques, and search materials, unless by so doing it can alleviate some of the company problems already described and thereby reduce overall corporate costs. Let me only cite the recent announcement by Documentation, Inc. of its forthcoming *Mechanized Index to Chemical Patents Literature* to be provided on magnetic tape at a cost of $12,500.

The third external development is the considerable thought and study now going into the development of compatibility on an even grander scale than we are considering — between large government, society, commercial, and regional information services. Everyone is aware of the need for compatibility or convertibility between media, machines, systems, and terminology. Anyone interested in compatible company systems should certainly watch these developments closely for what they will teach and for ways of tying in with them.

These are some of the situations which I think justify a study of compatible, company wide information and data systems. You will very likely wish to add other considerations to those which I have sketched.

TYPES OF COMPATIBILITY

But can we now give the concept of compatibility of information and data systems within a company more concrete meaning?

Within the framework of a corporate situation, such as that just presented, I would like to suggest that it consists of equalizing, normalizing, maximizing, and optimizing the dissemination of information among scattered, heterogeneous company parts; that uncoordinated information systems and services are incompatible with company interests if it can be shown that through some form of cooperation, sharing, exchange, or joint approach a greater amount of needed information can be more quickly or widely

disseminated or overall costs of acquiring, processing, storing, and disseminating this information can be reduced.

This is not easy to demonstrate without extensive study and, perhaps, actual test efforts. However, we can gain some insight into the potential rewards of such efforts through a study of the activities tabled in **Exhibit 1**. We should consider these activities as they might be separately conducted in the smallest, ill-equipped library to the largest, best-equipped information center of our imaginary company. We can try to identify any activities which we think

(1) entail wasteful duplication when conducted without coordination, and

EXHIBIT 1

Identification of Types of Compatibility

Activities	Is there problem of duplication?	Is there need for exchange?	Suggested corporate action
Management planning personnel selection, training, and use forms, methods and procedures systems engineering experimental studies other			
Acquisitions selection identification of sources ordering other			
Processing (manual or machine) bibliographic descriptions subject indexing or cataloging data indexing citation indexing abstracting translating vocabulary development coding programming storage other			
Reference identification of sources performance of searches research liaison and literature analysis other			
Dissemination current awareness service announcement of acquisitions union lists reproduction and display circulation bibliographic print out reports, charts, tables other			
Interactions between above			

(2) could be improved or reduced in cost through some sort of exchange, sharing, or pooling of staff talents, information resources, and services.

In a private communication to the author, Saul Herner noted that all systems are compatible to some extent. To nurture compatibility, system ingredients, he said, should be carefully analyzed and identified and common attributes and labors extended where possible.

I believe that the concept of compatible company systems can be applied to many traditional, as well as newer, information functions; that it embraces people, collections, equipment, systems, and services. The process of achieving compatibility starts with the earliest efforts of one company library to seek help from or give help to another company library. It moves on through varying degrees and types of coordination or integration of information activities, such as the familiar use of printed catalog cards. At the extreme end of the spectrum of compatibility lies complete standardization and centralization.

FACTORS BASIC TO COMPATIBLE COMPANY RETRIEVAL SYSTEMS

Many of the problems which might come up in our analysis of **Exhibit 1** are relatively easy of solution, once recognized, and for reasons of time I would like to ignore them in this part of our discussion.

The most challenging problems for company, as well as for society, government, or commercial services, are those of compatibility between systems for indexing, retrieving, and disseminating information and between the language of those systems. There is yet, however, no meeting of the minds even as to the meaning and purpose of such compatibility. For example, participants in a recent ASTIA meeting on compatibility between thesauri placed major emphasis on finding a means of "relating concepts from one system or thesaurus to another, no matter how the concept is presented verbally". There are other strong proponents of the universal language approach.

In a company situation, it seems to me that we should consider the capability for merging directly, or with nominal conversion, into a single retrieval system all or parts of certain indexes prepared at different locations. Indexing efforts could then be exchanged between sites; repeated indexing of the same documents could be avoided; searches of local indexes could be supplemented by central searching of pooled indexes; questions would need to be translated into only one system language for broad searching of information available throughout the company; innumerable man hours could be saved by joint, rather than separate, design of systems and preparation of vocabulary; indexers using the same system and vocabulary could easily be transferred from one indexing project to another with changing workloads or for training purposes; no longer would the users have to guess which of numerous indexes might contain the information they need.

Whether all this can be achieved as a practical matter is uncertain, but we will proceed on the questionable assumption that it can. On whatever basis you might undertake to develop compatible indexing and retrieval systems, you will wish to build in maximum flexibility and convertibility so that you can study and manipulate the system in many ways, adjust to changing requirements, and take advantage of improved techniques and equipment. Compatibility with the future should not be sacrificed for compatibility with all parts of the company. It is important to remember that attractive but irreversible decisions may beckon at every turn. A decision or action is totally irreversible if it cannot be altered wihout completely redoing past work. Such decisions should be made with cautious deliberation where costly operations, such as the analysis of documents by subject specialists, are involved.

It is no easy matter to finally determine which of your company indexes should be made compatible (in the sense of mergibility or convertibility, one to the other) and which ones should be kept separate; which courses of action will permit compatibility, and which ones will not. I have listed in **Exhibit 2** some of the categorical investigations and a number of specific questions which might shed light on these matters. In considering these questions, we should look for

(1) factors which are basic to the achievement of compatible systems, and

(2) decisions which might be irreversible.

A. What are the sources and special characteristics of your records which will affect the compatibility of their treatment within a single system and between company units?

1. Do some deserve more costly treatment because they are more valuable? What is the duration of their value? Which documents have local value only? Have some documents only intrinsic value?

2. Must your identification be accession numbers, page numbers, line numbers, test numbers, sample numbers, product numbers, run numbers, data sheet numbers, drawing numbers, or a combination of such? Can different identifications be merged into one system?

3. If data is to go into the system, is it repetitive (such as test or operating data), critical data, or random numerical information?

4. Are the same records duplicated in several types of documents?

5. Do you wish to treat interest profiles, questions to the system, specialized internal and external sources of information, or other nonconventional items as documents to be fed into the system?

6. What are the physical characteristics of the documents?

7. What are the sizes and expected growth rates of various segments of the collection?

B. What are the corporate versus local objectives or requirements?

1. Is the goal current dissemination, retrospective retrieval, or both?

2. Do you wish to retrieve data, information, or documents?

3. What free, auxiliary information should be captured? Do you wish to retain complete bibliographic detail, citations, author abstracts? How can this information be used now and in the future?

4. Do you need to index chemical compounds? For which collections and what purpose?

5. Must patents be indexed to permit retrieval from a legal point of view?

6. What operations will be performed upon the data or information in the system?

7. Will most questions be ones of recall of known documents or retrieval of unknown documents?

8. Where must information and data flow within the company? How will it be used? In what form should it be disseminated? Is print out of bibliographies and special reports required? Will you reproduce or circulate documents?

9. Should systems be user orientated? Is browsing capability needed? Is on-the-spot searching required?

10. What are the variations in time requirements and volume of input and output?

11. What are the variations in depth and specificity of search requirements?

12. What are the weeding requirements?

C. What system of indexing should be adopted for corporate use?

1. Do objectives and characteristics of the documents require several systems?

2. Is there considerable vested interest in existing systems? Should these be a model? If not, should they be continued, converted, or terminated?

3. Should you use coordinate indexing, permuted indexing, classification, or some other type of indexing? Is there an application for more than one type of indexing within one system? If so, how will one complement the other?

4. Should you use interfixes? What kind? Should systems which use interfixes be merged with those which don't? Can the same system of interfixes be applied to all types of documents covering many disciplines?

5. Can data and information be merged in one system?

6. Should you index chemical compounds by name, empirical formula, and/or structure? Can you adopt, modify, or combine some existing approach, such as that of Dyson, Wiswesser, the Biological Coordination Center, Dow, Garfield, Patent Office, etc? Should compounds be indexed into a general or separate system?

7. Will professionals or non-professionals do the indexing at each site?

8. How do you determine the optimum depth and specificity with which to index for overall corporate needs? Should each center index to meet its own or corporate requirements? Can documents which are shallowly or generically indexed be fed into the same system as deeply or specifically indexed documents?

9. Will the system chosen lend itself to machine indexing techniques?

10. Will the system be compatible with external indexing services of greatest importance to you?

D. How will you develop your vocabulary?

1. Should you choose Mooers' descriptor, Taube's Uniterm, or Herner's bound term approach — or a combination or compromise of these?

2. How will your choice affect your system of indexing?

3. How will you treat generics, logical relationships, synonyms, rarely used terms, etc.?

4. Can your vocabulary be integrated with, translated, related or converted to other vocabularies?

5. Can it accommodate new and changing terminology?

6. Can all subject disciplines and viewpoints be reconciled in one vocabulary?

7. How should you handle numerical data?

E. What format and method of storage should be used for the collection and for the indexes?

1. Does it matter whether inverted or non-inverted storage is used?

2. Should the index and document store be kept separate or combined?

3. What are the pitfalls of coding and fixed fields for print out, conversion, sorting, etc.

4. What consideration should be given to upper and lower case, abbreviations, special characters, sub and super scripts?

5. How do you avoid duplication of input to the system?

6. How important is space? Is duplication of document and index files justified at all sites?

7. Must you reproduce, display, transmit, or reorganize directly from the store?

(continued on next page)

8. Can the document store be organized in some way to supplement, rather than duplicate, the access points provided by the index?

F. How do you delete from the system?
   1. On what basis will you delete from the system? How often and how much? Will this vary between segments of the collection and between company units?
   2. Will weeding necessitate renumbering of items, reorganization of files?
   3. Should any data or information be retired into special lists, compilations, tables, handbooks, etc.?

G. What equipment should you choose to perform local and corporate requirements?
   1. Can any of the activities be handled more quickly, easily, or at less cost if machines are used locally or at a central corporate center?

If so, what types of machines are required? Are all types selected compatible as to input/output media, speed of operation, principle of operation, function, etc.?
   2. Are any locations committed to existing equipment? What are the limitations of this equipment?
   3. What can you do to provide the capability of conversion to newer and better equipment?

H. What the the interactions within the overall system?
   1. Does any new decision invalidate past decisions?
   2. Can work accomplished in one part of the system be reused in another part?
   3. How can you integrate all the information and data systems finally set up anywhere in the company so that in searching none that are pertinent will be overlooked?

These questions are not presented as a complete checklist for the study of compatible company systems. They are intended only to illustrate the types of questions that might be asked.

DIFFICULTIES — SOME GENERALIZATIONS

Innumerable factors would have to be considered before compatible, corporate systems could be put into operation. It is difficult enough to produce answers for a single user group. By the time a large corporate study could be completed, some of the early conclusions would already have been invalidated by changing circumstances. The increased study time required would invite criticisms from those anxious to get started. No information center ever seems to have enough staff to meet even the daily demands placed upon it. All those spending time on a grandiose, corporate scheme, uncertain of accomplishment and claiming benefits not yet quantifiable, might be considered impractical dreamers, ignoring the more immediate problems of their customers.

The intricacies of the approach are apparent. We are normally inclined to start with the simple and progress to the more complex only as necessity demands; but in the development of systems of maximum compatibility to meet maximum needs, we might have to do the opposite.

Variations in available funds, staff, and equipment would also create problems. For example, if local capabilities were too limited for participation in the corporate project, should a central center step in? Or, if corpo-

rate requirements were greater and more costly than the local requirements, who should pay the extra costs?

Inconsistency of input to the system by widely separated people having different viewpoints would certainly be a danger. What controls could be established to maintain equivalence in document analysis and interpretation?

Those fearing leakage of proprietary information might have just cause for their fears. Careful procedures would have to be worked out to guard proprietary secrets.

Documentation is a young art. For the past ten or so years, we have been preoccupied with the development of new techniques, few, if any, of which have yet proven themselves to the exclusion of others. Now, with small chance of consensus as to the best approach for a single situation, talk of compatibility emerges with standardization looming as its ultimate manifestation. Premature standardization on a large scale to systems which are not the best is entirely possible.

As clearly indicated by the earlier papers of this Institute, criteria for the selection of techniques have been the needs of isolated user groups. If we are now to combine the needs of many groups and service them from merged systems, new criteria for development of systems will have to be found.

The challenge is there. Some say it is insanity to think that each unit can continue alone; others, that compatibility can be achieved. So choose your form of insanity.

REFERENCES

[1] *Specialized Science Information Services in the United States*, National Science Foundation, 1961.

By Simon M. Newman
Consultant

15. Economic Justification –

Factors Establishing System Costs

THE ECONOMIC JUSTIFICATION for a proposed or existing mechanized information system, or even a partially mechanized one, is not simple, nor is it easy. Figures from normal cost accounting procedures are inadequate, not because the costs of any system cannot be computed, but because, without the knowledge of the contents of the output of the system, such cost figures will not provide the proper information for a valid justification. Why are such cost figures not helpful? There are several intangible and ephemeral factors, other than mere cost, which are more important in any evaluation of a system.

The search to find a figure of merit on which to base a decision to select a particular information retrieval system is of the same order of complexity as trying to select the best new model car for one's personal use. If one wishes to purchase the best car, does he make his standard of comparison, color, original cost, operating cost, or some such other factor? Concomitantly, how does he evaluate such factors as easy riding, easy turning or parking, bucket seats, protection against crash injuries, etc.? In the end, a rational selection of a car or a retrieval system depends on choosing a combination of cost and performance to meet existing requirements.

There appear to be four factors which affect the rational choice of a system. I have termed them: efficiency, utilization, availability, and operating speed. The most important and complex of these is efficiency.

EFFICIENCY

Efficiency is the ratio of the amount of pertinent information delivered by a system to the total amount of pertinent information in the original documents from which the system files were made, provided that proper correction for any false delivery of information is made. A system which is 100 percent efficient will deliver all, and only all, the information in the original documents in response to a query requiring that information. Any system, if economics are disregarded, can of course, reach 100 percent efficiency; one can search every document for every question.

But how can one measure efficiency. The yardstick has yet to be developed. Bourne,[1] of Stanford Research, has recently completed a six month preliminary study for the National Science Foundation of how such measurements might be made. Another study by Arthur Andersen and Company,[2] on the same subject, is about to be published.

Measuring efficiency includes, at least, a separate and detailed evaluation of how much information in the document file is found in the systems file, i.e., how much of the information in each document appears in the surrogates in the file which is searched. Of course, there is no loss where the entire document is placed in the file, e.g., as one at the University of Pittsburgh by Kehl,[3] as used in one of the programs for the General Electric Search Comparator,[4] and as proposed by Newman[5] for research on U. S. patents. But any system which uses surrogates has some loss, and such a loss should not be overlooked.

If surrogates are used, efficiency can be shown to vary directly with the depth of indexing, and with the sophistication of the indexing system. Such sophistication can provide, for example, the ability to search at different levels of generality and specificity, or from different aspects or viewpoints, or from both. One major hidden cost in the use of surrogates is the continuing expense of updating the search files, or the increasing loss in efficiency from failure to update. The constant growth of our knowledge causes the immediate deterioration of the retrieval value of any surrogate. A document may convey more information five years after publication because of new knowledge developed during the interim. Such additional information can be harvested only by re-indexing, if surrogates are used.

Efficiency is also lowered by noise, i.e., the so-called "false drops" or system output that is neither pertinent nor relevant to the question. This statement is made with the full realization that both pertinence and relevance are highly subjective terms, and that neither of them has been quantitatively measured.

A theoretical study testing efficiencies of retrieval systems has been done by Mooers.[6] Cleverdon,[7] in England, has released a preliminary report on his research in measurements of the relative efficiencies of different types of indexing.

Not every situation requires a high efficiency system. It is not necessary to use a forging press to swat a fly. Small or inactive files can often be serviced with modest means. Simple edge notched card systems will often perform satisfactorily for limited information requirements.

UTILIZATION, AVAILABILITY AND OPERATING SPEED

Utilization is the ratio of the actual use of a system to its potential use. A perfect system is not economic if it is not used. Mooers' Law[8] is not a facetious formulation; some people do not desire information. There are also people who do not use the system because they do not trust it, or because they do not know how to use it. Utilization can be increased and costs lowered by an educational campaign aimed at the potential users of the system.

Availability is a measure of the ease of accessibility to potential users. Physical arrangements for the system should be both simple and attractive. If the location of the user contact point is not close to his work, speedy and detailed communication between the user and the system must be provided.

The operating speed, i.e., the elapsed interval between the time a question is presented to the system and the time it responds with the requested information, should be minimal. A system will not be consulted if a user feels that he can get the information faster by doing the research himself. Mueller[9] found that typically there is a 25 percent loss of productivity by a worker awaiting a response to a query.

GENERAL OBSERVATIONS

Mueller has published the only cost study of an information retrieval system which I have been able to find. However, he includes in the input costs of his company's system, the costs of internally generated reports. Thus, these input costs include the cost of the original research as well as the expenses of editing and printing. Since these expenditures would have been made even if a report were not entered into the retrieval system, I question the value of this particular cost analysis.

Several theoretical studies[10] of cost analysis exist, in which a mathematical model of the retrieval system is created. This is done by formulating one or more equations which attempt to represent the operation of the system. Should the model parallel closely the operation of the system, the figure of merit yielded by the model will approximate the costs of the system operation. These models, although purporting to be of general application, seem to resemble the bookkeeping inventory type of information systems. The operation of such systems is so far removed from the information retrieval systems which we are discussing here, that the figures of merit which are developed in these studies are not helpful.

In order to justify a particular cost, one must have some measure of the value of the information which the system delivers. Quite obviously, such value varies from search to search, from question to question, and from user to user. The value of information developed for retrospective searching, which is often exhaustive, may be very different from that developed for a current awareness search. Engineers involved in technical development may require different types of information from scientists engaged in basic research, and from administrators of research, development and manufacturing departments. But even the same information developed for different uses may have different values for each of these uses.

Some researchers have approached the creation of systems, and of cost and efficiency studies by studying the users of information. Users' responses will often reflect the type or kind of service and system with which they are familiar. After some 33 years of experience, I am convinced that no user, no matter how sophisticated he may be, asks the question to which he wants an answer; instead, he asks the question he thinks the system can answer. It may be misleading to depend upon user reaction. Studying users and their habits requires a high degree of understanding of their problems.

Some help in pre-estimating operating costs can be derived from time measurements which most manufacturers list for operating sequences of their machines. We must first collect data on actual costs of operation of existing systems, such as that of Dennis,[11] before figures of merit for evaluation of information retrieval system costs can be developed. It is from a correlation of such sets of data from many sources, that systems for devising figures of merit can be designed.

REFERENCES

[1] C. P. Bourne, *et al.*, *Requirements, Criteria, and Measures of Performance of Information Storage and Retrieval Systems*, Stanford Research Institute, Menlo Park, Calif., 1961.

[2] *Research Study of Criteria and Procedures for Evaluating Scientific Information Systems*, Arthur Andersen & Co., New York, N.Y., March, 1962. N.S.F. Contract C 218.

[3] William B. Kehl, "Communication Between Computer and User in Information Searching", *Information Retrieval Management*, Data Processing Library Series, American Data Processing, Inc., Detroit, Mich., 1962, Chap. 11.

[4] *G.E. Search Comparator* (Advertising Circular), General Electric Defense Systems Department, Information Systems Operation (DSD-820), Dec. 1961.

[5] S. M. Newman, Rowena W. Swanson, and Kenneth Knowlton, *A Notation System for Transliterating Technical & Scientific Texts for Use in Data Processing Systems*, U. S. Patent Office Research and Development Report No. 15, U. S. Department of Commerce, Washington, D.C., May, 1959.

[6] Calvin N. Mooers, *The Intensive Sample Test for the Objective Evaluation of the Performance of Information Retrieval Systems*, Zator Co., Cambridge, Mass., RADC-TN-59-160, 1959.

[7] Cyril W. Cleverdon, *Interim Report on the Test Programme of an Investigation into the Comparative Efficiency of Indexing Systems*, College of Aeronautics, Cranfield, England, Nov., 1960.

[8] Calvin N. Mooers, "Mooers Law", *American Documentation*, XI, 3, July, 1960, p. 204.

[9] Max W. Mueller, "Time, Cost and Value Factors in Information Retrieval", *General Information Manual: Information Retrieval Systems Conference, Sept. 21-23, 1959, Poughkeepsie*, International Business Machines, White Plains, N.Y., 1960.

[10] *Mathematical Models for Information Systems Design*, RADC-TR-61-198, Magnavox Research Laboratories, Torrence, Calif., 1961.

[11] B. K. Dennis, "Financing a Technical Information Center", *Information Retrieval Management*, Data Processing Library Series, American Data Processing, Inc., Detroit, Mich., 1962, Chap. 9.

ADDITIONAL REFERENCES

A. Melik-Shakhnazarov, *Technical Information in the U.S.S.R.* (translated from Russian), M.I.T. Libraries, Cambridge, Mass., 1961.

Don R. Swanson, *An Experiment in Automatic Text Searching*, Ramo-Wooldridge, Canoga Park, April, 1960.

J. Verhoeff, W. Goffman and Jack Belzer, "Inefficiency of the Use of Boolean Functions for Information Retrieval Systems", *Communications of the ACM*, 4, 12, Dec., 1961, pp. 557, 558, 594.

By Karl F. Heumann
National Research Council

16. International Activities in Documentation

IN TREATING THIS TOPIC, I don't like to look back in history, because in a sense we are surrounded by history. In science information as in other areas we can observe the role and effects of nationalism and internationalism. When we see groups of people fighting and going through all the familiar steps to found independent countries in Africa we're seeing nationalism. When the United Nations, however, uses a variety of means to soften the forces of nationalism, then we are seeing internationalism.

Nationalism is extending the sites of international meetings into the far reaches of the world. An example is the 1960 conference of the International Federation of Documentation (FID) at Rio de Janeiro — it was the first regular conference to be held outside western Europe. According to a recent estimate, about 7½ international scientific meetings are started every day and we can expect further enlargement of the scientific world and its conferences.

One of the ways internationalism affects us is the need to gather documents from around the world for such meetings. In 1956 the number of abstracts and chemical abstracts from the USSR was nearly half the number from our own country.

As a consequence of this geographic scatter, language problems are sure to arise. In 1957 Peter Bernais and I made a count of the languages of the original articles abstracted in chemical abstracts. Russian language originals occurred about one-third as frequently as English originals. A more recent study of 1960 material shows that in some sections of chemical abstracts there were more Russian language originals than English originals.

It is estimated that two new scientific periodicals are founded each day. The fact that these journals start without regard for a total plan is obviously making our international information problems more severe. Founding a journal in one country can sometimes be defined as a nationalistic act.

It would be interesting to have statistics on the countries of origin of articles in professional journals. Some years ago the editor of a chemical journal made a study of this for one year. After the United States, the country from which the second largest number of articles came was Canada; but the third one may surprise you, it was Egypt. Since then an Egyptian chemical journal has been founded. This example rather suits both sides of my case because it shows the international sources of some of our leading U. S. journals. It shows also that nationalism can act to alter the pattern of these sources.

A trend that seems destined to continue is the increase of scientists traveling to international meetings both in and out of the United States. The 10th Pacific Science Congress held in Hawaii in the summer of 1961 had over one thousand scientists attending, about half of them from the United States. And there is the International Congress, to be held in Moscow this year, where there will be 125 Americans participating by giving papers.

We can look forward to increasingly complex international relationships with other countries having their effect on U. S. documentation, particularly having an effect on the raw materials for science information.

INTERNATIONAL ORGANIZATIONS

There are several international organizations concerned with documentation. Although most are professional associations, UNESCO is an intergovernmental organization which is giving limited but increasing attention to documentation through both its library and science offices. In my opinion the role of UNESCO should be studied further. It has the opportunity to draw attention to problem areas which may then be attacked by other organizations at the UNESCO level. For a variety of reasons, including political, UNESCO has not seen fit to operate vigorously in problems of documentation, with the exception of one good bibliography.

Among other intergovernmental organizations with active interests in documentation are EURATOM and the International Organization of Patent Offices. The latter is developing an intensive program of information exchange in Latin America.

Nongovernmental international organizations are often weak and have very little support. They also have the problem of infrequency of meetings as intergovernmental organizations do. The most important information activity internationally is the program of the International Federation of Documentation which is frequently referred to by its French initials, FID. The FID now has 43 national members, and has a secretariat in The Hague.

Until a few years ago FID was primarily concerned with the Universal Decimal Classification. Specialists in the United States have not been greatly interested in problems of classification, but in almost all other parts of the world classification is the normal way of dealing with scientific information. FID has had some 50 years of experience in promoting and refining a world-wide classification system. Recently the FID has broadened the scope of its staff and conference attention to the full scope of documentation problems.

The International Council of Scientific Unions is another important nongovernmental international organization. The primary activity of ICSU is abstracting. Its function is often misunderstood; it is not to provide the individual with abstracts, it is to help the editors of abstract periodicals in their own work. The abstracting program was started with physics only. An attempt was made to get the editors to contribute to abstracting periodicals regularly, to exchange pages by airmail, and to settle some standards in terminology and dialectics. Progress might seem slow, but I think it has been quite effective in the given field. In addition ICSU has now expanded into chemistry, and is on the verge of including the biological sciences.

The International Federation of Library Associations has an interest in international documentation. Another new organization with a related interest is the International Federation of Information Processing Societies (IFIPS) which holds its triennial Congress in Munich in 1962. IFIPS is especially concerned with electronic computers and associated equipment and the theory and technique for their effective use in processing data and information in other forms.

There are several United States organizations which have some relation to international documentation. A recent article in the FID Journal by Burton Adkinson is a comprehensive and well balanced statement: "Science Information in the Federal Government".

The Office of Science Information Service in the National Science Foundation is well known for the publication of a directory of nonconventional systems for dealing with scientific information. Within the Office of Science Information Service there is a foreign science information program concerned with the development and support of more effective international science communication. Dr. Adkinson, Head of the OSIS, has become the president-elect of FID. I think this is a reflection of the fact that the United States is becoming much more involved in the international exchange of information.

There is also in the National Science Foundation an Office of International Programs. It has been established recently, and its relationship to international programs is not yet crystallized. The National Science Foundation maintains an office in Tokyo, which is a very interesting experiment in attempting to get scientific information across international boundaries. It is probable that this program will be expanded.

The Department of State has a science advisor and several science attaches, who also deal with scientific information. The National Institutes of Health has recently established an Office of International Research, and intends to put a number of staff officers in various countries, the first of which is now in Paris, primarily to make sure that information about research supported by NIH in other countries comes back to the United

States. It is important to assure that the results of research support funds which we provide to other countries are reported back.

Other agencies of the Federal government which have foreign science information programs are Atomic Energy Commission, the Department of Agriculture, the Library of Congress and the Department of Defense. It is important to call attention to the dangers of a great many uncoordinated agencies dealing independently in information. A real problem is that scientists in other countries find themselves being talked to over and over and over again by a variety of people from the United States. It is possible that the science attaches of the Department of State can play a constructive central information and informal coordinative role for representatives of various agencies active in a foreign country or area.

I am associated with the National Research Council of the National Academy of Sciences. The Academy and Council are nongovernmental although they perform many services to government. There is in the Academy an Office of International Relations which is concerned with documentation as well as other topics. The Academy has a committee interested in the work of ICSU, which provides a channel from the United States into the International Council of Scientific Unions, largely through the Academy staff. The Office of International Relations also has a Committee on UNESCO and it is through this committee that many of the recommendations about scientific affairs, and in fact international affairs, are made to our U. S. National Commission for UNESCO. The Academy also in its Office of International Relations has an active Latin American program which includes some aspects of information work.

The United States recently has changed its adherence to FID, so that the Academy could become a U. S. national member for the Federation. In common with other adherences of the Academy to the international organizations, we have formed the United States National Committee for FID. This committee has as its purpose broad representation inside the United States, so that there is a better channel between the people in the United States interested in this topic and the International Federation of Documentation. The committee is made up of thirteen representatives of professional societies, eight governmental organizations, several members at large, the Secretary of the Academy, and all the people in the United States who are elected officers of FID.

I would like to close by citing four topics which should be the subject of some concern. First, there is not enough continuing study of international trends in scientific information. There are individual studies, but they tend to be fully individual and not to have long term substantive value. Second, we have information about information centers in the United States, but we do not have adequate information about centers in other countries that might well provide service to us.

Third, I think there is a lack in the use of international patent information and that the International Organization of Patent Offices could well be prevailed upon to make this kind of information more readily available. And, finally, as a personal matter, I am interested in some day having an International Union of Documentation rather than the tremendous scattering of activities found in our present situation.

By Saul Gorn
University of Pennsylvania

17. Computers, Communications, and Science – Extending Man's Intellect

IT IS AMAZING TO ME how the subject of this paper crops up again and again and how relevant the material is to different types of audiences. I have used this material in addressing management people on the impending shift in manpower, and in addressing high school teachers on the impending changes in educational ideals. It is material which appears in sections of introductory courses that might be called "computer appreciation". It is concerned with specialization in science and how it is related to the development of more and more interdisciplinary areas. In the way that is most relevant to the area of computers we have introduced it into the introductory course in the curriculum toward Master and Ph.D. degrees in the Computer and Information Sciences at the University of Pennsylvania's Moore School of Electrical Engineering. I call it "a philosophy of communication".

THE DEVELOPMENT OF MACHINES AND THEIR CHARACTERISTICS

The general attitude in this philosophy of communication comes up very naturally in an introductory course. Visualize it as given to a group of students who are going to be professionals in the field of computer and information sciences. I first go through a rapid review of the history of computation. This field appears to have developed at a pretty slow pace over the ages until the 20th century. At the point of the middle of the 20th century I talk about the influence of the war in accelerating the need for computations. I indicate that production itself was outstripping information about what was being produced at that time. A specific instance is the case during the war where guns and ammunition were being produced at a faster rate than the tables needed to fire them accurately. This prompted the Defense Department to ask Moore School of Electrical Engineering to give a general training program on computation, so that more people could help out in this situation. Right next door to this training group was a group of people working on pulsed digital techniques for radar. Somebody, probably Eckert and Mauchly, got the idea that since radar involved very rapid counting of pulses, perhaps these techniques could help the people with the bothersome computation problem.

The turning point of putting electronics into computers was conceived in that way, resulting in ENIAC, and then a long series of other computers whose names ended in *AC*. After the *AC's* came all the numerical series — the 700s, the 1100s, the 1400s, etc. By the end of the first hour the blackboard in the classroom shows an enormous growing tree of different types of computers, all digital. Then I say: "Now wait a minute! How many firing and bombing tables do we have to compute? How can we explain this sort of an explosion?"

The explanation has two sides. Somehow these machines had certain properties which were just what was needed at the moment. This would explain the development from nothing to more than a billion dollar industry in only fifteen years. Conversely, what was there about society and its structure that made this happen and that made this just the thing that was needed at the moment?

In talking about the machines, we point out that it was unfortunate that they were called computers. The French simply invented a new word "ordinateur" for the purpose. We point out that these machines are really general purpose symbol manipulators or information transformers. They allow one to do incredibly complicated syntactic processing of groups of symbols, where these symbols may be interpreted in any way one pleases. We rapidly get into the idea of loop control, which makes the machines general purpose. A key feature of this loop control is the common storage of instructions and data, which makes it possible for the machine to shift the interpretations of what is in the storage so that at one instant a word might be an instruction where, at another, it will be data. The machine is capable of changing its own instructions as it proceeds. The result of this is the ability to simulate the self-referencing subtleties of speech and thought.

SOCIETY AND THE INFORMATION PROBLEM

Now what about the picture of society? Why did it need just that kind of instrument at that time?

Let us consider a cybernetic picture of society. The definition of cybernetics as Norbert Weiner gave it (just about fifteen years ago) is the "theory of communication and control in animals and machines". That title itself was considered very dramatic at the time. Actually it was rather conservative, because one can look upon any growing organism in a cybernetic fashion: human society, a culture, a company, a language, a technology, language systems, domains of knowledge, etc.

In a famous essay by J. B. S. Haldane, called *On Being the Right Size*, the author begins by remarking that it is fortunate for humans that insects do not grow to the size of elephants. He then remarks that, considering the almost mechanical breathing system an insect possesses, the internal communication system for its oxygen, if you will, it is physically impossible for such a system to develop enough pumping energy to control a musculature (the control system) beyond a certain size.

COMMUNICATION AND CONTROL

An important feature of organisms that can be studied in this cybernetic fashion is

then the relationships between their internal communications and their internal controls; every growing system maintains willy-nilly a balance between communications and control, even if that balance means the death of the system. Those cultures, those civilizations, that became unbalanced on the control side developed a kind of stupidity, in which information necessary to intelligent behavior arrived too late. Like the dinosaurs, they died. Those civilizations that were overbalanced on the communications side could understand everything perfectly but could never do anything in a suitably coordinated way, like the Greek civilization or some of the past French Republics. They also died. If we look at the development of human cultures as far back as we can, we find that there are certain critical times when there were vital changes in the structure, in the whole organization of society. These vital changes or revolutions seemed to come in pairs. I submit that the first of each pair was a control revolution, and that rapidly following after it, within a few hundred years, there was a resulting communications revolution.

Far back in history there was the agricultural revolution which was a control revolution. Mankind became able to control his physical environment considerably more than he had previously. This was followed by an urban revolution within less than a thousand years. This was a communications revolution. The same thing has happened more recently. About 150 years ago there was a control revolution called the industrial revolution, when men became capable of a much greater control of the physical and social environment because the machines took over large scale routine labor. The rapid expansion of the population which could now be supported created an imbalance on the control side. A crisis has developed which has created a need for a reorganization of the communications system. People concerned with scientific information are generally acutely aware of this problem. They refer to it as the information crisis. Others in our society express it by saying: there is too much red tape, too much paper work, there is too much traffic, there is too much specialization.

The effect of the first industrial revolution was that the machines took over large scale routine labor. In the second revolution the machines are now taking over large scale routine thinking. These symbol manipulators, these information transformers, have made it surprisingly, sometimes painfully, evident that the biggest part of what we have considered to be thinking was in fact routine and therefore mechanizable.

MANPOWER AND EDUCATION

The result of each of these violent changes in social structure was a change in manpower distribution and types of manpower needed. There was a corresponding change in educational ideals because a different distribution of manpower needed a different kind of educational system. Thus in the first industrial revolution the large mass of unskilled labor that the large societies had come to depend upon seemingly became at the time unnecessary. Actually this mass was freed for even more work that did result later. The time lag was painful, but it was only a time lag. While the unskilled laboring classes became by and large unnecessary, there was an enormous class of white collar workers (that had not been needed before) which were now needed. The corresponding shift in educational ideals was from an emphasis on teaching techniques in some kind of guild system to teaching everybody reading, writing, and arithmetic. Just at that time it became economically important and economically feasible to provide universal education. This also accelerated the communications crisis that resulted.

Since the machine is taking over large scale routine thinking, there is now another corresponding shift in educational ideals. Teaching reading, writing, and arithmetic universally isn't enough. Machines can do such things. In many cases they can do them better. We now need a different kind of personality, a person who is going to decide what a machine ought to do, or to ask a machine to do tremendous jobs for him. When programming a machine for a problem, a person must consider all the ramifications of what, say, 15,000 clerks may have handled separately, for the machine is the equivalent of a staff of 15,000 clerks. Therefore, his type of thinking must be not the mechanical clerical type any more, he must use executive ability and creative thinking. Suddenly we are faced with the fact that we must educate most of our population to be executives and creative thinkers.

Further, the trend toward specialization must erase itself too. The reason for specialization in the first place was that there was too much detailed information about the world to be crammed into any one head. Therefore, this knowledge had to be split into domains, with different people cramming in different kinds of information. However, the storage and retrieval of that information and most of the work involved in it was a mechanical job. If the machines can take over that mechanical portion then the reason for the specialization disappears. But then you have to teach everybody the broad principles of every domain of knowledge, and the arrangement of the domains of knowledge in a taxonomic tree. They would have to go on from there to retrieve any details they needed; but they would program a machine to handle that retrieval for them. In other words, we must now learn how to educate a whole generation of Leonardo da Vinci's. Do we know how to produce even one?

Even proving theorems in geometry is by and large a mechanical job. When I talk to mathematics teachers I point out that the way geometry is being taught presents a worm's eye view of the subject. They have been making the students act like machines in step by step proofs without ever understanding how that which they proved was conceived of in the first place. One has to balance off this worm's eye view of mechanical proof with almost instinctive flashes of insight obtained by a bird's eye point of view of what a subject is like and what is likely to be true in the field.

STRUCTURAL CHANGES IN DOMAINS OF KNOWLEDGE

Let us now consider the particular causes of these periodic violent changes in the structure of a growing organism. The simplest example is the development of the sciences; how they grew, why they grew, the order in which they developed and the way that each one individually developed. The biological principle "ontogeny recapitulates phylogeny" seems to be applicable here. We remember that this principle points out that the development of an individual animal from conception on takes it roughly through the same stages that evolution took among the species until that of the animal was reached. Similarly, the history of the development of each individual science seems to have followed the same pattern as the history of the development of the sciences as species. The phases and changes in each science, to my mind, are due to an information retrieval problem. In talking to management people, I would characterize the problem as the growth of a file and what has to happen to it.

What happens is that there must be a balance, as the file grows, between the retrievability of the information and the needed communication flow of the information; the control of the information due to the structure of its arrangement must balance the method by which it is communicated. What has happened, then, is that the continuum of a domain of knowledge when a revolution is due, either splits into distinct fields or changes phase radically by a change in the structure of its arrangement. That is, once the mass of information got beyond the critical mass, usually either fission or fusion occurred. Fusion is the change in the structure of the individual science itself to make it a much more compact carrier of information; for example, general laws are highly compact bouillon cubes of information. Fission is the breaking up into various areas of specialization, which we have already mentioned. The fission or fusion occurred in each case because the information got beyond our capacity, and its former control began to require too much time to retrieve. In order to be able to retrieve the information, you either have to have separate specialized lumps or have a violent change in structure.

A CLASSIFICATION OF SCIENCES

Let us, then, look at the ontogeny and phylogeny of the development of the sciences. This particular point of view was that of the positivistic school of philosophers and scientists led by Auguste Comte over a hundred years ago. Since they were developing a new field called sociology and they considered themselves philosophers, they put the different sciences in a scale with philosophy and social science at the top. Mundane sciences like physics and mathematics were at the bottom of the scale. However, they did agree that mathematics had a more crucial value than that indicated by being at the bottom of the scale. In my scaling of the sciences I consider

that philosophy has a special role (as you might guess from the tone of this talk), and, further, that mathematics has a special role also (as you might have guessed if you know my background).

Originally the wise men of the tribe in a small cultural unit had to carry all the basic information, the natural philosophy that the tribe needed at critical moments. This was all one domain. Knowledge was considered, as it should again be considered, as one continuous domain. However, because of the ever repeating information retrieval problem, this knowledge was fragmented into different domains. History indicates a natural chronological sequence.

Mathematics seems to have been the first field to have split off and to have developed a life of its own; then physics developed. The more powerful the mathematics available, the faster the physics developed. Then there was chemistry, and the more powerful the understanding of physics, the faster chemistry developed. Next in order follow the biological sciences, the psychological sciences, and the sociological sciences. It seems reasonable that these sciences should have developed in this order when we examine the unit of discourse in each of these sciences. The unit of discourse in physics at one time was the atom, a rather small unit. However, that has been fragmented recently, fission and fusion again. The unit of discourse in chemistry is a molecule composed of atoms. You have to have sophisticated knowledge from physics in order to begin to get certain very basic knowledge in chemistry. The unit of discourse in biology is the living cell, an incredibly complicated group of molecules. Consequently you have to have very sophisticated information in chemistry before you can begin to get the really basic information in biology. The unit in psychology is the individual, and a human being is an incredibly complicated concatenation of biological cells. The unit in sociology is a structured group of individuals with some kind of communication and control structure among them. Again we have to have rather sophisticated information in biology before you can get very basic information in psychology. In fact, the pressure of the needs of information in psychology are such that it had to develop in two directions at once. The psychologist looking from the point of view of a sociologist developed into one kind of school. The psycho-analysts are an example of this. The psychologists' thinking of the individual as a biological system developed the other point of view; deterministic psychologists, for example, developed here. They both have to work at the same time because of the pressure on both sides.

MATHEMATICS AS AN EXAMPLE OF ADVANCED DEVELOPMENT

Mathematics happens to be the oldest of the sciences, and since I believe that the ontogeny-phylogeny principle in biology is really a principle of the development of growing organisms of any kinds, we should see that principle at work in mathematics. If we look at the phases in the development of mathematics, we can see what is happening and can begin to predict the sort of thing that will be happening among the other sciences.

Originally, even within the memory of man, mathematics was talking about the real world. Originally, of course, there was the question of control of communication about the environment. Since one type of new society was then agricultural, there had to be information about continuous quantities. That is, they were concerned more about measurements than about counting. When the Nile overflowed and the boundary lines were wiped out, they had to be able to get the boundary lines back again after the flood subsided. Or they had to construct a pyramid with an exact right angle, with one side pointing due east and west and another due north and south, etc. If the society happened to be not primarily sitting in one place to control the environment but moving around and communicating, then the emphasis was on counting discrete items. For instance, nomadic groups had to be able to keep control of numbers of goats or the number of members of a tribe. Thus they stressed counting; the other society stressed measuring. In the urban revolution both had to develop together for the purposes of commerce.

COLLECTION OF DIRECT FACTS PHASE

Thus the rules that were used in both counting and measuring were directly connected with physical entities. They had to file away the facts that two sheep plus two sheep was four sheep, even this is already an

abstraction, and two dogs plus two dogs was four dogs, and two beans plus two beans was four beans in the information system. This filing system soon became unwieldy. They must therefore contract the structure by creating the abstract concept, 2, and in the filing system they have just the one statement 2 plus 2 equals 4, and then also they have a large list of digitalized phenomena to which counting applies: dogs, sheep, cattle, people, and so on. Now they have in a very compact space, many sentences replaced by one sentence, and a list of appropriate replacements in such sentences. That long list together with the one sentence took up much less information space or retrieval time than the original did. This achievement of compactness indicates the general pattern.

At this first level of abstraction, these concepts, numerical concepts for example, were still considered rather concrete. As mathematics goes these days they are close to a concrete level, mathematics being only rarely fascinated by particular numbers. In those days there were different schools of thought for the rules to be used with these first level abstractions. For example, in constructing a right angle, there was a school of thought that claimed that if you take a rope and tie two knots in it and form a triangle with the three portions three units long, four units long, and five units long, respectively, then the angle at the knot that is opposite the side that is five units in length will be a right angle. Further, any one in his right mind would know that that is the way to arrange things if he wants to get his pyramid squared away. There might easily have been another school of thought which went in for sides which were five, twelve and thirteen units in length. This school might have believed that with these bigger lengths they were bound to get a more refined right angle than with the 3, 4, and 5 system. It is conceivable that they got into arguments and occasionally killed each other in the course of these arguments; they took these things seriously in those days. It is a recorded fact that the Pythagoreans killed a member who revealed to the outside world that, contrary to their doctrine that all nature harmonized by having all quantities ratios of natural numbers, the square root of two was irrational.

Thus this fact was added in the mathematical filing system and the amount of information about right triangles began to pile up: 3, 4, 5; 5, 12, 13, and so on. The filing system began to get to the point where it developed a critical mass and either fission or fusion had to occur. In this case it was fusion, the Pythagorean theorem. The result was not a list of what can be substituted for the lengths of the three sides of the triangle but rather a statement about the relationship the numbers in such a triple must have. Thus we have an infinite number of potential facts in that one sentence — a terrific condensation of information. Now when this one sentence, the Pythagorean theorem, was put into the file, the structure of that filing system condensed remarkably. The average retrieval time was extremely fast, although in any particular case in addition to the looking up of the theorem you would have to pay the price of computation time to verify the numbers considered.

Recall that the first phase was just the collection of facts from experience. This was a file with the limited structure of a single sequence, wherein you are lucky to find something. You had to hunt through this linear file from beginning to end, the way a person of the Ancient Mariner type gives you advice. You ask him for advice, and he'll give you an autobiography; and when the relevant information that you really want passes by, you stop him.

After this (linear file) collection of facts phase, we evolved to the selection of the appropriate abstract concepts, in other words, the selection of the right grouping of things to be observed. We had to learn what it was that we ought to be perceiving. At this stage of the game it was decided that numbers were important, that measurements were important and that the concept "animal" was important, whether talking about sheep, dogs and so on. Just as a child has to learn that the concept dog is important when he sees Towser in one place and Fido in another place, etc. In the classification phase one is inventing, not discovering, the combinations and groupings that will permit a tighter and more compact arrangement of information. In botany it happened about 200 years ago with Linnaeus. A new language, a new jargon, was developed for that information. This language permits classification of millions of things in an appropriate fashion for an appropriate purpose; we call this the taxonomic phase.

GENERAL LAWS

This same thing was happening in mathematics when it was decided that the concept of an angle or a triangle was important. Thus there was developed a filing system in which a portion was concerned with right angles, with triangles, circles, etc. For example, a right triangle would be obtained if the three sides of the triangle had lengths of 3 units, 4 units, 5 units; 5 units, 12 units, and 13 units, and so on. Again the file began to get too big, fission or fusion had to occur. In this case it was fusion again so that we derived general laws which like the Pythagorean theorem cover a fantastic number of facts, actual or potential, in one statement.

The more pragmatic mistakes one makes in selecting the collections to be given abstract names in the classification phase, the more complicated the general laws become. The better your choice of taxonomic groups, the neater the general laws become. Very often after a certain amount of generalization has been done, it would be decided that certain previous concepts in the classification system should not have been considered to be the important ones at all. That is why I stressed the fact that classifications were invented rather than discovered. A grouping would be rejected if by using it the description of a situation or how to extend beyond it becomes much more complicated than when compared to what would happen if another grouping were used. Thus facts themselves change pragmatically, since the things that are to be perceived have to change; consequently there is a feedback between descriptions of experience about things perceived and the decisions on what should be perceived. Neither ideas in Plato's sense, nor objects in the sense of materialism, are merely out there waiting to be passively perceived. Perception and knowledge are together a dynamic interlocking process; asking which is prior, mind or matter, is as absurd as asking which came first, the chicken or the egg.

As classifications change properly, the general laws become neater. This is important, because it indicates why neatness and esthetics are the criteria used in the development of the world of communications, whose key creators are our artists and scientists. The function of the arts and sciences is to sharpen the tools and substance of communication. These creative communicators with their esthetic criteria are considerably closer together in aims than the world or they themselves realize. They are almost diametric extremes to the control type represented by executives, army generals, etc., whose working value system must be almost exclusively ethical rather than esthetic. It is the professionals such as doctors, lawyers, teachers, engineers, etc., who have the difficult task of transforming information into action.

DEDUCTIVE SYSTEMS

Now these general laws begin to pile up. We have the Pythagorean theorem, we have a theorem about base angles of isosceles triangles, and a host of other theorems. An enormous file beings to develop. Again it gets out of hand, and either fission or fusion must occur. In this case again fusion occurred. Euclid discovered that if one began with a few general laws and certain logical rules about how to derive new ones from the old, one could derive all the general laws. This was the development of deductive systems.

Portions of physics have gone through the deductive phase since Newton's time, the area called rational mechanics is an example. Most of physics has gone into just that stage now. Chemistry is only beginning to enter this phase. So is biology if one looks at the work of Rachevsky.

The deductive systems began to pile up during the 19th century. The big stimulus was the attempt to prove Euclid's parallel postulate; the best minds in the world were not able to do it. Then it was discovered there was a good reason why it couldn't be proved. This axiom was independent of the others. To show that it was independent, perfectly self-consistent geometries were discovered that were not Euclidean. Thus there were developed many different deductive systems in geometry alone. The latter half of the 19th century and the beginning of the 20th century resulted in a tremendous proliferation of deductive systems. Again we faced the information retrieval problem which is always with us.

FORMAL SYSTEMS

It became apparent that either fission or fusion had to occur. For a while it was fission

into various geometries, types of algebra, and types of analysis; but then it was discovered that many of these deductive systems could be made to fit into exactly the same forms. A divorce of some of the key mathematical concepts from the real world came in when one deliberately made some of the world used meaningless in order to obtain such formal identifications. Thus by putting different meanings into those words, one got different deductive systems from one system. This introduced *formal* systems, complete formalization. Pure science was completely formalized; applied science put some of the semantic content and meaning back into such syntactic formalized systems by assigning them to these undefined terms and checking whether the axioms became true. This was the new meaning of the word application.

For example, let us look at developments in projective geometry in which points and lines are considered meaningless (deliberately). The only permissible interpretations are those which can be obtained from the axioms alone. Proofs are derived from logical rules applied to these few sentences (the axioms). You are supposed to think of nothing else at the risk of bringing in an irrelevancy and not having a good proof. Yet one application to the real world of this formal system would be to have "point" meaning a position in space, and "line" meaning the path of a light ray. Another application would have "point" meaning a member of the board of directors of a company, and "line" meaning a subcommittee of the board of directors. If you take some of the first axioms of projective geometry with such an interpretation, lo and behold, you are reading the charter for the board of directors; for example, "Any two people of the board of directors must be on one and only one committee together". This is the same as saying "two points determine a line". And if you take the word "point" to mean a certain field in the country and "line" to be a group of fields to be dusted in one day, the axioms of the geometry now read like a crop dusting contract. There are many other applications of the same formal system.

Similarly, in algebra there are highly abstract systems for groups, fields, rings, and algebras. And for such systems there are theories on the structure of the set of subfields of fields, subgroups of groups, and how to extend them. It is this type of theory which can be important in solving the problem of how to make a taxonomic language grow under control in an information retrieval system. If you cannot expand such a system, it will rapidly lose its value.

Such then are the trends that we see in the development of mathematics; but we can also expect to see them appearing in all the sciences. Each will have to go through those various phases, if the principle of ontogeny recapitulating phylogeny applies to the various sciences. My claim is that over and over again it was the information retrieval problem in a given domain of knowledge which brought about these changes in phase. When the domain of knowledge got too big to be controlled by the old system, the whole communication system had to change, whether by fission or by fusion.

The picture of the sciences which I have just given, you can recognize, is a naive one because it seems to imply a linear arrangement. Further, you now see why I considered mathematics separately. As any science gets to a completely formalized state the completely formalized part is mathematics and is considered as such. And what is philosophy doing outside of this arrangement of the sciences? It is examining the basic concepts and axioms in all of the sciences, comparing them for consistency, sitting on the sideline being critical and sneering; a very important function. For sitting off at the sidelines as it does it can see if the basic concepts are not jibing properly, look clumsy, etc. It has had a tremendous effect, but nothing is harder to read than last year's philosophy. For if philosophy has done its job properly, we can no longer see the problems that it is discussing, having already changed our methods of perception in accordance with its criticisms. Philosophy has still a controlling influence on the structure of the domains of knowledge and how they fit together.

INTERDISCIPLINARY SCIENCES

But in this day and age we see the development of many interdisciplinary sciences. Thus there isn't a linear alignment of science as described above. We should actually be thinking of the domains of knowledge as originally thought of; a unified and continuous host of information. This information we quantize according to our needs, marking out those domains that seem to be relevant at any given time. Those domains also change with the times. Moreover, as scientific information becomes much denser, the lines of demarcation separating erstwhile domains are no longer as clear as, say, the separation of galaxies in a thinly populated universe.

Possibly more important now than the traditional separation of scientific knowledge into the classic sciences is the distinction between the pure formalized science (mathematics), the applied science, and pragmatics. The formalized is concerned with pure syntax, the relationships among symbols independent of their meaning. The applied is concerned with the semantics of the words used, that is, the relationship between the symbols and their meanings. We are also concerned, however, with the relations between the symbols and their users or interpreters. This is pragmatics. Computer and information sciences can be distinguished from the mathematical portions of science precisely in its concern with pragmatics. The emphasis is on how interpretation is controlled, and how interpretations shift.

The fact that I couched this general picture in information retrieval terms is due to the fact that I have been considering scientific information pragmatically. I believe you have, too. In this new domain of computer and information sciences we are studying a growing mechanical language. However, in order for us to know that we are studying pragmatically important concepts we need information from you. It is possible to carve out a concept which would not be pragmatically important and spend our days doing research on it. Yet, practitioners of information retrieval systems are the ones that have to meet pragmatic problems day to day. There are various studies of mechanical languages which are interesting and some which are useful. However, as matters stand, in studying pure theory, we are in the position of a man who was stuck with an elliptical billiard table two feet high, with a leopard skin top. He made one because someone had ordered it, but that person didn't want it any more and cancelled the order. The pure scientist is in the position of having a load of these tables. If anyone happens to want one, we have them.

By E. M. McCormick
National Science Foundation

18. The Management Process and Science Information Systems

THE USUAL MANAGEMENT CONTROL CYCLE is familiar to scientists since it is essentially the scientific method itself. The first part is the determination of goals and objectives for the system being considered. The second part of the cycle is concerned with evaluation. Here the existing system is compared with the goals and objectives of the system and a decision is made on action to be taken. This results in implementation of the revised system. As operation of this system continues, it is important to collect and organize information which can then be used for further evaluation by comparison with the goals and objectives to determine the value of the system. This may result in different goals, decisions, implementations, operations, etc., which cause the cycle to be repeated as often as required to set up the desired management situation and to maintain it under dynamic conditions.

The management control cycle can be considered in two ways with regard to science information centers. The first is as a part of the overall process involved in scientific research and development activities. Thus, the science information center is used for collecting and organizing the information for management decision. Further, the management situation must be one in which scientific and technical information are significant parts of the management process. As such, it represents the viewpoint of the boss or the manager of the science information center.

The second way of considering the management control cycle is in terms of the science information center itself. Thus, the goals and ojbectives are those of the center, not those of the overall activity. The operations are those of the center itself, etc. This is primarily the viewpoint of the manager of the science information center who is concerned with developing an optimum system to provide service to the overall organization.

As has been indicated, these viewpoints have much in common. Thus, much of the material presented here applies to both. However, it is helpful sometimes to consider whether any specific management situation pertains to the overall system or to the science information center itself.

Before the principal phases of the management control cycle are considered individually, it is necessary to review certain aspects of the management situation in which science information centers exist.

THE MANAGEMENT ENVIRONMENT

Just what is the situation which makes the management of science information centers of importance to management? Traditionally, the technical information function is handled by providing library services to the staff. In general, this is a relatively small part of management responsibilities. However, in many cases the handling of scientific information has become a much more significant problem in recent years. The reasons for this are discussed in some of the papers in this book. Briefly, business, government and industry have found that their products and services depend more on the information produced and used by scientists and engineers. Management itself finds that more of its decisions are based on technical decisions. Further, the cost of this information is increasing and its management becoming more difficult.

In these papers the emphasis is on the management problems which differ from the general management problems of scientific research and development activities. Thus, much of the material must be considered in terms of the existing management environment of scientific research and development activities. Further, the point of departure or reference standard in considering technical information centers is the conventional library. Most of the papers are concerned with how these centers differ from or compare to these libraries.

SCIENCE INFORMATION CENTER DEFINITION

The essential elements of a science information center are identified by several of the authors. The common factor in these definitions is the aggressive attitude toward information collection and distribution. This is contrasted with the comparatively passive operations of the usual library. The technical information center volunteers its expertise to the scientist. It offers a wide variety of services to its customers and is generally aggressively striving to render more and better service. In many ways, of course, it is a special library in that its collection is narrow in breadth, comprehensive in depth, and directed to sophisticated clientele. However, the technical information center is more likely to use nonconventional methods of handling information. This is probably due to the fact that the items in the collection and the demands made on the system are not always amenable to conventional techniques. In addition, these technical information activities frequently are originated to meet technical needs by technical people who are familiar with newer techniques for data processing and information handling.

GOALS AND OBJECTIVES

It is apparent that one needs first to determine the reasons for having a science information center. What is its purpose? How will its function contribute to the overall objectives and goals of the organization? Then: what must be the goals and objectives of the science information center itself?

Although obviously important, it is generally difficult to set meaningful goals and objectives for science information centers.

Many just grew from library operations. Yet the reasons for this growth need to be investigated to determine what it means in terms of the goals and objectives of the company. Perhaps they have also changed. This is illustrated by situations in which management has changed the fields of interests of a company without informing the library or science information center so that it would be prepared to serve these new needs.

INFORMATION NEEDS AND USES

The first requirement in setting up a system is to determine the need for the service. Yet this is quite difficult to do, and many systems are in operation with certain assumed needs for the service but where there is no good measure of the need. Some user studies have been made but these are not conclusive with regard to the need for information. It is pointed out that the way scientists use an existing system is not necessarily the way they would use a better system. Scientists are conditioned to respond to a system in anticipation of the system response. This results in their not asking the question they need an answer to but rather asking another question which they feel can be answered and from which the desired answer can be derived. This results in some doubt that the actual information needs of a system can be determined by the scientist himself. It would appear that market survey techniques could be useful in this situation.

In considering this aspect of objectives and goals it will be noted that three papers referred to Mooer's Law. This states that, "An information retrieval system will tend *not* to be used whenever it is more painful and troublesome for a customer to have information than for him not to have it". It is suggested that this law is not entirely facetious and merits consideration when planning the services a science information center is to provide.

EVALUATION AND DECISION

The next steps in the management process are concerned with evaluation of the system and the decision on a better system. Evaluation of an information system is fraught with difficulties. Yet these difficulties are not so different from those with which management is already familiar. Although objective evaluations are only rarely possible, subjective evaluations are frequently made for management purposes.

Evaluations are made in terms of goals and objectives. Thus, since science information centers are established to directly benefit the scientist in his work, evaluation is also concerned with the user. All systems provide for feedback from the user; quite often this feedback is informal. However, more sophisticated techniques are now being applied to this problem. Many system studies go beyond the "how did you like it?" type of survey. There must be dependence on opinion, but management has generally recognized the importance of intuition over logic in many complicated situations.

Management's interests are served somewhat indirectly, i.e., through the scientist. Thus, management must not only consider the user's evaluation but also whether the assumed user need is valid. Again it is quite likely that the informal information system may be much more significant in comparison with the formal than is sometimes presumed.

ECONOMIC JUSTIFICATION

The economic justification for information activities, especially in an industrial environment, is considered by several of the authors. In addition to the general factors which must be considered, the specific problem of justifying a mechanized information system is presented in some detail.

A part of this economic justification involved determination of what can and should be done within the company and what should be done outside. Many of the existing information systems are primarily concerned with internal information where general disclosure would be prejudicial to the company. Yet an increasing number of commercial activities are being established to handle nonproprietary information where there is an economic advantage in handling this common information. Since these endeavors are competitive and must be self-sustaining, their pricing of various information functions is helpful in management evaluation of the cost of information systems.

MECHANIZATION

Many of the problems in evaluating an existing information system and in making a decision on a new system are encountered when mechanization is considered. There is much management interest in the question. To what extent is mechanization the answer to many of the problems in processing technical information? This topic is considered thoroughly in one of the papers and referred to in others. The approach is the same as for automatic data processing systems for commercial applications. Of course, there are technical differences between these two fields, but primary management considerations are similar. The experience in data processing should be helpful for information handling. The successful application of mechanization in information must first meet the requirements for data processing. Beyond this there are additional requirements for information handling. The emphasis in most of the papers is on these special requirements. Again the presentations are in terms of the usual management situation in science and technology which presumes some knowledge and experience in automatic data processing.

IMPLEMENTATION AND OPERATION

After the existing system has been evaluated and a decision made on a new and presumably better system, there are many considerations involved in implementing this decision and in operating the system.

Organizational location

The position of the technical information system in the management hierarchy is considered in some of the papers. The importance of having it as far up in the organization as possible is stressed. The factors which result in the responsibility for this service being pushed upwards in the organization are also considered.

It is suggested that technical information centers do not automatically get the support of top management but rather earn it by demonstrating their value to the organization. On the other hand, these centers are more likely to be recognized and use made of them when it is known that top management solidly supports them.

Of course, there are situations where the center has developed to meet a special need comparatively low in the formal organization chart and have stayed at this level. However, there are also examples where the need has been recognized first by management and the resulting center was established to meet these needs.

In addition to position in the formal organization, the position in the informal organization is also important. This is one reason for having technical peers in the information center — it permits better access to the important informal organization thus getting around organizational lines which sometimes hinder the communication process.

Personnel administration

Personnel problems were considered by several of the authors. It was felt that there were special requirements in the technical information situation which merit special consideration.

There was general agreement that there is a need for technical personnel in the technical information center. These individuals should first have competence in the fields of science and technology represented in the center, and second should have skill in using the tools of the center. The principle need for this competence seems to be in handling the contacts between the center and its customers. It is deemed necessary for the customer to be able to deal with someone in the center who can talk his language and understand his problem. It appears that much of the benefit of this situation is not necessarily the actual technical competence of the representative of the information center, but that he is or represents a group that the technical customer would accept as a peer. This peer concept seems to be quite important in handling the basic communication problem between the center and the customer. Again the contrast to the usual library environment can be noted.

The peer concept indicates that the center representative is interested in the user's problem as such rather than in the integrity of the sources of information. The trend here is analogous to that in ADP — one obtains personnel who are primarily skilled in the technicalities of the business itself and then one trains them to use the tools of the service activity (ADP systems or technical information systems) which are of use to the business. This has obvious advantages in the integration of the service activity with the other activities of the organization.

There is a question, however, as to whether this technically competent individual should be identified as a subject matter specialist or as some form of information specialist. Some consider that there is or should be a profession of information specialists. Although they may have technical backgrounds, their main occupation is handling information competently. Thus, in a sense they would most resemble librarians although possibly trained in more of the new technology of information processing. It is also proposed that the technical information field needs personnel whose basic skill is in researching, analyzing, and documenting the significant aspects of various fields of science and technology. These writers would produce state of the art reports which would serve many of the basic information needs of scientists, especially with regard to sifting out the important from unimportant material.

The other end of the gamut is the situation where the information function is handled by a researcher who does not lose his basic identity as a researcher. Perhaps one member of a team would spend more time than the others in the information gathering and disseminating capacity. However, he would do this as a secondary activity and would probably not have any special training in information processes. Although this may be inefficient as compared to a technical information center, it is defended (at least in part) by the fact that the scientist retains his first class status by continuing to be identified as a scientist. Otherwise, as an information specialist, as such, he would become a second-class citizen. Obviously, the situation is different in various types of scientific and technical enterprises.

This peer concept, in its various forms, emphasizes the need for prestige and status for personnel in the technical information center. Of course, management recognizing this need can meet it by these as well as various other techniques.

Financial support

The relatively high cost of some information centers as compared to library services aggravates the problem of financial support. Most centers are supported as a part of the overhead account as service activities. However, in one of the papers there is a report on the problem of support of an information center and of obtaining some measure of the value of its services by making charges for these services. Only partial support of the center is attempted; the rest is a direct subsidy as is the usual practice in the operation of information centers and libraries. This technique has disadvantages as well as advantages; it will be of interest to see how well it works out over a period of time and whether other information centers adopt the idea.

Public relations

Libraries have a traditional image of service but do not normally engage in an aggressive campaign to sell their services. Yet science information centers seem to be characterized by an aggressive attitude toward the collection of information and toward the dissemination of information to the users. This results in selling, promotion and marketing activities which are not those usually associated with a library.

COLLECTION AND ORGANIZATION OF INFORMATION

In order to close the management control loop, it is necessary to collect and organize information about the operating system that will permit further evaluation, modification of goals, and revision of the system if necessary. Again the problem is familiar to management. Further, the need for obtaining valid cost information is obvious.

Cost information

The precedent for technical information service is the traditional library function. This was considered to be a necessary part of the overhead operation. As such its support was a relatively small percent of the overall cost. Yet as the technical information function has grown, the cost of the service has in some cases increased to several percent of the operating budget. Yet, there are no good measures of the value of the information which could be compared to the cost of information. Actually, in the cost accounting sense there is very little information on detailed costs of library operations. For that reason

one of the papers gives information on costs in a successful mechanized and integrated technical information center. The presentation here is costing in the sense that an operating profit-making activity must be conscious of cost. Conventional information activities normally do not sell their product, hence, are not in a position to be as cost conscious as they might otherwise be.

In addition, often many of the costs of technical information are hidden. When there is a well-defined information activity, it is possible to determine costs with reasonable accuracy. However, in many situations the information function and the research and development function are combined making it difficult to separate these costs. The policy of considering information to be an essential part of the research process tends towards this. However, efforts are being made to identify the costs of science information activities. At the national level some government agencies are identifying them as line items in their budgets and efforts are being made to have other agencies also do this.

Information consolidation

In collecting and organizing information about systems, it is suggested that the precedents from data processing experience may be misleading in science information activities. Data processing is generally successful in meeting the needs of management because it is possible to consolidate data in the system to correspond to the various levels of management. This enables management to judge data about the system used for data processing.

However, in science information centers the basic commodity is information which, in general, is not capable of being consolidated as in a profit and loss statement. It is generally only available to and useful to the scientists and engineers themselves, not to the higher levels of management. Thus, their information about an information center is not as certain as with data processing. This presents special challenges in gathering the information needed for the evaluation of information systems.

Bibliography

(The bibliography is selected from "Information Handling and Science Information — A Selected Bibliography", *American Institute of Biological Sciences*, Washington, D.C., B.S.C.P., 1962, and reproduced with permission of the Biological Sciences Communications Project of the American Institute of Biological Sciences and the Center for Technology and Administration of The American University).

Adkinson, B. W., **THE FEDERAL GOVERNMENT AND U. S. SCIENTIFIC INFORMATION.** J. Chem. Doc. 2(1):48-50. Jan. 1962.

In addition to presenting a general review of the scope of the Federal Government's role in research and development, and a review of the character of the Federal Government's scientific information activities, the article presents a review of the six-point program which has been developed by the National Science Foundation for improving the dissemination of scientific information, particularly among U. S. scientists and engineers. The author concludes that the dissemination of scientific information must be recognized as an integral part of research and development.

Adkinson, B. W., **UNITED STATES SCIENTIFIC AND TECHNICAL INFORMATION SERVICES.** Spec. Libr. 49(9):407-414. Nov. 1958.

This discussion of United States scientific and technical information services is divided into the following parts: the present situation in the United States; some of the reasons behind the current problems; the principal scientific and technical information activities of the Federal Government; and a proposed program to remedy this country's scientific and technical information ills.

Agard Evans, A. B., and Farradane, J., **TRAINING THE SCIENTIFIC INFORMATION OFFICER.** Internatl. Conf. Sci. Inform. Proc. 1958(2):1489-1494. 1959.

Points out the difference between the function of a scientific information officer and a librarian. A syllabus is presented for a post-graduate course of training for a student who is already a subject specialist.

American Management Association, Administrative Services Division, **ADVANCES IN EDP AND INFORMATION SYSTEMS.** New York, 1961. 187 p. (Report No. 62).

Papers in this volume are "based on material originally presented at AMA's Seventh Annual Data Processing Conference, held in March 1961". Partial contents: Advances in information retrieval and data acquisition: I. Progress in the design of information retrieval systems, by M. Taube, p. 51-63; II. Improved information storage and retrieval systems, by B. E. Holm, p. 64-74.

Asmonas, V., **SYSTEMS OF SCIENTIFIC AND TECHNICAL INFORMATION SERVICES: LONG RANGE PLANNING.** Rev. Doc. 27(2):81-85. May 1960.

A proposal for the establishment of an international technical information system which would be based on three main international centers (one for the Americas; one for Europe, the Near East and Africa; one for Asia and Australia). In addition, there would be a national center for each country, and a center for each scientific or technical discipline. The paper also includes discussion of problems which would be encountered in the development of such a system.

Atherton, P., and Clark, V., **A SUGGESTED CLASSIFICATION FOR THE LITERATURE OF DOCUMENTATION.** Amer. Doc. 12(1):38-48. Jan. 1961.

The classification scheme presented here had its origin in a class project undertaken by students at the University of Chicago, Graduate Library School during the spring quarter 1960. A description of the principal features of the classification with reference to David J. Haykin's six basic building rules for special classification is followed by two appendices: I. Classified Guide to American Documentation 1950-1960, vol. I-XI; II. Suggested classification for the literature of documentation.

Bach, H., **SCIENTIFIC LITERATURE USE: A SURVEY.** Spec. Libr. 48(10):466. Dec. 1957.

The author draws from reports by Bernal, Herner, and Urquhart on the ways in which scientific personnel gather information, some observations as to certain general practices and attitudes among scientists which he believes should be kept in mind by those who manage science libraries. ©ADI

Balke, S., **WIRTSCHAFT UND DOKUMENTATION** [Documentation and economy]. Nachr. Dok. 12 (1):1-5. Mar. 1961.

Fundamental problems of documentation are discussed from the professional and organizational point of view. It is stated emphatically that the expert must be provided with the material for his work whatever the financial cost. Development in documentation in West Germany must take the form of cooperation between institutions staffed by highly qualified personnel. Complete centralization as in the Soviet Union is neither possible nor desirable. Documentary activity will be coordinated at national level by the proposed Institut für Dokumentationswesen. ©ADI

Becker, J., **INFORMATION PROCESSING.** Washington, D.C., Amer. Inst. Biol. Sci., Biol. Sci. Commun. Proj., 1960. 13 p.

Describes the information framework in all special libraries, public libraries, and information centers as containing the following elements: the information received which is usually in printed form, the analysis of this information for indexing and cataloging, the index to the information, and the stored information or file of information. Discusses various efforts to mechanize each of the elements in the framework.

Bello, F., **HOW TO COPE WITH INFORMATION.** Fortune 62(3):162-167, 180, 182, 187, 189, 192. Sept. 1960.

. . . Information retrieval is reported to be in 1960 just about where electronic data processing was 10 years ago. A history is given of "modern" information retrieval, beginning with Vannevar Bush, head of the Office of Scientific Research and Development, with his article, "As we may think", in the July 1945 Atlantic Monthly. Since then, information retrieval has attracted two general types of enthusiasts, those interested in building machines and those interested primarily in theory, with the shift in the last few years to debates on indexing and retrieval theory . . . The article chronicles worldwide activities in retrieval from the Rapid Selector of Ralph R. Shaw to the Itek Corp. system of the Minicard type for the Air Force, the computer-produced index Chemical Titles of Chemical Abstracts Service, and the "biggest single abstracting service in the world", VINITI, the All-Union Institute of Scientific and Technical Information of the U.S.S.R. ©ADI

Bohnert, L. M., **NEW ROLE OF MACHINES IN DOCUMENT RETRIEVAL: DEFINITIONS AND SCOPE.** Inst. Inform. Storage & Retrieval, 3rd, 1961. Papers presented, p. 8-21. 1962.

A discussion of the role of machines in indexing and document retrieval, and a review of the recent research in this area. The article includes definitions for the terms "document retrieval" and "machine indexing", as well as a discussion of the limitations of machines in this field, and a presentation of three methods for accomplishing machine indexing.

Booth, A. D., **THE EFFICIENCY OF CERTAIN METHODS OF INFORMATION RETRIEVAL.** Inform. & Control 1(2):159-164. May 1958.

Methods are discussed for the retrieval of items of data which are stored as entries in a table in the store of a computer. The average number of look-up operations required to find an entry is computed for several methods. It is shown that if advantage is taken of the relative frequencies with which the different entries are looked up, the average number of look-ups may be substantially reduced. The results are applied to the problem of using a computer as a mechanical dictionary. Author.

Bourne, C. P., **THE HISTORICAL DEVELOPMENT AND PRESENT STATE-OF-THE-ART OF MECHANIZED INFORMATION RETRIEVAL SYSTEMS.** Amer. Doc. 12(2):108-110. Apr. 1961.

The last ten years of equipment development and the application of mechanization techniques are reviewed for each of several functionally separate approaches, such as punched card systems, computer systems, and magnetic media systems. Comments are made on the progress to date, and the degree of activity to be expected during the next few years for each of these approaches. Author.

Bourne, C. P., and others. **FINAL REPORT: REQUIREMENTS, CRITERIA, AND MEASURES OF PERFORMANCE OF INFORMATION STORAGE AND RETRIEVAL SYSTEMS.** Prepared for Office of Science Information Service, National Science Foundation. Menlo Park, Stanford Res. Inst., 1961. 132 p.

A preliminary study was made of the requirements, criteria, and measures of performance of information storage and retrieval systems. Using an interview guide and a methodology developed during this study, a total of 92 applied electronics researchers and 11 metallurgists were interviewed in an attempt to measure and rank several different requirements for information. It was found that some requirements could definitely be measured, and that there was general disagreement among the users about the relative importance of various information requirements. The methodology and the interview guide could be extended, with minor modifications, to other technical subject fields. In addition to the study of information requirements, three separate and complementary tools were developed for the analysis and evaluation of information retrieval systems: (1) a coarse screening procedure; (2) two different performance evaluation procedures; and (3) two cost analysis procedures that used computer programs to simulate the operation of candidate systems to determine their operating costs over wide ranges in operating conditions. A general functional model of a storage and retrieval system was developed for use by these cost analysis programs. A number of specific research tasks were also suggested to further develop the techniques for the determination of user requirements and the measurement of the performance of information storage and retrieval systems. Author.

Boutry, G. A., **THE ICSU ABSTRACTING BOARD: THE STORY OF A VENTURE IN INTERNATIONAL COOPERATION.** Internatl. Conf. Sci. Inform. Proc. 1958(2):1503-1515. 1959.

A brief history and description of the International Council of Scientific Unions Abstracting Board. Included in the paper are: a detailed discussion of the International Journal of Physics Abstracting and mention of future activities and proposals of the ICSU Abstracting Board.

Brossman, S. W., **THE CASE FOR CENTRALIZED INTERNAL COMMUNICATIONS.** Res./Devlpmt. 11 (7):17, 19, 21, 23. July 1960.

Discussion of the need for, and organization, operation and control of a communications office with authority not only over printing and distributing, group filing, report writing, and library cataloging, but also over manual writing, revising, and cutting, as well as communications systems and procedures.

Brownson, H. L., **THE DOCUMENTATION RESEARCH PROGRAM OF THE NATIONAL SCIENCE FOUNDATION. AUTOMATIC DOCUMENTATION IN ACTION.** Proc. 1959:1-9. 1961.

The article discusses the background of the National Science Foundation and names other government agencies engaged in or supporting research and development problems in documentation; the work of private foundations such as the Council on Library Resources; the publication of the Current Research and Development in Scientific Documentation pamphlet; the Research Information Center and Advisory Service on Information Processing at the National Bureau of Standards; several projects being supported in information storage and retrieval and five projects in the field of mechanical translation.

Bush, V., **PROFESSIONAL COLLABORATION.** Science 125(3237):49-54. Jan. 11, 1957.

In this paper on the responsibility and opportunities of the professions, particularly those of medical men and scientists, Dr. Bush foresees that the time is coming when the practice of medicine will rest upon a systematic understanding of the life-processes in all their complexity. The full integration of uncoordinated, empirical data may not come in our lifetime, however. There may be required new methods of thought, novel ways of recording and transmitting the accumulated experience of the race, ways as yet unconceived of bringing to bear on complex problems the interrelated efforts of diverse minds. We may witness new devices as powerful, versatile, and rapid as digital computers in the realms of computation and analysis, but capable of interrelating and ordering masses of primary and inexact observations into meaningful arrays. There may be means for communicating the knowledge of a group which will render obsolete the cumbersome writing of papers and the chaotic task of storing and consulting them. ©ADI

Cahn, J. N., **"B.I.T.S." — BUREAU OF INFORMATION FOR TECHNOLOGY AND SCIENCE PROPOSED AS "KEY STATION" OF FEDERAL "NETWORK" OF INFORMATION SERVICES TO U. S. FREE ENTERPRISE SYSTEM.** New York, 1962. 3 p. Excerpts of address delivered at Engineers Joint Council, New York, January 17, 1962.

Presents a brief background on government concern with the rapid growth of scientific information. The author proposes a two-fold plan for Federal action in this area: 1) the establishment of a Federal network of libraries and information centers consisting of voluntary collaboration among four main elements — the three great National library systems, the major inter-agency information systems, the major intra-agency systems, and the Federally supported information centers; and 2) the formation of a "Bureau of Information for Technology and Science" as the principal point for gathering and distributing tax-supported, non-classified information to all individuals requesting it.

Case Institute of Technology, **AN OPERATIONS RESEARCH STUDY OF THE DISSEMINATION AND USE OF RECORDED SCIENTIFIC INFORMATION.** Cleveland, O., 1960. 63 p.

A study of three aspects of the problem of dissemination and use of recorded scientific information. Part One is a study of the reading behavior of chemists and physicists using the direct observation method to determine what is read, why it is read, and the differences in reading behavior between groups. Part Two is an economic analysis of journal publications to determine the average cost of publishing journals of various types and to determine the cost per reader of the most frequently read journals. Part Three is a study to determine how condensation affects the comprehension of scientific articles.

Cattaneo, A., **L'INFORMATION TECHNIQUE DANS UNE GRANDE INDUSTRIE** [Technical information in a large industry]. Rev. Doc. 24(2):88-94. May 1957.

Presents the requirements of the information service in a large industrial firm and its organization at FIAT in Milan, as well as considerations for the improvement of technical information.

Clapp, V. W., **THE COMPUTER IN THE LIBRARY.** Computer Appl. Symp., 1960. Proc. 7:35-45. 1961. The author concludes that "computer applications will progressively take place in library work — in some areas more rapidly than others". He points out that such applications are challenging to those engaged in computer work "because they involve some of the most subtle and difficult factors affecting human activity and accomplishment — namely information and meaning".

CLARIFICATION, UNIFICATION & INTEGRATION OF INFORMATION STORAGE AND RETRIEVAL,
proceedings of Feb. 23, 1961 symposium, New York City. New York, 1961. 94 p. Ref.

The symposium was sponsored by Management Dynamics, Lincoln Square Chapter (N. Y. City) Systems and Procedures Association, and Science-Technology Group, N. Y. Chapter, Special Libraries Association. The speakers endeavored to limit the time given to history and to the blue-sky future. The effect, rather, is intended to emphasize the present state of affairs — concentrating on areas of opportunity for the user, the researcher, and the manufacturer.

Cloud, G. H., KEY TO PROGRESS — SPEEDY USE OF PUBLISHED INFORMATION. Monitor 2(3):4, 53. Ref. May 1957.

Contains brief description of the Houston Research Library, Humble Oil and Refining Co. Coordinate indexing is used for report literature. Some 1,600 reports are "deep" indexed by more than 26,000 entries, with 4,500 Uniterm cards in the subject index. LC classification is used for books. ©ADI

Coblans, H., SOME NOTES ON THE ORGANIZATION OF SPECIAL LIBRARIES. Unesco Bul. Libr. 12 (11/12):261-266. Nov./Dec. 1958.

Points out the main differences between general and special libraries; and discusses matters of documentary reproduction, acquisition policy, translations, abstracts and indexes, periodicals and reprints as they relate to special libraries.

Cohan, L., and Craven, K, SCIENCE INFORMATION PERSONNEL; THE NEW PROFESSION OF INFORMATION COMBINING SCIENCE, LIBRARIANSHIP AND FOREIGN LANGUAGE. New York, Mod. Language Assoc. Amer., 1961. 74 p. Ref., p. 42-43.

This study, conducted for the U. S. Office of Education with support from the National Science Foundation, describes "science information" as a new profession and the science information specialist as its practitioner; and includes description of work elements and job titles in the field. The staff requirements for science information personnel both current and anticipated in government agencies are tabulated, and a graduate school program leading to an M.S. degree in information is outlined.

Colmen, K. S., INFORMATION IN ACTION. Res. Devlpmt. 12(2):6-18. Feb. 1961.

One of the most important means of improving communications is by making our everyday procedures more effective as communication media. Communication of company objectives, R & D objectives, and philosophic approaches for effective communication within an organization are discussed.

Columbia University, Bureau of Applied Social Research, REVIEW OF STUDIES IN THE FLOW OF INFORMATION AMONG SCIENTISTS. New York, 1960. 2 v. Ref.

Prepared for the National Science Foundation. H. Menzel, study director; L. Lieberman and J. Dulchin, research assistants. The first volume of this two-part report presents a review and comparison of the various types of "User studies" (studies on the flow of scientific information) which have been conducted. The studies are arranged by topical organization of content, and refer especially to the behavior, habits, usages, experiences and needs of research scientists in obtaining scientific information. Volume II is a collection of tables which complements the information presented in Volume I.

COMPUTER APPLICATIONS SERVICE. Detroit, American Data Processing, Inc., 1962. 2 v.

Cordonnier, G., OPTIMATION DE L'ORGANISATION DOCUMENTAIRE [Optimization of documentation]. In Kent, A., ed. Information retrieval and machine translation, pt. 2, p. 1205-1237. New York, Interscience, 1961. Also in Rev. Doc. 27(1): 12-31. Feb. 1960.

This is a state of the art review of the various techniques in use for machine translation and information retrieval. Particular attention is given to systems which involve photostorage and the "Selecto" system.

Costello, J. C., SOME SOLUTIONS TO OPERATIONAL PROBLEMS IN CONCEPT COORDINATION. Amer. Doc. 12(3):191-197. July 1961.

Discusses the operational problems attendant to the functioning of coordinate indexes with emphasis on the intellectual and human considerations, those which determine system efficiency and output quality.

Coughlin, R. E., DOCUMENTATION FOR SCIENCE AND ENGINEERING. Burlington, Conn., Burlington Pub. Co., 1960. 177 p.

A review prompted by what the author regards as a major shortcoming of many of today's technical communications programs, namely the seemingly unchecked trend toward specialization at the expense of integration. It is contended that implementation of documentation programs for science and technology as a whole will offset the detrimental effect of over-diversification of personnel and facilities. Toward this end, details are given on practical matters of establishing a documentation program, including organization, administration, standardization, and education. ©ADI

DATA PROCESSING ANNUAL. 3. PUNCHED CARD AND COMPUTER APPLICATIONS AND REFERENCE GUIDE, 1961. Detroit, Mich., American Data Processing, Inc., 1961. 320 p.

Reviews of books in the data processing field, p. 210-220; Books in the data processing field, p. 221-226; Bibliographical index to articles in periodicals, p. 227-274.

DATA PROCESSING EQUIPMENT ENCYCLOPEDIA. Detroit, American Data Processing, Inc., 1961. 2 v.

Vol. 1, Electromechanical devices: punched card, punched tape, related systems. Vol. 2, Electronic devices.

DATA PROCESSING LIBRARY SERIES. Detroit, Mich., American Data Processing, Inc., 1962. 5 v.

DATA PROCESSING YEARBOOK. Detroit, Mich., American Data Processing, Inc., 1962.

Dennis, B. K., HIGH SPEED LITERATURE SEARCHING ON AN IBM 704. 25 p. In Information Retrieval Systems Conference, Poughkeepsie, 1959. General information manual [papers]. New York, Internatl. Business Mach. Corp., 1959.

A detailed description of General Electric's Flight Propulsion Division's Technical Information Center's high speed literature searching system which uses the IBM 704 computer. Also describes the Uniterm coordinate indexing system which was previously used and explains why the Technical Center decided to mechanize its searching system and why the 704 was selected for use in the new system.

Dubester, H. J., THE LIBRARY OF CONGRESS LOOKS AT MECHANIZATION OF INFORMATION RETRIEVAL. In Clarification, Unification & Integration of Information Storage & Retrieval; proceedings, Feb. 23rd, 1961 symposium, p. 37-45. New York, 1961.

Mechanization is used in several operations at the Library of Congress, such as those of the Order Division and the Loan Division. However, the management of the Library of Congress has many questions which they feel must be answered before all or parts of their information system are automated. The first of these questions is: "Is automation needed?"

Duyvis, F. D., DOCUMENT REPRODUCTION SERVICES; THEIR EFFICIENT ORGANIZATION AND MANAGEMENT. Unesco Bul. Libr. 14 (6): 241-259. Nov. 1960.

Twenty-five principles are enunciated and explained. They cover such matters as scheduling of work, laboratory maintenance, transport of docu-

ments to the camera, communication and control of orders, pricing, accounting, and standardization. The author recommends a series of case reports to provide comparative financial data, and the establishment of an international organization for reproduction services possibly under the auspices of IFLA and FID. A bibliography of more than 30 references is appended. ©ADI

Dyson, G. M., and Farradane, J., THE AIMS OF THE INSTITUTE OF INFORMATION SCIENTISTS, LTD. n. p., 1961. 6 p. Prepared for the General Papers Session of the Division of Chemical Literature, American Chemical Society, Sept. 5, 1961.

The authors recite the background which leads up to the formation of the Institute and then explain its purposes and plans for the future.

Edmundson, H. P., and Wyllys, R. E., AUTOMATIC ABSTRACTING AND INDEXING — SURVEY AND RECOMMENDATIONS. Commun. ACM 4(5):226-234. May 1961.

This report presents a new concept in the automatic analysis of documents: the relative-frequency approach to measuring the significance of words, word groups, and sentences, which employs as the primary criterion of a word's significance the contrast between the word's relative frequency of use with the document and its relative frequency in general use. This approach is discussed in detail, as are its applications to problems of automatic abstracting, indexing, and translation. The report includes a summary and comparison of the pioneering automatic analysis studies of P. B. Baxendale, H. P. Luhn, and V. A. Oswald, Jr. ©ADI

Engelbart, D. C., SPECIAL CONSIDERATIONS OF THE INDIVIDUAL AS A USER, GENERATOR, AND RETRIEVER OF INFORMATION. Amer. Doc. 12 (2): 121-125. Apr. 1961.

Urges the development of automatic systems for individuals which would be a way to store, retrieve, and manipulate the information within each individual's private domain, with information-packet sizes that match his actual needs (i.e., separate concepts, facts, considerations, etc.). This private automatic system could go far toward increasing the effectiveness of the individual's capabilities to the level needed for the extended and complex problems that are the pressing ones of our day. The author also describes such a system which he developed and named "micro-documentation".

European Productivity Agency, TECHNICAL INFORMATION AND THE SMALLER FIRM; FACTS AND FIGURES ON PRACTICES IN EUROPEAN AND AMERICAN INDUSTRY. Paris, 1958. 69 p. (Project 296/2).

This is the final report of the survey of the

methods used by small and medium sized manufacturing firms to obtain technical information.

European Productivity Agency, Division for Technical Action and Productivity in Agriculture and Food, **AGRICULTURAL DOCUMENTATION: THE RESPONSIBILITIES OF LIBRARIES AND INFORMATION SERVICES**. Paris, 1961. 77 p.

Report of a seminar, Apr. 20-23, 1960, arranged by the European Productivity Agency, and organized by the Ministry of Food, Agriculture and Forestry and the Research Council of Food, Agriculture and Forestry of Germany and the International Association of Agricultural Librarians and Documentalists.

Fairbairn, R. E., **INFORMATION METHODS: ADAPTATION TO GROWTH**. Aslib Proc. 9 (10): 301-314. Oct. 1957.

On the premise that information services cannot be planned ahead, but must be developed in close connection with the experience of services requested and rendered, the writer discusses the stages of development in information and related services; the differences between commercial and economic, and technical information and intelligence work; the management of an information service, and future expectations and realities. In the last, he cautions against the enthusiasm generated by the advent of microcopying techniques and computer systems as cure-alls for information problems. Also outlined is a suggested role for ASLIB in furthering information services. ©ADI

Farradane, J., **THE FUTURE OF INFORMATION WORK**. Aslib Proc. 12(5):191-199. May 1960.

The information officer, who is deputizing for the researcher in his reading, must necessarily be an information scientist. Few of his essential tasks have affinities with librarianship and newer developments in information work are still less related. Although the work may include in addition to the more usual activities of abstracting, indexing, keeping research workers informed on literature . . . and research in documentation, the author believes that the general standards are deplorably low, and that this is largely because managements and governments fail to appreciate their importance . . . Many problems can be solved only through collaboration and international cooperation. The hope for the future lies in raising standards, improving techniques, and thus attracting higher grade personnel, and in stimulating government and industry to greater awareness of the potentialities of information services. ©ADI

Foskett, D. J., **INFORMATION SERVICE IN LIBRARIES**. London, C. Lockwood, 1958. 142 p. Ref. (Crosby Lockwood's new librarianship series, 4).

Contains chapters treating origins of information service in libraries, role of the information officer, selection and acquisition of stock, arrangement and indexing, dissemination of information, reference service, educational role of an information service, reports and correspondence registries, training and qualification for information work, and further developments in information service including translation, documentary reproduction and microfilm. ©ADI

Francillon, M., **INFORMATION RETRIEVAL: A VIEW FROM THE REFERENCE DESK**. J. Doc. 15(4):187-198. Ref. Dec. 1959.

A view of the problems in information retrieval from the standpoint of the librarian as liaison between the researcher and information. The author believes that attempts to improve information retrieval must take into account this relationship. He emphasizes the idea by describing and presenting results of a study conducted from records of reference service in the IBM Research Library at San Jose, California.

Frank, O., **CO-OPERATION BETWEEN FIRMS IN THE FIELD OF INFORMATION**. Rev. Doc. 28 (3): 89-92. Aug. 1961.

Report on cooperation between firms in the field of information based on the author's practical experiences in the coordination of documentation and information work. The following points are discussed: Ways of disseminating information; necessity of good planning; inquiry into the amount, availability and presentation of information in a particular field; organization questions; compilation of the information; distribution of the information; cooperation with other information centers; savings through cooperation; and experience with cooperation in information.

Funk, C. E., **THE INFORMATION CENTER OF AMERICAN CYANAMID'S STAMFORD LABORATORIES**. J. Chem. Educ. 34 (10):507-509. Oct. 1957.

Describes the organization and operations of the Technical Information Section at Cyanamid's research laboratories, including the molecular formula index for company technical reports and screening programs. ©ADI

Garrett, P., **A CLASSIFICATION SYSTEM FOR ANY DATA BANKING (INFORMATION STORAGE AND RETRIEVAL) PROCESS**. Santa Monica, Calif., Benson-Lehner Corp., 1959, 11 p. Research report 59-6 on Contract Nonr-266600 with the Office of Naval Research.

Study was started to discover and state explicitly the fundamentals of data banking (more commonly called information storage and retrieval). A clear exposition of these fundamentals will be useful in directing the development of equipment to meet particular application requirements. A logical framework or hierarchical tree is displayed that includes all possible data banking processes and shows their similarities and differences. The basis of this framework is the organization of the store and the method of search, not the physical form of either the items of information or the search equipment.   Author.

Glass, H. B., and Norwood, S. H., **HOW SCIENTISTS ACTUALLY LEARN OF WORK IMPORTANT TO THEM.** Internatl. Conf. Sci. Inform. Proc. 1958(1): 195-197. 1959.

Report of a survey in which 50 biological scientists were interviewed to determine how and where they had learned of sources of information pertinent to their fields of interest.

Glimn, A. F., and Greenway, R. D., **INFORMATION STORAGE AND RETRIEVAL.** Part II, Equipment applications. Bethesda, Md., Defense Systems Dept., Gen. Elect. Co., 1960. 10 p. Ref.

Machines alone can never solve the fundamental problems of information storage and retrieval. They can only provide the means for implementing solutions which would not have been practical using manually operated systems. Thus, the solution to the problem of evaluating and specifying equipment for information storage and retrieval systems must be evolved by conducting a complete and exacting operations analysis study to determine the system parameters. This paper discusses the factors involved in evaluating the specifying equipment and equipment configurations for information storage and retrieval systems.

Goldman, A. J., and others, **MATHEMATICAL RESEARCH RELATED TO INFORMATION SELECTION SYSTEMS.** Washington, U. S. Natl. Bur. Standards, 1961. 58 p. (NBS Report No. 6883).

Mathematical research relevant to information selection systems is described. Three areas of mathematical problems related to mechanization of the information retrieval process are considered: (1) efficient formulation of search questions; (2) rapid classification of incoming documents on a given one-dimensional scale, and (3) categorizing and manipulating documents and their relationships.

Greenway, R. D., and Russell, M. V., **LET'S DESIGN AN INFORMATION SYSTEM.** Washington, D. C. Gen. Elect. Co., Defense Systems Dept., Inform. Systems Sect., 1960. 11 p. Ref. Presented as a contributed paper to the 18th National meeting of the Operations Research Society of America, Detroit, Mich., Oct. 10-12, 1960.

Discusses the complex inter-relationships which exist between techniques for indexing and devices for machine search and retrieval of indexed information. A generalized approach to indexing is used to show the equipment requirements as a function of system requirements. The future of mechanized information systems is discussed. It is imperative that every information system provide for collection, reduction, storage and retrieval, manipulation and presentation of information.

Griffin, M., **THE LIBRARY OF TOMORROW.** Soc. Tech. Writers & Pub. Proc. Annu. Conv. 8:66-71. Ref. 1961.

A projection of what the library of the future will be. To meet the increasing volume of scientific and technical information, the libraries will use machines for cataloging, indexing, abstracting, cross-referencing, and retrieving of information. The library will be part of a global network of communication centers. The technical writer will have the added task of adopting input material for machine scanning. Concludes with a plea that librarians must not be unprepared to load the machines or to retrieve from them when they are available for the efficient operation of the libraries of the future.

Hanson, C. W., **ORGANIZATION OF MATERIAL AND SERVICES IN A SMALL INFORMATION DEPARTMENT.** Rev. Doc. 28(3):105-109. Aug. 1961.

A discussion, from actual practice, of precisely what can be done by a small industrial firm to provide itself with an effective information service; how it can be done; and how much it will cost. The basic aims of this information service are: (1) to keep the staff informed of scientific and technical developments relevant to their work, and (2) to help them find solutions to specific problems as they arise.

Hattery, L. H., **INFORMATION AND COMMUNICATION IN BIOLOGICAL SCIENCE.** Washington, D.C., The Amer. Univ., School of Govt. & Pub. Admin., Cent. Technol. & Admin., 1961. 99 p.

Report of the Biological Sciences Communication Seminar, sponsored by the Biological Sciences Communication Project, AIBS, and held at The American University, June 19 to July 1, 1961. The purpose was to identify and review problems associated with the flow of biological science information from scientist producer to scientist consumer. Developments in the various areas of study are given in this report, along with the seminar program and procedure, a roster of participants, and a list of committees with their purposes and reports.

Heald, J. H., **TRANSITION FROM A MANUAL TO A MACHINE INDEXING SYSTEM.** Inst. Inform. Storage & Retrieval, 3rd, 1961. Papers presented, p. 170-190. 1962.

An account of the problems and requirements involved in the conversion of ASTIA's major information system from one of manual operation to one of automation. Included is a detailed description of the Thesaurus arrangement developed especially for this transition.

Herner, S., **THE RELATIONSHIP OF INFORMATION — USE STUDIES AND THE DESIGN OF INFORMATION STORAGE AND RETRIEVAL SYSTEMS.** Washington, D.C., Herner & Co., 1958. 30 p. Technical

Note No. 1 on Contract AF 30(602)1857.

A review is presented of the results of past studies of the information-gathering methods of workers in various fields, and the general applicability of these results to the design and improvement of information programs and systems is shown. Two cases from the literature are used to illustrate storage and retrieval systems that do and do not meet the requirements of their users, and to show the contrasting need of the pure scientist for mere references to information and of the applied scientist for direct access to actual information. Author.

Heumann, K. F., **THE BIG BLACK BOX AT YOUR BECK AND CALL.** Spec. Libr. 51(9):483-484. Nov. 1960.

Suggestions are given as to how a librarian should approach and utilize the capabilities of data processing systems. Manufacturers' representatives and programmers for the systems are recommended as people who can be of much assistance. The experience of a reference librarian, or of one skilled in indexing, classification, or subject headings, is said to be of much value in utilizing machine techniques for searching technical literature. ©ADI

Hillier, J., **MEASURING THE VALUE OF INFORMATION SERVICES.** J. Chem. Doc. 2(1):31-34. Jan. 1962.

A discussion of the value of an information service from the point of view of management. The author contends that: (1) Management's considerations must go beyond the provision of extra brains to perform functions which have grown beyond the capability of the individual, (2) the additional brain-power which is serving the creative individual must, in some way, operate in conjunction with the individual's experience-based optimization of his information input, (3) there must be a balance between a centralized information service and a dispersed system, where the service is performed by individuals who are an integral part of the research teams, and (4) we must undertake further studies to develop a more complete understanding of the relationship between information flow and creativity.

Howerton, P. W., **DOCUMENT SYSTEMS: TO AUTOMATE OR NOT TO AUTOMATE.** Washington, D.C., 1961. 12 p. Paper presented before the Interagency Records Administration Conference, National Archives and Records Service, Mar. 17, 1961.

Documentation problems started with the first recording of knowledge. Some of the solutions to these problems have been less than satisfactory. A satisfactory documentation system need not depend on complex devices to be useful, but it must satisfy the need of the customers who will use its services. In such a system, machines are powerful tools which, under the guidance of human judgment, can do routine operations that free the creative talents of man.

International Business Machines Corporation, **REFERENCE MANUAL: INDEX ORGANIZATION FOR INFORMATION RETRIEVAL.** White Plains, N.Y., 1961. 63 p.

A simplified presentation of the methods and patterns of organizing indexes. It is geared mainly to systems personnel in an effort to help them understand the problems to be encountered in organizing information for retrieval. A glossary of terms and a bibliography on information indexing are included.

INTERNATIONAL CONFERENCE ON SCIENTIFIC INFORMATION. Washington, D. C., Nov. 16-21, 1958. Proceedings. Washington, D.C., Natl. Acad. Sci. - Natl. Res. Counc., 1959. 2 v.

This conference was sponsored by the National Science Foundation, the National Academy of Sciences — National Research Council, and the American Documentation Institute. The discussions covered seven different areas: 1. Literature and reference needs of scientists: knowledge now available and methods of ascertaining requirements; 2. The function and effectiveness of abstracting and indexing services; 3. Effectiveness of monographs, compendia, and specialized centers: present trends and new and proposed techniques and types of services; 4. Organization of information for storage and search: comparative characteristics of existing systems; 5. Organization of information for storage and retrospective search: intellectual problems and equipment considerations in the design of new systems; 6. Organization of information for storage and retrospective search: possibility for a general theory; 7. Responsibilities of a government, professional societies, universities, and industry for improved information services and research.

International Federation for Documentation, **MODERN DOCUMENTATION AND INFORMATION PRACTICES; A BASIC MANUAL** edited by Dr. O. Frank. The Hague, 1961. 225 p. Ref. (FID Publication 334).

This manual, published with the assistance of Unesco, "deals with the fundamentals of documentation and information work, and especially with the organization of documentation and information centres". Contents: Chapter I. Introduction, by O. Frank; 2. Organizational forms and purposes, by O. Frank; 3. The need to organize, by J. W. Holmstrom; 4. Intake and outflow, by G. S. Stekhoven; 5. References and storage of documents, by H. Elsner; 6. Ready made references, by J. E. Holmstrom; 7. Information retrieval, by J. E. Holmstrom; 8. Mechanization using manual apparatus, by H. A. Elsner; 9. Mechanization using electrical apparatus; by J. E. Holmstrom; 10. Reproduction, by O. Frank; 11. Internal organization, by J. E. Holmstrom; 12. Overcoming language barriers, by J. E. Holmstrom; 13. Human factors, by J. Koblitz; 14. Co-operation and co-ordination, by J. Koblitz; Appendix 1. Recommended books and articles; Appendix 2. Organizations concerned in the promotion and improvement of documentation and related practices.

Jeanmaire, R., **ROLE D'UN SERVICE DE DOCUMENTATION DANS UNE GRANDE ENTREPRISE INTERNATIONALE** [Role of a documentation service in a large organization]. Nachr. Nouvelles 35(5): 153-158. Sept./Oct. 1959.

A documentation department can make an important contribution to the creative, and advisory activities of an organization: the documentalist can make of his department a laboratory of ideas, suggest methods of analysis or reveal descriptions of processes in furthering experimental work, assist commercial development by surveys of possible markets, the setting of high standards in publication, contribute to good public relations, etc. ©ADI

Kent, A., **EXPLOITATION OF RECORDED INFORMATION. I. DEVELOPMENT OF AN OPERATIONAL MACHINE SEARCHING SERVICE FOR THE LITERATURE OF METALLURGY AND ALLIED SUBJECTS.** Amer. Doc. 11(2):173-188. Apr. 1960.

Describes the background, plans, initial stages, and problems of the operational mechanized searching service in metallurgy and allied subject fields. The article is based on the experiences of the Center for Documentation and Communications Research at Western Reserve University which is supported by the American Society for Metals and the National Science Foundation.

Kessler, M. M., **AN EXPERIMENTAL COMMUNICATION CENTER FOR SCIENTIFIC AND TECHNICAL INFORMATION.** Lexington, Mass., Mass. Inst. Tech., Lincoln Lab., 1960. 19 p. (Report No. 4G-0002). Contract AF 19(604)5200.

A discussion of the problems of scientific communication and some of the thinking and research recently performed on this subject at Lincoln Laboratory. The report stresses that the evaluation of new ideas and components must be made in a system environment and not in terms of parameters unique to each component. A distinction is made between scientific message units and their mode of propagation. The message units (scientific talks and papers) are considered adequate for their functions, but they are encountering increasing losses and delays in propagation. The analysis indicates that the most critical item in need of research and invention is an indexing or addressing scheme that will direct papers to readers. Valid directional indexing should be sought in the operational history of the author and the intended

reader. A communication system for experimental purposes is briefly outlined. The three principal channels of the systems are (1) Non-interrogated broadcasting, (2) Interrogated point to point transmissions, and (3) Non-interrogated point to point transmission. It is stressed that the critical need at this point is for a deeper understanding of the logic of scientific information and its flow habits. It is recommended that a pilot system of scientific communication be established to serve as a test bed for components development and systems research. Author.

Loosjes, T. P., **ORGANISATION UND DIENSTE DER HOLLÄNDDISCHEN DOKUMENTATIONSZENTRALE FÜR DIE LANDWIRTSCHAFT** [Organization and services of the Netherlands Documentation Centre for Agriculture]. Nachr. Dok. 10(2):59-65. July 1959.

A description of the Netherlands Documentation Centre for Agriculture, as an example of centralization of documentation effort in a subject field. Activities and services of the Centre, and some details of operational costs are included in the article.

Lowry, W. K., **AUTOMATIC EQUIPMENT FOR INFORMATION HANDLING.** Automatic Documentation in Action. Proc. 1959:51-57. 1961.

A description of the application of 9 pieces of electronic equipment to information handling functions at the Bell Telephone Laboratories. The philosophy behind these applications is that the greatest advantages will be realized from using machines for clerical operations in the information service. The author concludes that although they have barely scratched the service in applying machine techniques, they have already realized a great reduction in space requirements and are able to offer much better service on engineering drawings.

Lowry, W. K., and Albrecht, J. C., **A PROPOSED INFORMATION HANDLING SYSTEM FOR A LARGE RESEARCH ORGANIZATION.** Internatl. Conf. Sci. Inform. Proc. 1958(2):1181-1202. 1959.

The authors have designed this information center with a large research organization in mind, but most of the approaches and procedures may also be applied to smaller groups. It is advocated that this (or any other) system be centered around the information requirements of the group involved, in order that collection and maintenance of superfluous materials be avoided.

Luhn, H. P., **SELECTIVE DISSEMINATION OF NEW SCIENTIFIC INFORMATION WITH THE AID OF ELECTRONIC PROCESSING EQUIPMENT.** Amer. Doc. 12(2):131-138. Ref. Apr. 1961.

Describes a service system of dissemination of new scientific information in which machines are used.

MACHINE INDEXING: PROGRESS AND PROBLEMS.
Papers presented at the Third Institute on Information Storage and Retrieval, February 13-17, 1961. Washington, D.C., The Amer. Univ., School of Govt. & Pub. Admin., Center Technol. & Admin., 1962. 354 p.

The purpose of the Institute was to explore one attack on the problem of communication of scientific and technical information — that of machine indexing. The twenty-one papers presented are intended to provide a composite report of the state of the art in 1961.

McCormick, E. M., **DIGITAL COMPUTER PRIMER.** New York, McGraw-Hill, 1959.

McCormick, E. M., **THE RESEARCHER AND INFORMATION STORAGE AND RETRIEVAL.** In Clarification, Unification & Integration of Information Storage and Retrieval; proceedings Feb. 23rd, 1961 symposium, p. 79-83. New York, 1961.

Discusses three general points pertaining to the subject which " can be summarized as a consideration for more systems analysis in information storage and retrieval". Points are: (1) existing studies for systems evaluation, (2) association of ideas, and (3) "the amount and type of information interchange there is or will be between information storage and retrieval systems".

McCormick, E. M., **WHY COMPUTERS?** Inst. Inform. Storage & Retrieval, 3rd, 1961. Papers presented, p. 220-232. 1962.

A discussion of computers based on the assumption that they are, could, or should be considered the ultimate in information processing devices. The author cites reasons for their use, and discusses their advantages, limitations, and application.

McGuire, H. G., and Stoddard, T. L., **INFORMATION PRESENTATION SYSTEM.** Bethesda, Md., Gen. Elect. Co., Defense Systems Dept., 1960. 14 p.

Machine-controlled information presentation subsystems used for displaying information at electronic speeds are the subject of this paper. The over-all effectiveness of the display subsystem depends on the net effectiveness of its three complimentary elements: Men, Machines, and Methods. These elements are interdependent, and their arrangement in a proper relationship involves balancing the capabilities and limitations of each element in order to achieve the objectives of the system.

Maizell, R. E., **INFORMATION GATHERING PATTERNS AND CREATIVITY; A STUDY OF RESEARCH CHEMISTS IN AN INDUSTRIAL RESEARCH LABORATORY.** Amer. Doc. 11 (1):9-17. Ref. Jan. 1960.

A comparison of creative and "noncreative" research chemists with respect to the ways in which they use their professional and technical literature. The creative chemists differ from the "noncreative" in that the former read more technical literature on the job, are less reluctant to use literature of greater reading difficulty, are less influenced in their independence of thought, read more extensively and consult more frequently the older material, are more inquisitive and have broader cultural interests. The findings of the study are believed to be helpful in planning library and information services, in refining future inquiries into the ways in which scientists use recorded information, and in improving tests for the identification of creative ability among chemists. Author.

Melik-Shakhnazarov, A. S., **TECHNICAL INFORMATION IN THE U.S.S.R.** Translated from the Russian by B. I. Gorokhoff. Mass. Inst. Tech. Libr. Libr. Monog. 3, 122 p. Ref. 1961.

Under a grant from the National Science Foundation, the Libraries of the Massachusetts Institute of Technology are sponsoring a series of studies by Boris I. Gorokhoff of the dissemination of scientific and technical information in the Soviet Union. This project is part of a foreign science information program of the Foundation's Office of Science Information Services, which include critical and descriptive studies of the organizations and activities of information services abroad . . . It has therefore been decided to incorporate in the Library Monograph Series of M.I.T. this translation of A. S. Melik-Shakhnazarov's Nauchnotekhnicheskaia informatsiia i propaganda v mashinostroenii (Technological information in machine building), published in Moscow in June, 1960. Notwithstanding its title, the book is actually the most comprehensive review of the Soviet technical information system to appear in the U.S.S.R. in recent years. Foreword, page v.

Mooers, C. N., **THE "TAPE TYPEWRITER PLAN", A METHOD FOR COOPERATION IN DOCUMENTATION.** Cambridge, Mass., Zator Co., 1960. 22 p. (AFOSR-TN-60-532). Contract AF 49(638)-376. Also in Aslib Proc. 12(8):277-291. Aug. 1960.

The "Tape Typewriter Plan" makes possible widespread cooperation in documentation between libraries, while at the same time facilitating the internal clerical and cataloging operations at individual libraries.

Mueller, M. W., **TIME, COST AND VALUE FACTORS IN INFORMATION RETRIEVAL.** 12 p. In Information Retrieval Systems Conference, Poughkeepsie, 1959. General information manual [papers]. New York, Internatl. Business Mach. Corp., 1959.

This paper deals with a study conducted by the Operations Research Division of the Lockheed Aircraft Corporation (California Division) with the specific intent of unearthing some of the economic factors behind the library information handling system in a typical engineering organization. While many of the findings are still of a preliminary nature, they show the need for further development of the commodity concept and provide some interesting design criteria for improved information systems. Introduction.

Murdoch, J. W., and Simpson, G. B., **PRACTICAL INFORMATION HANDLING.** Indus. Res., Apr./May 1961: 41-43.

An optimum information system must provide for the following: the user must guide the selection of inputs; information processing time must be held to a minimum; information, and not references to information, must be immediately available; the user will not be able to state his information requirements exactly; and the user must be able to proceed easily from one segment of the system to another.

Myatt, DeW., and Upham, T. E., **A QUANTITATIVE TECHNIQUE FOR DESIGNING THE TECHNICAL INFORMATION CENTER.** J. Chem. Doc. 1(3):18-24. Nov. 1961.

Based on their definition of a technical information center, and their assertions as to what the mission of an information center should be and the relation between the resources which the center must collect and the people served by the center, the authors present 4 guide-lines for designing and operating an information center. In conclusion, they urge that anyone designing an information center begin by looking at the situation with the greatest perceptivity.

Opler, A., and Baird, N., **EXPERIENCE IN DEVELOPING INFORMATION RETRIEVAL SYSTEMS ON LARGE ELECTRONIC COMPUTERS.** Internatl. Conf. Sci. Inform. Proc. 1958(1):699-710. 1959.

Report of research into the use of large electronic computers for information retrieval systems. The research was conducted by programming an IBM 702 Electronic Data Processing Machine for the search of two chemical files. Results are reported from the viewpoint of all those concerned with retrieval systems — the user, the documentalist, and the administrator.

Samain, J., **CLASSIFICATION AND INFORMATION RETRIEVAL.** Automatic Documentation in Action. Proc. 1959:273-282. 1961.

First, this is a discussion of the problem that the information stored in the system is very often expressed in very different terms from those used in the question asked of the system. Second, the consequences of this problem which confronts every documentation system are drawn. Third, this describes the organizational scheme based on this problem and which has been applied in the National Center of Scientific Research (C.N.R.S.) of Paris.

Schultz, C. K., **RESEARCH IN INFORMATION RETRIEVAL — SOME RECENT CONTRIBUTIONS.** In Clarification, Unification & Integration of Information Storage and Retrieval; proceedings, Feb. 23rd, 1961 symposium, p. 47-55. Ref. New York, 1961.

An informal survey of research in information retrieval as found mainly in published reports.

Sewell, R., **TECHNICAL INFORMATION SERVICES IN GERMANY, LUXEMBOURG, BELGIUM, AND HOLLAND.** Aslib Proc. 11(10):240-265. Oct. 1959.

A report of a three weeks' trip to 22 technical information centers on the continent of Europe. The three aims of the trip were: 1) to examine methods of operating information services, 2) to study the attitude of industrial management and research toward technical information, and 3) to contact some of the leading people in the technical information field in Western Europe. Each center visited is fully described, and its available information and library services are given.

Shaw, R. R., **A MEDICAL INTELLIGENCE PROGRAM FOR THE NATIONAL INSTITUTES OF HEALTH.** n.p., 1961. 117 p.

Report of a survey of library and bibliographic services at the National Institutes of Health with recommendations for optimum services . . . Chapter X, Bibliographic Intelligence Services, is of particular interest. In it is outlined a section offering services tailored to the needs of particular research projects together with a screening service and special indexes for techniques, instrumentation, and news of medical research. ©ADI

Singer, T. E. R., ed., **INFORMATION AND COMMUNICATION PRACTICE IN INDUSTRY.** New York, Reinhold, 1958. 304 p. Ref.

A compilation of chapters presented as guides to subject fields such as operations research and the technical information program, chemical research file departments as information services, patent searching, abstracting, indexing, training the literature scientist, etc.

Spitzer, E. F., and McKenna, F. E., **THE INDUSTRIAL INFORMATION DEPARTMENT.** In Singer, T. E. R., ed., Information and communication practice in industry. p. 1-53. Ref. New York, Reinhold, 1958.

A general description of the organization and operation of industrial information departments. The description is rather short, but the reader is guided to more detailed information on the subject through the bibliography provided with the article.

U. S. Armed Services Technical Information Agency, **CONTROLLING LITERATURE BY AUTOMATION.** Presented at the IV. Annual Military Librarian's Workshop sponsored by Armed Services Technical Information Agency . . . 5-7 October 1960. Washington, 1960. 130 p.

Contents: Preparing for automation, by Lt. Col. W. Hammond; Selection, training and relocation of personnel, by L. R. Barnes; File conversion, data cleanup and inventory control, by F. A. Keller; Human aspects of ADPS, by E. S. Pope; Building an information retrieval system, by H. Rehbock; Impact of automation on the organizational structure of ASTIA, by H. Miles; The road ahead — integrated data processing, by W. A. Barden; The tape typewriter plan, by C. Mooers; and, A generalized computer method for information retrieval, by C. Schulz.

U. S. Congress, Senate, Committee on Government Operations, **CO-ORDINATION OF INFORMATION ON CURRENT FEDERAL RESEARCH AND DEVELOPMENT PROJECTS IN THE FIELD OF ELECTRONICS.** An analysis of agency systems for storage and retrieval of data on ongoing work and of views of private companies on indexing and communication problems. Washington, Govt. Print. Off., 1961. 292 p. Ref. (87th Congress. 1st Session. Committee Print).

This publication is a companion print to Senate Report No. 263, 87th Congress, 1st Session, issued May 18, 1961. The present print narrows the focus of the preceding publication. It explores in the one field of electronics the type of problem which the earlier print surveyed for all scientific fields — namely, how to manage information on research and development work in its prepublication stage. — from Senator Humphrey's Letter of Transmittal. In addition to the main body of the report this publication contains the statement and findings of Senator Humphrey, chairman of the Subcommittee on Reorganization and International Organizations, and the Summary and Recommendations of the Consultant, J. Stern.

U. S. National Science Foundation, Office of Science Information Service, **CURRENT RESEARCH AND DEVELOPMENT IN SCIENTIFIC DOCUMENTATION, No. 9.** Washington, Govt. Print. Off., 1961. 270 p. Ref. (NSF-61-76).

This is the 9th in a series of semi-annual descriptive reports on current research and development in scientific documentation.

U. S. National Science Foundation, Office of Science Information Service, **NONCONVENTIONAL TECHNICAL INFORMATION SYSTEMS IN CURRENT USE, No. 2.** Washington, Govt. Print. Off., 1959. 66 p. (NSF-59-49). The information in this report supersedes, for the most part, the information given in publication No. 1 of the same title. Supplement to No. 2 (NSF-60-14) issued in 1960, brings the information up to date.

Describes technical information systems currently in operation which embody new principles for the organization of subject matter or employ automatic equipment for storage and search.

U. S. National Science Foundation, Office of Science Information Service, **SPECIALIZED SCIENCE INFORMATION SERVICES IN THE UNITED STATES; A DIRECTORY.** Washington, 1961. 528 p. (NSF-61-68).

A directory to 427 physical and biological sciences information services in the United States as compiled from information collected by questionnaires. Designed as a reference aid for working scientists, engineers, librarians, and document lists.

INDEX